BOOK 4

WE ALL HAVE OUR DEMONS

CHRISTIAN DELIVERANCE

This book was originally going to be entitled
"DISCERNING HUMAN NATURE", then
"REVEALING THE MAN OF SIN"

(Let no one deceive you ... for the Day of Christ's
COMING will not be before ... The Man of Sin is
revealed ... 2 Thes. 2:3). Yes the Truth will set us free,
but nobody said it would be easy. Can you handle it???

PETER HOBSON

1st Editiion 2002

National Library of Australia
I.S.B.N. 0 947252 14 2

Printed in Sri Lanka
by New Life Literature (Pvt) Ltd,
Katunayake.

FOREWORD

I am especially delighted and honored to be able to write the Foreword to this book for two reasons: 1. I consider Peter Hobson a friend and deeply respect him and his commitment to a much maligned and much needed ministry which the Lord Jesus Christ has initiated, 2. because I feel **this is the "crown jewel" of Peter's writings. I think this is the best book he has done so far.**

Peter and I have both spent roughly three decades sacrificially ministering to God's hurting people. I have been both amazed and excited to see how close our thinking is (although our words and spelling might differ slightly), even though we are geographically so far apart... that is the work of the Holy Spirit - we have both had the same Divine Tutor.

Peter has shared revelation in this book which confirms things that most of those of us, who have ministered deliverance, have suspected and come to believe. We have suspected, and Peter has laid out the scriptural case to prove, that *everyone has demonic problems,* unless they have actively sought and received deliverance from them.

The revelation and scriptural proof offered that the *disease of Sin* is a nest of spirits, often referred to in Scripture as "the old man," "the strong man" or "the man of sin," is a mind-opening truth from God. Likewise his explanation of the *disease of pharisaism* is a reality which I have also observed in operation in the States.

Peter's message and warning rings loud and as clear as the clarion call of a trumpet..."Everyone has demons and needs to seek the Lord for deliverance and healing from them, while the opportunity remains," because shortly there will be the sound of another trumpet...and we all want to be ready!

I cannot recommend this book and the ministry of its author too highly.

William D. Banks (or Bill Banks)
President, Impact Christian Books Inc.
KIRKWOOD MO 63122 U.S.A.

DEDICATION

This publication is dedicated to THREE "people" precious to me.

First and foremost it is dedicated to all those dear Christian saints who desire to make themselves ready for the Bridegroom Christ and the Wedding!

Second, it is dedicated to my incredible wife Verlie who, like the apostle Paul, bears the marks of Jesus in her body (Gal. 6:17). It is Verlie that has prayed and fasted, ministered, suffered and interceded on her prayer couch and whose mouth the Lord has filled with discernment and power over many years, thanks be to God!

Finally, it is dedicated to the memory of my theological professor, Dr D.B. Knox who, after serious discussion said "Well Peter, you may one day make a significant contribution to the Church with your interest in the healing ministry". Such encouragement was rare in 1966.

PREFACE

While I realise that the revelations contained in this book are absolutely essential for the preparation of the Bride for the Wedding of the true Church, nevertheless I am deeply concerned that, because they touch on the personal spiritual condition of each one of us, they may be distressing to many people.

However I am not saying anything that is putting a problem upon you or condemning you in any way; what I am doing is diagnosing personal (hidden) problems with the Spirit of Truth, so that the healing and the cleansing made available through the blood sacrifice of the Son of God can be received by the human beings He has created - you and me.

This book is not for your cursing but for your blessing, and there is no need to fear because in Christ Jesus we have the Victory (Col. 2:13-15).

I have been accused in the past of encouraging demon chasing and seeing them under every stone. Well, I can't see them if they aren't there but I do understand the concerns of the "average" Christian. There are two ways to chase demons:

(i)   We can become obsessed with seeing demons in the lives of people without balancing it with love for the sufferer. This can become an exercise in faultfinding, destructive criticism, malicious accusations and fear mongering. This kind of discernment is itself unclean, and the person who does this needs MORE deliverance ministry than their targets.

(ii)   We must ALWAYS see sufferers who are seeking help as the Lord Jesus would see them, with the motive of rescuing them (which is what the word "deliverance" means). Clearly this should not degenerate into turning a "blind eye" by ministers.

We are to prosecute the war as the Lord's commandos with a policy of **search and destroy**. No war was ever won with a "I don't go looking for the enemy" strategy. If a person with emotional, mental or physical problems comes to us for help we should be seeking to discover the spiritual and physical sources of the problem.

How else will the Wise Maidens (Matt. 25:1-11) be ready for the Bridegroom??

The main things are that we Christians:

    (i)   *Understand the problems of human nature.*

    (ii)   *Get ourselves into the Lord's End-Time cleansing program.*

    (iii) *Help others to also get ready for Him.*

    (Iv) *Understand how the Man of Sin (Lawlessness) operates, because this book reveals him.*

Now I say again to EVERY reader - do NOT be afraid but begin to see your situation from God's viewpoint. You were created by Him and for Him, not to be controlled by His enemies, the powers of darkness, but by His HOLY Spirit within you.

The blood sacrifice of the Son of God was the HUGE price that was paid (Col. 2:13-15)

—FOR YOUR FREEDOM!

Read this book with FAITH, not fear. You are not alone. Spiritual warfare is coming out into the open more and more. Choose whose side you want to be on - Christ's or anti-Christ's, the wise or the foolish, the winners or the losers?

As for me and my house, we will serve the Lord Jesus Christ!

- and we hope you do, too.

28 February 2001

APPENDIX

If you read Book 3 **"Walking in Victory"** you may remember the Epilogue in which I expressed the view that this Book 4 (the intended title of which was **"Discerning Human Nature"**) will be for many *"the most penetrating book, outside of the Bible, they have ever read "and make sure you get or borrow a copy".* Well, here it is!

Regrettably much criticism of past Church leadership is necessary, but I hope it is constructive and will encourage true repentance and Godly change for the blessing of God's people - leaders/shepherds and sheep.

Please remember at all times that the motive for this book is NOT to tear down the good, or dishearten the saints but to bring an unprecedented level of repentance, change, true discipleship and Christlikeness, as we approach the end of the Church Age, and the coming of the Bridegroom.

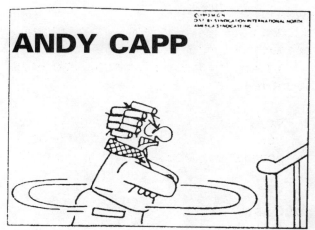

CONTENTS

BOOK 4 WE ALL HAVE OUR DEMONS!

INTRODUCTION

LEVELS OF DEMONISATION ON THE RISE

I don't think there will be any doubt amongst Christians in the Holy Spirit Renewal movement that the levels of demonisation throughout the nations are rising rapidly, especially amongst the one-time Christian nations.

Once upon a time, just after World War II, Australians looked forward to peace and happiness. The sky was blue, the beaches clean, as people recovered from the hurts and ravages of war. Young people everywhere looked good - straight-limbed, clear-eyed, full of laughter and hope. And why not, with good wages and job prospects and the sun shining?

However, by 1993 we saw the ravages of another problem on every side. Drugs, sexual licentiousness, occult pursuits, unemployment, disease and pollution of the creation etc. have produced an unbelievable ugliness of soul and mind reflected by mental and emotional illnesses, violent crimes, unmarried mothers and their fatherless children.

Ask anyone dealing with the public. Ask transport drivers and door-to-door salesmen, ask nurses helping hospital patients, the policeman on the beat, Post Office staff, store check-out girls etc., what they really think of the behaviour of the general public today.

Even Hollywood can't find good-looking, fresh-faced, clean "stars" anymore. So many of the new leading men have brutal faces and the leading ladies have snaky eyes. Where are the Robert Taylors and Olivia de Havilands of yesteryear? Consequently film stars today remain romantic leads into their fifties, because "beautiful" new stars are very hard to find.

This increase in the level of demonisation in the West has been mainly caused by the **entertainment industry** promoting non-Christian ideals, and **Universities** which produce articulate humanists who have found their vocation in **politics** and in the **media** (print, television and radio) where the real power in a democracy lies. Consequently humanists (who believe there is no God for man to answer to, so man is God) have been able to paint glorious and rosy pictures of the future, for mankind to look towards while doing its own thing.

They do not know they are under a curse (Jer. 17:5-6) and they themselves are slaves to sin (2 Pet.2:17-19, John 8:34) so that all their glorious pipe-dreams will turn to ashes.

It is the same kind of deception with which the communists were duped for 70 years until the Soviet empire collapsed under the weight of its own foolishness, for does not the word of God say **"The fool has said in his heart, 'there is no God'"** (Psalm l4:l, 53:1)? It is well known that the Soviets taught "scientific atheism" through their schools for years.

It is established in the Word of God that the activities of demons are as follows:

SIN

Gen. 4:7 (lit.)	Matt. 12:38-45	(Are you free
1 Kings 22:19-23	Eph. 2:2, 6:12	from sin?)
Hosea 3:4, 4:12	Rev. 18:2-5	

FALSE TEACHING

Acts 13:8-10	James 3:14-16	(Know anyone
2 Cor. 11:3-4	1 John 4:1-3	whose teaching is
1 Tim. 4:1-2		perfect?)

DECEIVING MIRACLES

Matt. 24:24	2 Thess. 2:1-10
Acts 16:16	

CORRUPTION OF WORSHIP

Lev. 17:7	1 Cor. 10:20-21	(See chapter 3)
Deut. 32:17	Gal. 4:3-9	
Ps. 106:36-38	Rev. 9:20	

SICKNESS (Physical and Mental)

Luke 8:35	Matt. 12:22	(Wow! What a
Luke 9:39	(cf. Matt. 9:32-33, 17:15	minefield!
Luke 13:11	Mark. 5:4-5, 9:17-25)	see 1.3)

While it is true there are many good and wonderful things happening in the Holy Spirit Renewal movement, it is unfortunately also true that OUTSIDE of this move of God, the world, and those sections of the Churches which are chained to tradition and/or their own comfort are sinking under the weight of demonic attack - sin, sickness, false teaching and worship with mind and form, rather than operating by the alive (human) spirit aided by the Holy Spirit (John 4:24).

Perhaps the most important single message of this book is to show **the Bible teaches you can get a demon out of ANYONE.** Or perhaps I should phrase it the other way around. By "you" I mean any deliverance minister (i.e. Christian "exorcist" in popular language) can find a demon or unclean spirit in ANY living human being, and if they can find (discern) it, they have authority in the mighty Name of Jesus to bind or to loose it.

I want to say in the plainest possible way that the Bible teaches this truth. It is not discoverable by men through scientific observation alone because scientific experiments still require interpretation of the evidence and men can only interpret data or information according to the limits of their finite, natural, polluted minds. The **reincarnation of the human spirit** theory is a classic example of this. It is only when we bring the truth of God's Word to bear on the reincarnation evidence that we can see how the reincarnationist has been deceived through lack of the knowledge of the truth of God's Word and thereby misinterprets the evidence available from various case histories and experiments. We will be looking at the reincarnation deception closely in chapter 6.

EASY WAYS TO INCREASE OUR DEMONISATION

This is probably the easiest thing in the world to do. I know of nothing so easy as to increase the level of my personal demonisation; all I have to do is what comes naturally, pursuing *the lust of the FLESH, the lust of the EYES and the PRIDE of life* by living a WORLDLY life (1 John 2:16).

If I ignore Christ's teachings and that of the Apostles, all of which carry the MORAL LAW of God from the Old Testament into the New Testament, for today, I will just get spiritually sicker and sicker, and physically sick also.

SEX

Let me illustrate from the LUSTS of the FLESH, and in particular SEXUAL lust. The New Testament plainly teaches that human beings are to *"abstain from fleshly lusts which war against the soul"* (1 Peter 2:11). Did you understand that powerful message? FLESHLY LUSTS hurt your SOUL, that is, your feelings and emotions, your inner well-being, the hidden YOU! This is where we know love and hate, fear and lust, anger and pleasure. We know that SIN (which is a SPIRITUAL disease) dwells in the flesh (Rom. 8:3) and no good (spiritual) thing dwells in the flesh (Rom. 7:18). Our soul is our area of SPIRITUAL activity (James 3:15) and is located IN our flesh (Rom. 8:3, 1 Peter 2:11), in our bloodstream, to be more precise (Lev. 17:11,14 lit. Hebrew), which includes our mind, heart, nervous system, stomach, bowels and bladder etc..

When we are joined together with someone in sexual intercourse we become ONE (body, flesh) with them, bound and fused together as one unit. It is probably unnecessary for me to add that at such times the transference of unclean spirits from body to body, soul to soul, is the easiest thing in the world - with the flow usually from the more heavily demonised person to the one less polluted.

Some lustful men are so stupid that when they see a mentally retarded or drug damaged woman they set about sexually assaulting her, thinking that with such a helpless victim no one will understand her or believe her if she complains.

But as the Bible says *"Be sure your sins will find you out"* (Num. 32:23) and the penalty is extremely great as unclean spirits flood into the attacker from the afflicted woman. The one-flesh sexual unity makes demonic transferences so easy during immoral or evil conduct. (cf.1 Cor. 6:16)

It's true. The transfer of demons from soul to soul is often effected during lustful (unclean) behaviour and **any type of fornication is an open invitation to the powers of darkness to enter our soul** and to twist us up emotionally and spiritually.

God did not set His moral laws in place for (His) fun, or to be a spoil-sport, but in order to protect YOU, His precious creation, from the attention of your spiritual enemies. (Deut. 10:13, cf. Rom. 8:28).

This is the main reason people usually reject those who have had a lot of sexual experience from being potential lifelong partners. There are exceptions, of course, amongst those who are already heavily demonised, but people with extensive sexual histories usually experience rejection and loneliness. **Each different sexual contact reduces our ability to form a one-flesh unity as God intended.** The apostle Paul warns us that *"... he who joins himself to a prostitute becomes one body with her. For as it is written, The two shall become one flesh"*. (1 Cor. 6:16). If that is true with a prostitute then it is true for all.

This means a man can become one-flesh with many women but, of course, the cumulative effect of such conduct is to weaken and DESTROY the unity that God desires for a man and woman. It is designed to be a PERMANENT ONE-flesh unity - not a collective string of half-baked relationships linked together by sexual gratification - and unclean, demonic linking of lust and animal spirits at that![1]

---

1. It is not our purpose here to discuss the wide range of behavioural causes of society's ills. Our publication **"Sex, Demons and Morality"** does, however, attempt this in relation to sexual behaviour.

GLUTTONY

I am sure I don't have to remind you that the FIRST lust of the flesh with which the human race was tempted was - FOOD! (Gen. 3:6). What I am not sure about is whether Eve and then Adam were tempted with food because it is a more powerful, continuous human need than sexual activity, or because there were no other human beings around with which Eve or Adam could indulge in "hanky panky" (sexual games).

The Gluttony spirit causes all sorts of physical infirmity and is so easy to increase, like your weight!

DRUGS

John Phillips, founder of the **Mammas and the Pappa's** rock group explains in a television documentary:

> *"I was just a mess, you know. It's funny how drugs turn all your priorities upside down, especially heroin - er, narcotics.*
>
> *The things that you feel are really important in life, your family and your job, the relationship with your fellow man, cleanliness and truthfulness, and all the boy scout virtues and everything else get turned upside down.*
>
> *The first thing you think about is "scoring" and you don't care who you have to screw to do it.*
>
> *I guess if I hadn't been arrested in 1980 we wouldn't be here today, talking, because I was really on my final legs - I was just a mess ....!"*

Illegal drugs are, of course, a huge source of **mind and personality altering** experience today, because taking them invariably and often dramatically increases a person's level of demonisation. Although some such drugs may be used medically under clinical conditions, their social use is illegal because "wrong" and over-use is very dangerous. Let us be clear that mind-altering occurs when unclean spirits enter the soul and take over control, and they do not care whether their entry has been achieved by illegal or legal drugs.

Social addictions such as alcohol and nicotine are also very destructive and spiritually inspired. The **Salvation Army** have it right when they preach against **"The Demon Drink!"** We repeat the message of the Word of God - **"abstain from fleshly lusts which war against the SOUL"**

To the world, Phillips was a musical genius. When he died in March, aged 65, he was lauded by obituary writers as one of the original creators of the flower-power generation, a legend who wrote such classics as *California Dreamin'*, *Monday, Monday and San Francisco (Be Sure To Wear Some Flowers In Your Hair)*.

ACCIDENTS AND VIOLENCE

Physical damage caused by road, sport and workplace accidents and incidents of physical violence can also cause changes in personality for the same reasons expressed above. Doctors may diagnose brain damage but why does damage to the brain often affect personality? We can understand it affecting mental performance, memory and even physical skills, but why do some "sweet" people become profane or blasphemous or violent - or just plain ugly??

There has been a take-over, and it's not just a matter of pain or malfunctioning of flesh, ligaments and their skeletal frame.

THE OCCULT

Occult activity, of course, is a major source of (increased) demonisation. Because it practises FAITH in the WRONG SOURCES, the demons involved will create UNBELIEF in the RIGHT SOURCES, that is, in the Bible and its revelation of our Father God, His only begotten Son Jesus, and the Holy Spirit. When someone has trouble believing the main truths of the Bible you can be sure there is a spirit of unbelief in residence, and probably because of earlier occult interests, perhaps ancestrally.

The dangers of promoting the Occult can be gauged from the effect of a number of new television shows featuring witches and unclean supernatural activity is having on teenagers. A survey conducted by *Western Sydney University* and commissioned by the *Australian Broadcasting Authority* shows that ***"girls are taking television programs such as Buffy the Vampire Slayer so seriously that they are forming witches covens in schools".***

"Charmed" and *"Angel"* were reported to be two other influential programs in this trend. "Charmed," of course, promotes witchcraft. It may be that "Buffy ...." and "Angel" are intended to depict the victory of good over evil, but according to the report Professor Nightingale was astonished how seriously girls took all such programs, and the article implies the major interest is in the evil side.

While this trend may cause widespread damage to those who WATCH this kind of "entertainment" we should not forget the curse that comes upon those who participate in its production, unless they get things VERY right!

It is one thing to be a part of a show which presents evil as evil. It is altogether another thing to present evil as funny or good. Did not the prophet **Isaiah**, speaking for the Lord, declare:

> ***Woe to those who call evil good, and good evil; Who put darkness for light, and light for darkness. (Isaiah 5:20).***

If you doubt the Almighty, the everlasting God HATES occult practice[2], just read Deut. 18:9-13!

It seems that each actor who has played **Superman** on film, a kind of substitute Christ (anti-Christ) to whom mankind can turn to save them when all human help fails, has suffered tragically. In recent times it has been **Christopher Reeves**, bound to a wheel-chair after a tragic fall from a horse.

Superman? I believe Christopher's role as Superman opened the door to evil attack. The other actor known to me was also named Reeves. **George Reeves** died from a gunshot wound, adjudged to be self-inflicted, in 1959. Thirty years later **Lenore Lemmon,** his girl-friend at the time of his death, has gone on record as saying, **"What made him commit suicide was "Superman". It's as simple as that!"**

Everybody needs a Saviour at some time in their life. With Christ Jesus it requires a whole new start with God, involving change. With the anti-Christ **Superman** (or **Hulk** or **Spiderman** etc.) the fantasy is that of a Saviour who requires nothing from us - so we can continue in our rebellion against God and His ways. Are you getting the message?

---

2. See also Book 1 **"Make Yourselves Ready"** Chapter 1.3 (i)

PEARLY GATES

EVERYONE WANTS TO LIVE LONG, BUT NO ONE WANTS TO BE OLD...

NO ONE LIKES THE STIFLING HEAT, BUT WHO WANTS THE BITTER COLD?..

MOST PEOPLE WANT TO BE HAPPY, YET FEW ARE SEEN WITH A GRIN...

EVERYONE WANTS SALVATION... AS LONG AS THEY STILL CAN SIN!

By kind permission of Ian Jones, Pearly Gates Promotions
Email: pgp@interworx.com.au

So also **Elisabeth Montgomery** played a "good" witch in *"Bewitched"* and became an early cancer victim. Her co-star **Dick York** also suffered serious infirmity while playing opposite her and died before she did.

Bill Bixby played *"The Hulk"*, another supernatural super hero, and also died early of cancer. Likewise **Carolyn Jones** of *"The Addams Family"* died very early and had to be replaced, while **Sharon Tate** was murdered by **Charles Manson's** group after she starred in *"The Fearless Vampire Killers"*.

All the above is only from my memory banks and Hollywood documentaries. I feel sure that if someone were to do thorough research on this disastrous trend much more information and confirmation would result.

We close this little section with a reminder of Moses' exhortation:

"... keep the Commandments of the Lord, and His Statutes which I am commanding you today

FOR YOUR GOOD!" (Deut. 10:13)

It is important to realise that people often engage in occult activity without realising they are doing so. For example HYPNOSIS is condemned as **"charming"** (Deut. 18:11), whether it is practised by entertainers, amateurs or those involved in mental health therapy. It is probably responsible for many false Recovered (or Repressed) Memory Syndrome (R.M.S.) cases.

Modern Western societies are riddled with hypnotic influences such as rock music (drums) and media saturation of the average home. The old saying "If you repeat a lie often enough it will be believed" is proving true every day. Lying spirits (1 Kings 22:22-23) are everywhere and hypnosis, indeed ALL occult activity, is about deception and unbelief.

PROFANE (FOUL) SPEECH

Reproduced by kind permission of Planet Media

The following newspaper report[3] is of great interest, not only because it identifies chronic swearing as *"Tourette's Syndrome,"* but also because it spells out that some people cannot control their speech. Why?

Any unclean spirit which takes over human beings and controls their actions, whether it be a spirit of *profanity* or *anger* or *panic*, can safely be called a CONTROL spirit - what the Word of God calls a ruler or authority (1 Cor. 2:8, Eph 6:12).

---

3. Daily Mirror 22 Feb 1990

And although the article quotes a psychiatrist as saying there is no cure, praise the Lord we know better:

> *"A woman who can't stop swearing has been found a new home after neighbours petitioned to have her evicted.*
> *Carmen Ferrolla suffers from a disorder which makes her swear uncontrollably.*
> *As she spoke about her 20-year ordeal with the disorder, termed Tourette's Syndrome, she suddenly broke into a tirade of swearing.*
> *"It has been hard ...., I'm a .... - sorry. I can't help it." She said.*
> *"It will be hard leaving here." She said, "But the house has new furniture."*
> *Then she inexplicably shouted: "Bitch, ... "*
> *But no matter where she lives, like the one in 3000 other Australians who suffer from the disorder, Carmen can only expect loneliness and sadness.*
> *She has battled the rare disorder since she was 14.*
> *Dr Preminda Sachdev, of Prince Henry Hospital's Neuro Psychiatric Unit, who treats Carmen, said there was very little which could be done to stop the continual outbursts.*
> *"There is no cure ..."*

Probably the easiest way of all to increase our demonisation is to deliberately cultivate foul language. As the Lord Jesus said, **"The mouth speaks out of the abundance (fullness) of the heart"** (Matt. 12:34).

As we use foul language our heart is entered and re-filled continuously with spiritual pollution, so that speaking profanity becomes easier and easier, until we no longer realise how ugly we sound and lose all sense of guilt concerning our speech.

Indeed some of us cultivate profanity in order to become more acceptable to others. As a young man in the Citizens Military Forces in Australia some 50 years ago I (stupidly) made a point of learning to swear a little so as to fit in with all the other young men in my Artillery Regiment. As one young corporal put it, "A little bit of bulls ..... goes a long way". He seemed to have a point (at the time) but the price was really too high. It took me years to realise the unclean spiritual inspiration behind "colourful" language and how I had yielded my heart to unclean control; and even more years to get rid of the bastards. (I use that word in the literal, spiritual and scriptural sense, not in the profane sense - Heb. 12:8 - to describe unclean spirits which were once sons of God but had defected to become children of the devil - Job. 1:6, 2:1, Rev. 12:7-9, 1 John 3:10).

See also **"spirit of blasphemy"** in chapter 1.

CORRECTING TRADITIONAL ERRORS

For twenty years or more people, including fine, mature, Christian teachers have been pouring polite scorn on the notion that anyone outside of a small, poor, disadvantaged minority of our civilised culture could possibly have a demon. Large sections of the Christian church have taught, and still teach, that a Christian CANNOT have a demon. It would be nice if it were true, but unfortunately it is not true. Indeed this teaching is probably the single most destructive teaching in the church today because

(i)   it means that every demon within a Christian is safe from exposure and "free" to carry out Satan's missions without serious or effective warfare being waged against it. No wonder some churches are in such a mess.

(ii)   This teaching prevents a Christian from correctly diagnosing the source of his or her problems.

(iii) It therefore prevents the application of Christ's solution to the problem.

(iv)   The Christian is thus hindered from fulfilling the high calling the Lord has placed on their life and can never truly take their place in the Lord's army as He intended.

(v)   The promised Victory Life can never be attained because the enemy has a foothold, or perhaps much more than a foothold, within the human soul.

(vi)   The command of the Word of God to Christians to be cleansed and purified INWARDLY can never be obeyed or achieved (2 Cor. 3:18, 7:1, 2 Tim. 2:21-22, James 4:8, 1 John 3:2-3, cf. Matt. 5:8.)

(vii) It follows from this that the Christian's place in the five (5) wise maidens (Matt. 25:1-13) is greatly at risk!

This book is all about presenting the evidence to you in support of the major revelation that **the Bible teaches EVERY human being has indwelling unclean spirits,** and God's will and solution for you in this matter. There is no need to be frightened by this for the Bible says that we, our human spirits, have authority over them, and because we Christians have the Holy Spirit indwelling us we also have the Lord's POWER to bring against them for their removal.

It is strange, but true, many Christians have no difficulty in accepting that every human heart carries the disease of SIN (Rom. 7:20-23) but cannot accept that every human heart carries unclean spirits.

Even evangelicals have settled for a fairly innocuous interpretation of the disease of sin, whereas we have a very powerful definition at the first mention of sin in the Bible. "**Sin is a demon lurking** ..." (Gen. 4:7 lit.), which definition we will be looking at more closely in chapter 5.

Others deny the existence of sin as a disease of the human heart, teaching that all men are basically good, yet others water it down to external behaviour only, even though the great **apostle Paul** tells us that it dwells within him (Rom. 7:17,20,23,25).

> **The Oxford dictionary of the Christian church** tells us that *"Since the end of the 17th century there has been little further development of the doctrine of sin... More recently the recognition of demonic forces in contemporary civilisation has led to a renewed theological emphasis on the gravity of sin..."* (page 1260).

For nineteen centuries now the Christian church has blamed most human shortcomings and moral failures on **sin** and **the flesh.** That is not wrong because this is what the Bible seems to do. It is just that having recognised the source of human problems as sin and the flesh we have not bothered to look any closer at what "sin" or "the flesh" means, nor have we tried to peel back the cloak of mystery and examine where and how demonisation slots into the scheme of things: For example what is the relationship between:

> sin and the flesh?
> sin and demons?
> **flesh and demons?**

and how do we know what source to blame for our failures? We will be presenting a simple explanation to all these questions. Indeed I propose to show from the Word of God that the disease of SIN is in reality a nest of unclean spirits whose ruler is sometimes described as **the old man,** or **the strong man,** and even **the man of sin.** If you feel shock waves blowing your mind at this point please remember that we live in the End-Time period and time is running out for this Age. The Heaven and the earth are being shaken by Almighty God and that includes you and me. Please keep an open mind and test everything in this book with the Word of God.

CHANGE YOUR CHURCH !?

Nearly 30 years ago I heard a fiery Pentecostal preacher telling his flock that it was time for all Christians who truly loved the Lord to leave their historic churches and denominations and move into Pentecost.

"**Come ye out from among them**", he thundered, "**and be ye separate, says the Lord.**" (2 Cor. 6:17). At the time I was just getting into Renewal and thought he was a little premature. I hoped, like many, many others, to bring renewal to the whole body of Christ as it was then, and God's purposes have certainly been served by this. Many people in historic churches have been touched by the Holy Spirit and sometimes whole congregations have been blessed.

However, the sad truth is that the power brokers and others in hierarchal leadership have generally permitted a minimum of change - enough to encourage the faithful and keep them hoping for more, when in fact they have applied the political religious cork to the bottleneck and have no intentions of letting any more spiritual fizz or life into their churches.

I have been disappointed to see the spirit of deception at work here. Many a time I have noted an historic church minister's reaction as the Holy Spirit sought to break out in Renewal for his flock. It goes something like this:

Step

1. He resists Renewal and preaches against it because it cuts across his traditions, and Christians in Renewal make so many mistakes!

2. After a short period of attempted adjustments by both sides, those who have been touched by the Holy Spirit leave to join a Pentecostal style church. This can leave quite a gap in his church's workforce.

3. Over a period of time the minister sees his flock diminishing and gets desperate to (i) stop the drain away to Pentecost, and (ii) have departures replaced by newcomers.

4. The minister begins to make Renewal gestures and noises. He brings in some worship music from the movement, with guitars and keyboard ("That seems safe"). He talks about the Holy Spirit but always points out the dangers of "going overboard", which can be quite a fair criticism but can also cloak negativity.

5. He introduces healing prayer, perhaps once a month (God help the sick who may have to wait for the set day to come around!).

6. With Renewal music, his healing line and his messages on the Holy Spirit he is now thought of as a Charismatic by some of his patient and trusting flock, who believe their church is on the move. He keeps some of his young people and he holds his loyal senior people. He keeps his hierarchy happy. All seems well.

There are just a few little things wrong with all of that. He is a fraud. He has no intention of moving ahead with the Spirit of God. He is giving his people false hope under false pretences. God knows his heart and that he is motivated, not by seeking the perfect will of God for himself and his people but by numerical and financial survival. He is still a traditionalist and a boot-licker of the men who run the system and not a true servant of the Lord. The demise of his congregation seems to have been averted, but it is really only temporary. The Lord will not leave that flock under that shepherd for long. Other assemblies with apostolic vision and power will soon be birthed nearby and God's hungry people shall be satisfied (Ps. 63:5, Matt. 5:6).

How do you know who is a counterfeit or fraudulent charismatic minister?

There are probably many ways but I can suggest three indicators that may help:

(i)   He allows worship songs to be sung only once. Genuine charismatics know that people have to stop singing with their heads and begin worshipping with their (human) spirits (John 4:24). This usually involves singing a worship song more than once - perhaps several times - as the WORDS sink into the spirit. Many with **intellectual** faith find this quite difficult, even irritating.

(ii) He never gives the REAL Head of the Church the opportunity to break into the meeting with a Word of prophecy for His people.

(iii) He is not interested in having deliverance ministry in his assembly, notwithstanding the Word of God's command to Christians to be cleansed (2 Cor. 7:1, James 4:8 etc.). Somehow he reads the words *"psychiatrist"*, *medicine* and *"drugs"* into the New Testament - a strange miracle indeed!

Change your church? Long ago I would have said not to change your church unless you really felt a strong leading to do so, but now, when most churches have had many opportunities to move with God, I would say:

"If you can't change your church - change your church!"

- especially if your Pastor/Minister/Priest continues to believe, and persists in believing, against ALL the evidence, that a Christian cannot have a demon.

"'My people are destroyed for lack of knowledge' says the Lord" (Hosea 4:6), and the good Lord knows that we are going to need ALL His gifts and graces in order to survive and emerge victorious from the spiritual warfare that lies ahead.

The devil knows if he can persuade Christians nothing unclean dwells within them (notwithstanding the apostle Paul's testimony that *no good thing dwelt within him, his flesh* - Rom. 7:18) then those unfortunates will not set about cleansing themselves (2 Cor. 7:1) nor make themselves ready (Rev. 19:7) for the Bridegroom.

If these Christians are still alive on earth when the Trumpet blows (1 Thes. 4:16-17) then they are in real trouble. Unfortunately half the nominal "membership" of the Body of Christ will be caught in this position (Matt. 25:1-13), but we hope and pray - not you!

It will not be good enough to say "Lord, we didn't know!" - because He will say *"Friend, you didn't listen, you were lukewarm (Rev. 3:16), you ran out of the oil of the Holy Spirit (Matt. 25:6-9), you presumed on the Grace of God (Num. 15:30-31, Psalm 19:13), and although you made a good start you did not bear much fruit (Mark 4:3-20) and were not truly my disciple (John 8:31-32). You did NOT continue in my Word but set your heart stubbornly in your traditions (Mark 7:6-9). Depart from Me..."*

If your spiritual leaders are blind to the Renewal of the Holy Spirit, if they are blind to the salvation NOW being revealed in the last time (1 Peter 1:5), AND you have sincerely and fervently prayed (James 5:16b) for their eyes to be opened (2 Kings 6:15-17) - without success, then it is TIME TO CHANGE YOUR CHURCH.

You do not have much time in which to put your own house and affairs in order with the Lord. Get into a cleansing program as quickly as possible, even if you have to begin one in your own home. You cannot afford to miss out on God's great RESTORATION PROGRAM.

DISCERNMENT

I have tried to present at least 75% new material in every book we have published. Obviously some Biblical information and revelation is common and important to several deliverance topics, but to the best of my knowledge I have only rarely included the same material in three (3) different titles - and only where to omit such material would have left the text unbalanced and seriously impaired.

Likewise this book, although being the fourth in a series on how to cast out demons, stands on its own, with some material utilised from **"Your Full Salvation"** and **"End-Time Deliverance"**. Obviously some fundamentals in the exercise of the gift of discerning of spirits (1 Cor. 12:10) have already been covered by the first three books in this series on **Christian Deliverance**[4] and it would not be appropriate to go over so much material again.

---

4. See Apendix A

However I would judge that at least 80% of the material produced in this book has not been presented in our other publications.

Any similarities with books on the subject of Deliverance by other authors is purely by the sovereignty of the Holy Spirit. I have deliberately only glanced at other publications so that I might be completely UNINFLUENCED in the area of discernment and give you a fresh view on this vital End-Time weapon. However I am glad to acknowledge the encouragement received from **Dr Derek Prince's** earlier booklets and tapes in the very beginning, more than twenty five years ago, and *the enormous input by my wife* **Verlie** *over the past eighteen years.*

Are you **fully** committed to the Lord Jesus Christ? Are you prepared to be shaken - to be picked up by the Holy Spirit by your collar and tail and shaken until all your traditions, your self-importance, your pet-theories, your unclean habits and practices, indeed ALL your SIN has been shaken free and fallen to the ground? Are you prepared to follow where He leads you? Mentally? Geographically? Spiritually? To become a child? (Matt. 18:1-4)

If so, then I ask you to consider the evidence contained in this book without prejudice. Begin at the beginning with an open and teachable heart and try to put out of your mind all pre-suppositions and traditional doctrine. I have no doubt that some readers will manifest uncleanness while reading this book - anger, unbelief, mockery etc., and others will not only manifest but also get "spirit releases" as something unclean takes fright and departs.

But there is no need for any Christian to fear. Jesus is Lord. Jesus is Lord of YOUR life, your heart, your soul, your mind, your body. Just make sure that you overcome the anger, the unbelief, the mockery etc., and that your heart is submitted to Him (James 4:7) and you can only receive blessing. Trust Him - now, and throughout your studies here.

This book is about the most basic problems that have troubled mankind since Adam and Eve. It is about overthrowing SIN and DEATH, the hereditary spiritual diseases within each one of us.

I hope you enjoy this book, but more than that, I pray the Spirit of God will sweep away the veils from over all our eyes that we may SEE, and having hearts set on fire, and clothed with spiritual armour, achieve the mission or vision that each one of us has received from the Throne of God.

CHAPTER 1

WHAT ON EARTH HAS GOT IN TO US?

1.1 OPENING A CAN OF WORMS

Have you ever opened a can of tinned food and found in it a seething mass of maggots and worms. It happened to me once, and that is enough!

I believe this to be an accurate description of the human soul. The **apostle James** tells that **earthly wisdom,** which you and I share with our families, friends and acquaintances every day, **is "soulish and demonic"** (James 3:15).

Even when human behaviour reaches its lowest, beastial, cruel level, we only ever see the tip of the ice-berg in daily life. It requires the Word of God to reveal to us the true wickedness of the human heart. As the **prophet Jeremiah** declared:

> **"The heart is deceitful above all and desperately wicked. Who can know it?"**

> Jeremiah goes on to tell us in the Lord's Name:

"I the Lord search the heart ..." Only He who made us is able to know what a can of worms we are, but we can get a good idea of the real situation when we look around us and see the enormous range of demonic activity.

There is violence, fear, illicit sex, perverted sex, selfishness, crime, profanity, blasphemy, sickness (emotional, mental, physical), disease, disobedience, occultism, drugs (social, religious, medical), lies, domination, gluttony, greed, murder etc.

Some people may think that describing the human soul as a can of worms is too harsh, even untrue, but **the Lord Jesus** Himself describes the fallen human spirit (dead in trespasses and sin - Eph. 2:l) as a **worm** (Mark 9: 44,46,48) and **John the Baptist** describes his listeners as **snakes** (Luke 3:7) - so take your pick.

TACKLE THE RULERS

When I first began to cast out demons on a regular basis (back in 1973) I was both very excited about the ease with which most of them came out, and also perturbed about how many there seemed to be, even of one kind or type (name).

I began to keep lists, counting each spirit that left (yawn, cough, etc.) by putting strokes on a pad. I ended up with large lists of names and high numbers of unclean spirits which I was most uneasy about showing to other clergy or those in leadership, because I myself found them hard to believe.

I offered such details, so painstakingly gathered over twelve months or more, to some of my church leaders and was quite relieved when they showed no interest.

Years later I discovered that other deliverance ministers had also made long lists of names of the types of spirits they had encountered. **Frank and Ida Mae Hammond,** who wrote *"Pigs in the Parlour"*, came out with a comprehensive list of groupings each under a sub-ruler, and other top deliverance ministers and authors known to me, such as **Bill Banks,** did the same thing, quite independently. Most deliverance books published expose certain spirits revealed to the writer by the grace of God and there are many major revelations, such as the Hammond's revelation of the complexity of the kingdom of *schizophrenia.*

All of these revelations of the enemy have been mightily helpful, praise the Lord, but if we continuously pursue this kind of exercise, pressing for more and more revelation beyond which the Lord deems necessary, we will (as mentioned in Book 1) end up with a list as long as the telephone book, and just as boring.

These huge lists of unclean names will also drive ministers to despair of the heavy workload involved with just one sufferer (let alone a whole assembly) and discourage their perseverance until victory.

So what do we do? We sit down and think. We plan a campaign, appropriating the wisdom of Christ Jesus as Commander of the Lord of Hosts (Joshua 5:13-15).

We realise the enemy is an army and that the kingdoms of sin and death within the human heart (I hope you will not remain in doubt about this, after all the evidence I will give you from the Word of God) are made up of many divisions, regiments, battalions and smaller units (squads, patrols).

We realise that when we begin ministering deliverance against this spiritual army we are not going to come up against the rulers and authorities quickly, even if we name them. **Before we can defeat a general we have to defeat his army**.

If we name the general (ruler) he will send out his army to do battle for him, and they will be the first to go.

It is like any other war, a war of attrition. The officers will fight to their last man (spirit) and the general will fight to his last officer (spirit). If you only attack the infantry, you will need continuous and complex discernment forever, but if you name the general, he will send out his army ahead of him, hoping to divert or weary you long before he has to come forth out of his hidden concrete bunker (cf. Hitler).

So, **away with long lists**. They have been useful in exposing the complexity of the human condition and the range of spirits polluting the world, but we don't need them any more.

What we need is the names of the enemy's generals (rulers) in every human heart seeking the cleansing of Christ.

A great gift of sharp discernment is not so necessary if we know the basic composition (make-up) of the kingdoms of sin and death.

These basic kingdoms and their generals/rulers are very similar for EVERYBODY (e.g. fear, infirmity, lust etc.) but obviously in widely different MEASURES.

I believe the Bible reveals these generals. All we have to do is to study the character of the devil in the Word of God (Gen. 3:1-6, Isa. 14:12-17 etc.) and a few other very special sections (Matt. 12:22-45, Rom. 1:18-32, the five key deliverances in the New Testament and the lists of deadly sin, (e.g. Mark 7:21-23, 1 Cor. 6:9-10) in order to have a very good idea. These, and perhaps other texts, will give us the devil's character, and **the character of his rulers.**

We can thank the Pharisees and Sadduccees for revealing to us the nature of **self-righteous and religious spirits** which we will be looking at soon.

Only when the general within the human heart has lost all his army can he (the strong man, the old man, the man of sin) be removed. There is a picture of this once powerful figure, who has lost it all, painted for us in **Isaiah:**

> **"Those who see you will gaze at you, and consider you, saying: 'Is this the man who made the earth tremble, who shook kingdoms, who made the world as a wilderness and destroyed its cities, and did not open the house of his prisoners?"**
>
> **(Isaiah 14:16-17).**

How the mighty have fallen - praise the Lord!

Conclusion? Go for the rulers and authorities, and you will get them all.

1.2 SPIRIT OF FEAR

The amount of spiritual pollution in the human soul is mind-blowing. Let us consider FEAR for a moment. A psychiatrist could probably give you a list of different types of fears (phobias) as long as your arm. Fear of heights, fear of water etc. etc. are all part of our **spiritual** problems because the Word of God tells us that **fear is a spirit** (2 Tim. 1:7). Indeed we are told that when you became a Christian **you did not receive a spirit to AGAIN make you a slave to fear** (Rom. 8:15). This suggests that we have ALL been demonised with a spirit of fear BEFORE our conversion to Christ. However the receiving of God's Spirit of adoption, that is, the Spirit of God or Christ (v.9), should release us from a large measure of our various fears as we enjoy reconciliation with our heavenly Father.

Is there anyone you know who has not suffered from spirits of fear and infirmity in one form or another? Is there anyone you know who does not suffer from at least one of these spirits right now?

The following are the preaching notes from a message preached by one of our Deacons, **Eric Etienne:**

FEAR: *(Oxford Dictionary): An unpleasant emotion caused by exposure to danger, expectation of pain, a state of alarm (be in fear), feel fear about/ towards (a person or thing) feel anxiety or apprehension about, cause to hesitate, to shrink from fear.*

Results of **FEAR:** Fear creates: NEGATIVITY, INDECISION, INFIRMITY, WORTHLESSNESS, RESENTMENT, HURT, SADNESS, LONELINESS, FRUSTRATION, BITTERNESS, UNBELIEF, MISERY, GRUDGES, MIGRAINES, INSOMNIA.

OVERCOMERS enjoy: **PEACE, JOY, HAPPINESS.**
PHOBIAS:

CLAUSTROPHOBIA	- Fear of Confined Spaces
AGORAPHOBIA	- Fear of Open Spaces, Public Places
AEROPHOBIA	- Fear of Flying
ACROPHOBIA	- Fear of Heights
PYROPHOBIA	- Fear of Fire

ALGOPHOBIA - Fear of Pain
AQUAPHOBIA - Fear of Water
AUTOPHOBIA - Fear of motor vehicles (accidents)
NYCTOPHOBIA - Fear of the night (Darkness)
ASTROPHOBIA - Fear of Celestial Bodies
XENOPHOBIA - Hatred or Fear of Foreigners
HOMOPHOBIA - Hatred or Fear of Homosexuals
THANTOPHOBIA - Fear of Death
TECHNOPHOBIA - Fear of Technology

COMMON EVERY DAY SAYINGS REGARDING FEAR;

Fear and Trembling, Panic attack, Press the panic button,
Quake with fright, Tremble with Fright, Fear for one's life,
Frightened to death, Scared out of one's wits, Change colour with fright
Go white as a sheet, Turn ashen, Cower with fright.
Be horrified, terrified, Shrink with fear, Get cold feet,
Rooted to the spot with terror/fear, Feel one's hair stand on end,
Be on edge, Have second thoughts,
Scared half to death.

In addition, although I have met men who claimed to have no fear, I think it is true to say that they were not aware of the truth when saying they were afraid of nothing at all, but they know no fear of the things that most people are afraid of such as heights, storms at sea, sharks, alligators, lions and death.
Fear is the opposite to, and the enemy of, FAITH!

FEAR OF THE CHURCH

One hidden fear that must be revealed, even though it would seem to be "church-bashing" is "**fear of the church**". It is unfortunately true that discipline exercised over young children and students by some sections of the Body of Christ in the past far exceeded what we think of today as "tough love". Indeed at times there was no love in it at all, but pure sadism and cruelty which was enjoyed by the perpetrators.

This often created a fear and dread in the students and a literal holding of the breath. As the spirit of fear entered the soul and built up into a sizeable kingdom, the student would develop breathing problems, the true cause of which would escape diagnosis.

The result? Later in life even slight anxiety could produce panic attacks resulting in emphysema and even asthma attacks.

The solution? Correct spiritual diagnosis and total removal of spirits of *"fear of the church"* by means of the Lord's deliverance ministry. This also frees up the student theologically and promotes the pursuit of true Christianity rather than a fearful and blind acceptance of traditions.[1]

The **fear of the church (organisation, run by sinful men)** must not be confused with **the fear of the Lord.** A major reason why western developed nations are running into social and economic chaos is because they have lost their fear of the Lord, with rebellion and evil accelerating on every side. When the good Lord brings judgement upon the nations He will restore the fear of the Lord, **which is clean** (Psalm 19:9)!

The fear of the church (organisation, run by sinful men) is largely based upon false teaching, and therefore unclean. This gives us the clue as to how true disciples (John 8:31-32) can avoid confusion. We need a good working knowledge of the major themes of the Word of God, especially the New Testament. The Word of Truth is our final authority in matters of faith and morals.

When I was asked by a deliverance minister if I was afraid of anything I answered, *"Not that I know of, except heights."* It was several years before I discovered some HEREDITARY FEAR in me when nightmaring. My father was awarded the Military Medal for bravery in the field during the horrendous carnage of the first World War, and I know from my dreams he must have been very frightened (we will say more about this later).

INSOMNIA

Many people can "sleep like a log" and are the envy of others who suffer from insomnia. Sleep deprivation is a cruel infirmity, turning people into desperate pill-poppers.

Most counselling on this subject today embraces dealing with fear, panic and terror caused through traumatic experiences (personal or ancestral), horror movies etc.

I would suggest seeking a Christian pastor or counsellor with a view to working through a **Renouncing Prayer** before the Lord, for example:

---

1. See chapters 4 and 5.

Dear Lord Jesus ...
I renounce all spirits of fear associated with ...... I take authority over them in your Name, and command them to loose me forever ...

Such a prayer should be taken slowly, thoughtfully and with necessary detail. The conclusion should always be to pray for a fresh fullness of the **HOLY Spirit,** to replace the unclean control spirit.

It is not wrong to repeat such a prayer often, as often as necessary. We have to get it through the unclean spirit's thick head that this is not just a formula we are saying, hoping for the best. We say what we mean, and we mean what we say with **FAITH.** We will resist the devil UNTIL he flees from us (James 4:7).

Also please consider targeting spirits of **panic, anxiety, terror** etc. when ministering to sufferers with a kingdom of fear.

Faith is the enemy of fear! Praise the Lord!

1.3 SPIRIT OF STUPIDITY

One of the important pieces of discernment that nearly every Christian will need to apply fairly regularly is that the vast majority of people have **a spirit of stupidity**, no matter how high their I.Q.[2] measures. You know that there are some very clever men and women in this world, people with photographic AND retentive memories, with an enormous capacity for minute detail and also the ability to articulate their wealth of knowledge so that you and I can (sometimes) understand what they are talking about.

For example, there is a well-known Federal politician whose mind operation would put a computer to shame, and is also reputed to be a "good guy" who cares about people. Nevertheless some of his opinions are contrary to the Word of God and to that extent, like all of us, he lacks **wisdom**.

Cleverness and wisdom are two different things and it would be nice to have both. **Stupidity** is the opposite of **wisdom** and both are more of a moral (spiritual) quality whereas **cleverness** is more to do with the functioning ability of the brain - a physical quality. Obviously, like so much human behaviour, the **spiritual** (wisdom or stupidity) and the **physical** (brain cleverness) can be mutually inclusive so it can be difficult to know what is going on without some discerning of spirits.

---

2. Intelligence quotient

The Bible says that if **anyone** does not believe in a Supreme God he or she is a fool, regardless of how clever they are (Psalm 14:1, 53:1). The Bible goes on to say that **"The fear of the Lord is the BEGINNING of wisdom"** (Psalm 111:10, Prov. 9:10, 15:33). From this we can deduce that someone may recognise the existence of a Supreme God, but **if they do not understand His awesomeness and fear Him, they remain in a state of stupidity,** because the fear of the Lord **is only a beginning** down the road to wisdom.

Many Christians are afraid to call someone a fool because of Jesus' warning **".... whoever says 'You fool' shall be in danger of hell fire"** (Matt. 5:22). It is good to be cautious about this because Christians should not normally speak offensively to others, but nevertheless the fact remains *the apostle Paul accused the Galatians of stupidity* (Gal. 3:1, cf. Luke 24:25, Rom. 1:22, 1 Cor. 15:36, Eph. 5:15) and he can do so because it is the truth - they have been stupid! The point is, if you are going to call someone stupid in order to shock them out of their error(s), **make sure you are right, and doing it for Godly motives.**

The Old Testament book of **Proverbs** is a great book of Wisdom but if you were to sum up its main message you would have to say that it distinguishes between the behaviour of a stupid man and a wise man, and how one should relate to each of them. We have in Proverbs a large Biblical book written by a man famous for his wisdom, half of which is devoted to the stupidity of mankind.

The wisest man of his Age, **King Solomon** actually tells us that **we are all born with a large dose of stupidity,**

> *"The heart of a child is bound up in foolishness,* but the rod of correction will drive it far from him." (Prov. 22:15).

It seems apparent that this scripture is directed to male children in the first instance, probably because it is young boys who want to run and jump and climb and yell, experimenting with their voice to find out all the various noises they can make, unless they are corrected effectively.

Such wild and unrestrained behavior is, of course, stupidity, which can border on hysteria. It is the exact opposite of bringing up a child in the way he should go (Prov. 22:6) in the fear and nurture of the Lord, and as we have just recorded from the Word of God it is THIS fear that starts us on the road to Wisdom.

Many parents have been talked out of using the rod of correction by a society that pays more heed to some psychologists than the Word of God. Consequently **children with hearts full of stupidity grow up to become adults full of stupidity**, and so the vicious cycle worsens with each succeeding generation, as we head towards the close of the Church Age.

The Hebrew people are a brilliant, innovative race, producing more geniuses per head of population than any other nation on earth, yet because the fear of the Lord is the beginning of wisdom the apostle Paul blames their rejection of the Lord Jesus Christ as their Messiah on a SPIRIT OF STUPOR (Rom.11:8).

So, you see, **being stupid,** is not really an insulting term (to be applied only to unbelievers) but it is more **a description of a spiritual state caused by an unclean spirit, from which we have all suffered. Indeed, for people to take this teaching and use it to hurt others would itself be a stupid action, revealing the need for deliverance from spirits of mockery and/or ridicule, and perhaps cruelty!**

It is a spiritual state of stupidity which causes mankind to repeatedly make the following disastrous mistakes and believe deception century after century:

1. *Man is basically good and can work out his problems by reason and consultation.*

2. *Man can avoid the Cross of Christ because Salvation is by good works.*

3. *Just as all roads lead to the top of a hill so all religions lead to God.*

4. *The unity of Labour is the hope of the world.*

5. *A loving God will never send anyone into Hell. His love is unconditional.*

The Word of God reveals how totally wrong these notions are:

1. Man is a sinner (Luke 13:1-5) and can do no good thing without Christ (John 15:5).

2. He who believes in the Son has everlasting life; and he who does not OBEY the Son shall not see life, but the wrath of God rests upon him (Matt. 20:28, John 3:16,36; 5:24, Acts 4:12).

3. Jesus said *"I am the Way, the Truth and the Life. No one comes (goes) to the Father, except through me* (John 14:6, Acts 4:12).

4. Jesus Christ is the Hope of the world (Rom. 15:12-13). **All substitutes are antiChrist.** Ask the fragments of the Soviet Union, the Bulgarians, Czech's, Poles, East Germans etc. if the unity of Labour did them any good. Man's best efforts without God always fail (Jer. l7:5-8).

5. The love of God and the righteousness of God must always be seen as indivisible. The Cross of Jesus manifests both **the Love of God** for the world in providing a blood sacrifice (solution) for sin, and also **the righteousness of God** which was satisfied by His sacrifice (John 3:16, Rom. 5:8, 1 Pet. 3:18, 2 Pet. 2:4-9) in paying the price for OUR sins. His love is NOT unconditional, as we shall see in the section discussing Religious spirits.

To reject the sacrifice is to reject the love of God, which spells disaster, no matter what people believe or do not believe.

The Word of God also teaches us that it is impossible for an adult fool to be set free from his foolishness by physical methods (Prov. 27:22) but what is impossible for man is not impossible with God (Matt. 19:26), and the FEAR of the LORD is the BEGINNING of wisdom!

It is as **Archbishop William Temple** said early last (twentieth) century: *"In the Bible, the majority is always wrong!"* It follows therefore, that Democracy must be undergirded by Christian laws and Christian faith if it is not itself to become a great deception, and its parliaments become forums of ignorance and stupidity instead of wisdom.

1.4 SPIRIT OF REBELLION

Having shown that all people who do not believe in the existence of God, and all those who DO believe but do not fear Him, have at least ONE unclean spirit (the spirit of stupor), it should be added that the New Testament also confirms that **every non-Christian has a resident spirit of rebellion (disobedience); indeed we were ALL born with it!**

"And you He made alive when you were dead in your trespasses and in your sins (V.2) in which you then walked according to the age of this world, according to **the ruler of the authority of the air, of the spirit now operating in the sons of disobedience (V.3) among whom we all also then conducted ourselves** *in the lusts of our flesh, doing the will of the flesh and of the mind, and were by nature children of wrath as also the rest (of mankind)." (Eph. 2:1-3)*

What a powerful statement this is. It really spells out the world, the flesh and what appears to be Satan's spirit—all linked inextricably together and producing the result of sins and putting the sinner under the wrath of God—and the **spirit of rebellion,** probably referring to the **"old man"** or **"strong man"** within us all.

It is, of course, addressed to Christians who have therefore come out of the darkness of this Age and into the light of Christ, but nevertheless it explains the CAUSE(S) of the darkness. I believe the following points are found in the passage:

1. The **human spirit is in a kind of "dead" state** before it is made alive by the Holy Spirit (i.e. born again).

2. Those not born again into the New Covenant-keeping family ALL behave according to:

    (i)   the lusts of their flesh
    (ii) the will of their flesh
    (iii) the will of their mind

3. We were therefore **by nature** (soulish instinct) **ALL children of wrath** like ALL mankind, before receiving the saving grace of Christ.

4. This polluted and disastrous spiritual condition of original sin in our lives causes us to behave **according to the ways of the world—**

5. Which puts us (our minds and flesh) under the control of the (spiritual) **ruler of the authority of the air** (airwaves—media? sound—music?)

6. —as well as being under the control of the **spirit of rebellion** (against God) which operates **IN** the sons of disobedience.

7. **Therefore original sin is caused by a spirit of rebellion within us, inherited from Adam (Romans 5:12).**

Clearly the apostle Paul tells us *everyone who has NOT received the HOLY Spirit and therefore been born again in their HUMAN spirit is under the control of an unclean spirit of rebellion or disobedience.* This makes them very vulnerable to the ways of the world with its satanic music and media influences. Our sexual natures are particularly vulnerable to such corruption by spiritual forces, even before we were born (the first time).

It is sad to have to write that the vast majority of Christians who are genuinely committed to the Lord have never really dealt with their spirit of rebellion. Most of them do not even know it is there, in their soul, and others think that it disappeared when the Holy Spirit first came into them at their conversion.

But it is not as simple as that. Rebellion is only removed through brokenness, through self being crucified with Christ, through walking in the footsteps of Jesus along the road to Calvary, and through specific, determined, deliverance ministry.

The spirit of rebellion is the root cause of cancer and is the reason that Christians are only slightly less prone to cancer than non-Christians. As most people know, cancer is wild, chaotic cell growth which is a manifestation of rebellion against God's natural order. It is not hard to perceive that such a manifestation often has a *spiritual* source (Eph. 6:12). We discuss this further in chapter 2.

1.5 SPIRIT OF SODOMY

The full details of this kingdom of spirits are revealed to us in Romans 1:24-31 and we have discussed this in *"Sex Demons and Morality"* and *Book 2.* I only want to point out here that this enemy comes into our heart and soul through the original problem of idolatry (Rom. 1:21-23) but then, doesn't everything?

Sodomy is sometimes partnered by **confusion** and **destruction** and can lead to MULTIPLE PERSONALITY DISORDER (M.P.D.) which we will examine in chapter 8.3.

1.6 SPIRIT OF EPILEPSY

Have you ever wondered about that phrase in Psalm 121:6? "THE SUN SHALL NOT SMITE YOU BY DAY, NEITHER THE MOON BY NIGHT".

We all know that sun-stroke or heat stroke can be very nasty. I myself suffered from it for many years, but MOONSTROKE??? What possible damage can the moon do to us?.

Well, to make it brief, a full moon causes many older ladies all over the western world to become a little strange, even unbalanced, at night. Doctors know it, Nurses in hospital wards especially know it and watch out for it. It may happen to men also, but because the ladies generally outlive the men, it is far more noticeable among the fairer sex.

When do witches covens practice their evil rites? Certainly the night of the full moon is very common. They are certainly moon-struck, perhaps without knowing it. Let us add to all this one very important revelation. The word **"MOON-STRUCK"** is used in the New Testament (Matt. 17:15) describing the young lad with the seizures, and is accurately translated as **EPILEPSY** (R.S.V.). The Concise Oxford dictionary defines "moon-struck" as *"deranged in mind."*

So what do we learn from all this? Very simply that epilepsy is a form of being **demon-struck** and again the problem has its roots in the occult. Please study the passage carefully (Matt. 17:14-21, cf Mark 9:14-29).

1.7 SPIRIT OF SUPERSTITION

The literal meaning of this word as used by the apostle Paul is **"demon-fearing"**. (Acts 17:22). Sometimes it is translated **"religious."** **Superstition is an awareness and fear of the activity of invisible (spiritual) forces around us.** This awareness may be purely soulish and instinctive without any reference to logic or the five physical senses. Hence the term **"sixth sense"** is a way of describing that we sense something but we don't know how.

Again, this is a religious problem related to witchcraft and the occult. Unfortunately some historical church buildings are choking with it under the delusion of historical numinous.

However we should keep in mind that **Christians also have a "sixth sense"** which may be inspired by the indwelling Holy Spirit, for **"as many as are led by the Spirit of God are sons of God"** (Rom. 8:14).

1.8 SPIRIT OF BLASPHEMY

Nearly every section of the church has a particular secret enemy within its ranks - that of blasphemy. **Protestants** and **Roman Catholics** have for centuries thought of each other as performing acts of worship or believing certain doctrines which are blasphemous in character. Before the present ecumenical climate they spoke their minds plainly, but unlovingly. Today, such things are often left unsaid, but nevertheless held quietly in the heart in trust that the love of God will overrule and eventually correct those in error. The **World,** of course, is full of blasphemy. I do not think there has ever been a time in human history when so much that passes as entertainment is designed to evoke blasphemous laughter from the "customers". One doesn't need the gift of discerning of spirits to know that laughter which responds to blasphemous "jokes" is not "human" laughter but demonic.

Most people are not aware of the enormous level of blasphemy being practised around us and through us by the powers of darkness. For example,

Emmanuel is the name of our Saviour (Matt. 1:23), So what does the por-nographic movie trade do? It produces sex movies about a sex siren named Emmanuelle. But the days of subtlety have disappeared and blasphemous movies are becoming far more blatant. Some sections of the film industry will have a lot to answer for.

Once it was lascivious jokes, now it is religious jokes. Once it was only protestant ministers who were ridiculed – now it is any minister or priest. In the eyes of the business world, actors representing ridiculous ministers are good for a laugh in any advertising commercial. Puns on the Word and the Spirit (for motor fuel) are commonplace as is the use of distorted scriptures. ***"Man shall not live by bread alone but also needs blah blah blah!"*** If one has a food product that one wishes to advertise as being very tasty and irresistable, a comic-like clergyman making a pig of himself over the said product is not uncommon.

Restraint of blasphemous language, of course, is virtually a thing of the past, with the widespread use of blasphemous language through the television and video medium, and the misuse and distortion of words like Christ, Jesus, God etc, into Crikey, Cripes, Jeez, Jeepers, Gee whiz, sheesh, Cor, Gor blimey (God blind me) etc. etc. The swear word "bloody" is not normally considered blasphemous - some people don't even think of it as **profanity** or swearing and so in Australia it has been referred to as the "Great Australian Adjective" with some kind of unclean "macho" pride.

People say angrily "Give me the bloody thing!" or "The bloody thing let me down!"- not realising that their unclean nature (the Old man - Rom. 6:6, Eph. 4:22) with all its demonic components (See Chapter 5) is manifesting blasphemy *against the blood sacrifice of the Son of God.*

It is a demonic travesty or slur, and a degrading allusion to the battered and bloody body of our Saviour as He hung upon the Cross. Demons hate the blood of the Cross because by it Jesus has triumphed over them, and so they work at disparaging that Supreme Sacrifice as much as they can by using it as a common expletive. It is not normally intended this way by the swearers, but by the unclean sin in them. We humans are simply the dummies that allow ourselves to be used to denigrate Jesus' saving blood. Beware the message of Hebrews 10:29!

> *"How much worse punishment do you think will be appropriate (for) the one who has:*
>
> (i)   *trampled on the Son of God*
> (ii)   ***deemed common the blood of the Covenant*** *by which they are sanctified?*
> (iii)   *and insulted the Spirit of grace?"*

But all this kind of blasphemy is of the world. Bad as it is, what should concern the Christian even more is blasphemy within the Body of Christ - by blood-bought Christians - and it often flows from **"mature"** Christians, Christians who are mature in the Word. As a young catechist (trainee) part of my duties included supervising a singalong after church on Sunday nights. We used to gather around the piano in the minister's home but when I reflect on it now, it was mainly an exercise in blasphemy and mockery, I am ashamed to say. The youngsters were laughing and giggling, but not with the joy of the Lord. We sang well-known revival hymns and choruses with magnificent words depicting the holy and glorious saving acts of God but for the vast majority of those present, we may as well have been singing "Roll out the barrel" in the local public house. Either words or tunes or both were distorted carelessly – and without thought, and I as leader lacked the perception, and therefore the motivation to put the kids right.

There is no question in my mind that satan loves to place an agency of blasphemy in Christian preachers and teachers. Probably half the jokes told from the pulpit have a blasphemous base to them. By that I mean teaching from the Holy Word of God is lightly spoken of in order to produce laughter. Sometimes the preacher is not to blame. I once heard a tape of Renewal pioneer **Bob Mumford** who has a beautiful sense of humour. He drew many laughs from his audience but the one thing that has stuck in my memory is the raucous cackle of someone in the auditorium, fairly close to a microphone. These spirits of mockery and blasphemy laughed at anything and everything as they strove to tear down the message Bob Mumford was giving. The principle is simple for this kind of unclean spirit. If you don't like the message, destroy its impact by laughing at it, especially in all the wrong places. Virtually every discerning preacher has experienced inward alarm when audience laughter has become unclean.

The most obvious danger for serious Bible students is the misuse of God's Holy Word. I stress HOLY. What God has said is not to be laughed at, but we do it all the time. Our minds are so full of God's Word that we find it popping out of our mouths in every kind of situation **used as the Lord never intended it to be used** - rarely in the right context and almost always with some kind of distortion of the words or their meaning. Consider these five (5) danger signals:

(i) *Examine your jokes carefully – are you creating laughter about HOLY things?*

(ii) *When you say "For God's sake" do you really **mean** "for **God's** sake" or are you just saying that for emphasis?*

(iii) Are you quoting God's Word without distortion?

(iv) When you sing praises are you singing loose words, or carelessly out-of-tune, or both?

*(v) Beware of introducing something with "...**and I say with all reverence**..." Blasphemy CANNOT be said reverently.*

We discussed PROFANITY in the INTRODUCTION

1.9 SPIRIT OF DISTORTION

Apart from distortion of the Word, which we have seen to be unclean, it is safe to say that ANY distortion is unclean. Distortion of the truth, distortion of God's Creation, distortion of our health, our bodies, our minds, God's living standards (morality) etc. etc.

An obvious area of illustration would be **Art.** Distorted pictures are often thought of as symbolic and they are – they symbolise distortion and ugliness. Pagan countries of the world often specialise in wood carvings and we need to take note of the faces and the expression carved on the faces and see how sin in man distorts God's creation. Why does satan delight in reproducing images of man that are ugly, distorted and disfigured? Simply because he is a destroyer. He tried once to disfigure and destroy Jesus and now he works unceasingly to disfigure and destroy "man, made in the image of God." Perhaps he thinks that in distorting man he is insulting man's Creator!

One only has to look at what tribal natives, committing atrocities under the domination of spiritism and witchcraft through their leaders, do to themselves, disfiguring their faces and bodies, in order to understand the destructive nature of the spirits controlling them. Even in civilised countries some young people are persuaded to have themselves heavily disfigured with tatoos – which most deeply regret at a later stage - and it is interesting to note how many times SNAKES are featured, and in what way (cf. Levit. 19:28).

This is why deliverance and cleansing is so vital for today. There is disfigurement, disease, sickness, distortion, corruption, spoiling (defilement) and death on every side – more so than for any other generation in history. We dare not shun the Lord's delivering grace in these critical days.

These are just some of the areas the Church can be made aware of right down from the leadership and through to the rank and file members. No hurt or offence is intended by any of these observations and I pray that they will bring a blessing to YOUR heart, as the TRUTH is faced squarely and honestly, so that THE TRUTH can set us free.

1.10   SPIRIT OF BITTERNESS

Have you noticed how many fights and brawls take place in, or just outside, places which sell **alcoholic drinks?** News item after news item brings this information to us almost daily. There are a whole range of spirits related to violence. To name a few: violence, blood-lust, anger, murder, hate, bitter–ness, resentment, destruction. Let me comment on one or two.

(i)   Destruction

When a school teacher sees one or two children disrupting an otherwise well – behaved class and **destroying** a teaching situation, you don't have to be brilliant to discern a spirit of **destruction** at work.

Likewise violent or physical sport usually goes hand in hand with alcohol (but not during training!), and drunkenness is often an opportunity for someone's dark (demonised) nature to take control.

(ii)   Murder

Murder is the third heaviest sin[3] mentioned in the Word of God. It carries with it a heavy curse because it is considered to be an attack on God Himself (Gen. 9:6). There is to be no (earthly or human) mercy or pity for a murderer in a Godly society (Deut. 7:16, 13:8, 9:13,21, Rom. 13:4) although God's forgiveness and Paradise are still attainable through faith in the Lord Jesus Christ (Luke 23:34, 39-43). Praise the Lord!

(iii)   Anger

This is a very common and major spiritual problem which has spawned a whole new psychological focus called **"Anger Management"**. However, by the grace of God we can expect to do better than simply manage (control) the spirits, we can actually get rid of them - the whole Kingdom.

It is as well to understand that by the time a person seeks to deal with their anger problem it is usually a sizeable Kingdom of spirits in the soulish area and, like so many things, they will rarely experience a quick-fix.

---

3. After speaking against the Holy Spirit, and unbelief in the Lordship of Jesus Christ.

As **Proverbs 19:19** informs us:

"(A person of) great wrath will suffer punishment, for if you deliver them, you will have to do it again."

There has been an unverified suggestion that anger not only creates health problems in the head and heart but also the feet (cf. Rom. 3:14-15).

What is not normally realised is that ANGER in the heart is **spiritual murder.** Just as lusting for a woman in the heart is considered **spiritual adultery** (Matt. 5:27-28) so also anger in the heart brings the same condemnation as the act of murder. Check it out for yourself. (Matt. 5:21-22a).

(iv)   Bitterness

The Lord responds in a devastating way to bitterness, and his Word tells us that it is a ROOT problem. I take that to mean it is a RULING spirit in many human hearts, with many off-shoots or offspring.

We are told about gall and bitterness (Deut. 32:32, Acts 8:23) and the **ROOT of bitterness** (Deut. 29:18, Heb. 12:15). Proverbs tells us that **"the heart knows it's own bitterness"** (Prov. 14:10), and of course, the story of Israel's murmuring against God in the wilderness is well known to many Bible students (Ex. 15:22-27).

Bitterness is also related to **jealousy** (Num. 5:12-31) and **envy** (James 3:14) so we can see that it spawns or keeps company with the nastiest part of our human nature.

Some people love being bitter and won't let it go. There are few things more self-destructive than an unforgiving nature and bitter people often end up with serious skeletal problems, prime candidates for a wheelchair. **"Envy is rottenness to the bones"** (Prov. 14:30b, cf. 15:30, 16:24).

(v)   Accusation

The company of many people is avoided because they make others defensive with their critical and/or accusing nature. They are often very hardworking and conscientious because they themselves fear criticism. Why? Because they were severely criticised in their youth or childhood and have bitter memories.

In the same way that being emotionally hurt can produce grief, and grieving turns to resentment, then anger, bitterness and finally hatred, so also a critical or accusing spirit is often the result of hurt and bitterness.

People who cannot handle constructive or even gentle criticism or correction need a lot of healing. It would help a great deal if they could diligently and regularly apply the principle of removing the beam in their own eye before trying to remove the splinter from someone else's eye (Matt. 7:1-5). As is so often the case the removal of an unclean spirit must be accompanied by improved behaviour, attitude and speech lest the spirit return with many ugly "friends" (Matt. 12:43-45).

1.11 SPIRIT OF LUST

When most people hear the word "lust" they usually think of sexual lust because it seems to be the most difficult natural drive to control, for most people. However, there are at least three (3) lusts in the Word of God with which we have to deal. How would you interpret the following scripture?

".... all that is in the world, the lust of the flesh, and the lust of the eyes and the pride of life, is not of the Father but is of the world". **(1 John 2:16)**

Some very vivid explanations have been **"Sex, Money and Power"** and **"Gals, Gold and Glory"**. Perhaps in these days of so much violence shown by the entertainment industry, and "drunk in" by those who want "action" films, the gorier the better, that last phrase should now read **"Gals, Gold, Glory and Gore"**.

But good (and memorable) as these comments are, they seem to omit what I believe to be a major lust of the flesh, something that is even more enslaving or tempting than immoral sex, and that is GLUTTONY, - the lust for FOOD!

When we look at that successful temptation of Eve and then Adam in the Garden of Eden, we see a three-fold attack on our original ancestors in **Genesis 3:5-6.**

(i) Pride, (Power and Glory)

The serpent says to Eve **"You will be like God (or gods)"** ...(v.5) Pride was satan's (Lucifer's) original problem (Isa. 14:12-16) so it should be no surprise that he would test Eve through pride, glory-seeking and power-seeking.

(ii) Gluttony

The woman experienced the lust of the eyes. She **"saw that the tree was good for food, that it was pleasant to the eyes ..."** (V.6).

(iii)   Sex

It is only after Eve, and then Adam, have been successfully tempted by the serpent that sexual desire comes into the picture. Their eyes were opened to know both good and evil, so that they realised they were naked. With their sexual awakening they sewed fig leaves together and made themselves coverings. (V.7)

Which is the greater area of sin and pollution for mankind - sexual lusts or gluttonous lusts? The answer is that *they are both areas of potentially enormous uncleanness and defilement.*

The sexual nature of human beings is such a vulnerable (and therefore polluted) area of our lives that we have written a separate book **"Sex, Demons and Morality"** to examine many of it's manifestations. For example, when the **apostle Paul** lists a number of deadly sins for the Corinthians, **four out of the first five are sexual sins** (1 Cor. 6:9-10).

However, when Christians defeat (control or have removed) their unclean sexual desires, it is not unusual for them to experience **gluttonous spirits** seeking to neutralise or destroy them, after the manner described in James 1:13-16.

This is why both Christians and non-Christians support a whole range of business products, exercise and diet programs designed to get us fit, not fat. Keeping our bodies fit and healthy is big business today.

Lurking hidden behind the more obvious sex and gluttonous spirits is SELF, with all its pride, power and glory-seeking, the Old Man, the strong man, -- YUK!

Is it any wonder the Lord has called His disciples to PRAYER and FASTING (Matt. 9:15, Mark 2:20, Luke 5:35, cf. 1 Cor. 7:5), that the true disciples of Christ should discipline their bodies and bring them into subjection (1 Cor. 9:27).

1.12   SPIRIT OF DEATH

For most people death is an experience they put off for as long as possible and prefer not to think about, and in this sense death is thought of as a physical experience. Death is the cessation of life within our physical bodies.

The Bible says we die (physically) because there is a deposit of death transmitted down from Adam (and Eve) to all mankind. Sin and death entered into mankind together and have since infected and affected EV-ERYONE (Rom. 5:12) down through the Ages.

Not only is death demonstrated physically by the cessation of life, but as we grow older the deposit of death within us manifests itself more and more through our lives and our appearance. We sometimes undergo personality changes, and if the grace of God is not making us sweeter people we become impatient, frustrated and crotchety (hence the perpetual generation gap where we can become critical of young people doing the same things we ourselves did at their age).

We slow down, becoming less mobile, and find it harder to climb onto our roof to repair it. Our eyesight loses it's sharpness and our hearing is not so acute. Our skin begins to wrinkle, men's hair disappears and our teeth show signs of decay. The doctors tell us our organs are not functioning so well because they are wearing out (what they call degenerative disease) but it is only a term of description to cover the situation. It is not a disease in the normal sense and, scientifically speaking, nobody knows why we wear out. There is no **logical** explanation for it, only a **biblical** one – that **the spiritual kingdom of death gradually overtakes the whole living organism** – usually over a span of about 70 years (Psalm 90:10) in normal circumstances.

Across the western world huge Life Assurance Companies pay good com-missions to their Life Agents who sell Life Insurance to people. Why? Because although life Insurance makes very good sense, especially to men with family responsibilities, people normally don't want to talk about the subject of death, especially their own.

Everybody knows they are going to die. They know they should make provision for their dependants in the event of their untimely death but it is not easy to find someone who will sit down and talk about it. That most people sense death is a spirit is confirmed by interpretive drawings of **"The Grim Reaper"**. Such drawings or paintings are usually in the form of a skeleton shrouded in a monk's hood and habit, and holding a long-bladed sickle (for reaping).

Biblical evidence that death is a spirit is found in Romans 5:12 where we are told that death passed from Adam to every man but, of course, what is transferred to us is plainly not physical or removable by science.

We are informed that death should NOT continue to reign (as a king) in Christian believers (Rom. 5:14,21, cf. Rom. 6:9) and that instead of the spiritual personality of death coming to collect us when our time on earth is up, the spiritual person of the Lord Jesus Christ will come for us instead (John 14:2-3).

So it seems clear that death is not some nebulous, abstract, philosophical concept or theory but a personality. Not a human or fleshy personality but a spiritual entity or being. It seems a strange thing to say but it is an angel spirit (in the sense that "angel" means "messenger") and an unclean ruler.

This spirit is extremely arrogant. I have heard one say (before it was cast out) *"You will all bow the knee to me, one day. I'll get you all in the end!"*

As you would expect, this is a big distortion of the truth where Christians are concerned. **He doesn't get US! – Jesus Does!** And some of us won't even taste death at all! (1 Thess. 4:17).

This spirit does not even fear satan but eventually meets the same fate as him (Rev. 20:10,14). In fact it is interesting to note the **apostle Paul** writes that **"the last enemy to be destroyed is death"** (1 Cor. 15:26). This confirms that the devil himself goes into the lake of fire **before** the ruling spirit of death, as do the beast and the false prophet. Indeed death is the last enemy to be destroyed, with Hades (Rev. 20:14).

Two points in conclusion:

(i)   *We can say with the apostle Paul:*

      "Death is swallowed up in victory (Isa. 25:8).

      O death, where is your sting?

      O Hades, where is your victory (Hos. 13:14)

      The sting of death is sin, and the strength of sin is the law. But thanks be to God, who gives us the victory through our Lord Jesus Christ."   *(1 Cor. 15: 56-57)*

(ii) If death is a spiritual entity deposited in every human being since Adam, and the Lord has now reinstated His deliverance ministry within the Body of Christ, *can this spirit be removed from Christians by deliverance?*

      The answer is obviously yes.

The possible consequences of this answer are absolutely mind-blowing but should be considered together with Romans 6:23 and 1 Thess. 4:17. For the moment I suggest you note these comments, try to keep your mind open, and move on.

1.13 SPIRIT OF INFIRMITY

We have discussed this spirit in an earlier book of this series.[4] Let me quote you one paragraph:

> *"Infirmity"* is a broad word covering every human flaw in body (flesh, bones), mind and soul (emotions). It literally means weakness, frailty or sickness in any part of a living creature and you will remember that a spirit of infirmity had to be cast out of the daughter of Abraham before her deformed spine could be healed (Luke 13:10-13).

Please remember that ANY part of you which is less than PERFECT indicates some form of weakness (infirmity). It means that you have been robbed of your perfection by the spiritual nature of sin and death (Rom. 5:12), by the robber spirit (John 10:8-10). The Lord Jesus Christ brings to us a full salvation including healing and deliverance so that all the devil has robbed from us might be RESTORED (1 John 3:8b). **By Jesus' bruise we are HEALED!** (1 Peter 2:24).

This is obviously an ENORMOUS area of demonic activity!

1.14 SCHIZOPHRENIA

Australia has been reported as having one percent of people suffering from schizophrenia at a financial cost of $1.5 billion annually, but when we include the less severe and the closet (undiagnosed) cases it is more like 10 percent with a corresponding financial blowout, probably not measurable.

One of the saddest things about schizophrenia is the burden and concern carried by the loved ones close to the sufferer. At the moment there seems to be no light at the end of the tunnel for them and they understandably feel they are not listened to or understood when they do get an ear, probably because unless we are "in their shoes" we can only sympathise, rather that empathise.

However, there is reason for hope. There are some hard things to say, but better the hard truth with hope of healing, rather than darkness and hopelessness. Now is their time, not for talking, but for listening.

---

4. Book 1 **"Make Yourselves Ready"** Chap. 3.7(iii).

KING SAUL

I would like to say a few things about schizophrenia as sensitively as possible. We will establish, I trust, that we ALL have our demons according to human testimonies, and notwithstanding some historic church opposition. We have also to argue the place and meaning of SIN, and what the Word of God has to say about all of this.

I believe we find a classic case of **paranoid schizophrenia** in the person of **King Saul,** the first King of Israel. He experienced a love/hate relationship with his armour-bearer **David** who was to become King in due time. Saul was jealous of David's popularity, saw him as a threat to his kingship (1 Sam. 18:5-9) and sought to kill him (1 Sam. 19-20) in spite of David's continuing loyalty (1 Sam. 24).

When David had Saul at his mercy but spared his life, Saul relented of all his bitterness but it didn't last long. Saul's problem had begun a lot earlier when an unclean spirit would manifest in Saul's personality until David's Godly music would drive it away (1 Sam. 16:22-23).

EXPOSING THE HIDDEN

Anyone can suffer from schizophrenia, the same as cancer. Just as cancer is the outward manifestation of a spirit of rebellion, producing rebellious cell growth in our flesh, so also schizophrenia is the manifestation of that part of our soulish nature which is at variance with God. Both Christians and non-Christians can suffer cancer and schizophrenia but statistics have shown that fully submitted adherents of a religion are less likely to suffer cancer. However, many Christians have not really dealt with their inner rebellion and some are therefore more vulnerable than others, but generally speaking **submission to God reduces the probability of cancer, and indeed, any sickness**.

Our rebelling against God increases our vulnerability to evil (Mark 2:9-12, Eph. 4:26-27).

Although schizophrenia has been defined as dislocation between thoughts, feelings and actions, hence the sense of a split mind, it actually takes place when the dark side of the soul (the spiritually unclean side of human nature) exposes itself to the natural, physical world. It is like an island being created in the middle of the ocean. The land was always there under the sea but hidden from sight and apparently non-existent. Suddenly it emerges in the middle of the ocean - and may disappear just as suddenly - but it is always there. The Bible calls this spiritual uncleanness sin and death. All human beings suffer from this to some degree (Rom. 5:12) but people diagnosed as schizophrenics no longer have the "disease" always hidden below the water.

The Problem

Today as westerners delve more and more into the Occult and meditational religions, follow more promiscuous sexual habits, experiment with drugs and become addicted to the hypnosis of heavy rock music (with extra bass sound) it should not surprise us that the spiritual uncleanness within us is strengthened and encouraged to manifest itself without restraint, and indeed, take over completely. Obvious demonstrations of this unclean spiritual power are well known through the exercise of animalistic martial arts, rock hysteria, drug trips, hypnosis producing so called evidence of re-incarnation (the hypnotist never contacts the human spirit, only the unclean spirit) primal screams and the altered states such as produced by eastern mystics like the Bhagwan or Maharaj Ji Guru etc.

This "invisible" ugliness of human nature can actually be seen on some people's faces, if one is very observant. Almost all of us have a "good" side to our face and a not-so-good side as illustrated (diagram).

Now you see a little about how your ugly side looks to God! He didn't make you that way but through the victory of the Cross of Christ, He offers to release you from all your uncleanliness. The problem is spiritual.

THE HEALING SOLUTION

The first step in the healing process is to see that, just as the problem is spiritual, so is the solution. If you are looking for a scientific, medical solution you are wasting your time. Doctors may, in due time, discover some physical weakness to which schizophrenia can be attributed such as defective genes or stress, but even if they do, one disease or problem is always replaced by another. For years many people who hear voices within them have been told that they are imagining things, when the real solution is to warn them the voices are not gods or God, and the sufferer is not to do **anything** that these voices say at any time, especially when they are being cast out by Christian ministers. Again, the problem is spiritual.

Frank and **Ida Mae Hammond's** classic *"Pigs in the Parlour"* has a very helpful revelational section on schizophrenia. It contains very detailed discernment and the chapter on this subject closes with the challenge:

"The Schizophrenia deliverance is the deepest, most involved and most determined deliverance that we have encountered.

**A normal type
human face**

**when we mirror the
"good" side, we get:**

**but when we mirror the
not-so-good side we get:**

Secondly God, through the Lord Jesus Christ, is the answer. The Bible tells us that He died on a rough, brutal Cross in order to defeat and overcome every unclean spirit that attacks you and me (Col. 2:15). The purpose of our existence is to determine whether we (each one of us) will join forces with Christ or the antichrist. If we belong to Christ we can be freed from the power of the antichrist. If we do not belong to Christ we already belong to antichrist and there are no satisfactory answers for any of our chronic mental or emotional problems. Most illness is either caused by our hereditary soul pollution known as sin and death and/or our life-style. Nothing is accidental. There is no such thing as luck.

The Cross of Christ gives us a **legal** victory over every unclean spirit inside and outside of us, but this victory has to be pursued and grasped by the sufferers, or those caring for them, if they wish to experience it.

Briefly, they must:

(i)   **WANT to be helped**
(ii)   *put their total trust in Jesus of Nazareth*
(iii) *obey the counsel of the Lord's servants who are ministering to them.*

Schizophrenia CAN be beaten! Praise the Lord!

CHAPTER 2
CANCER AND DEATH

2.1 CANCER IS REBELLION

We have yet another two vital revelations to share with you in this chapter, and it is to do with two deadly maladies which cause a death somewhere, every moment of every day. **Cancer** and **heart disease** are alleged to be the two greatest killers of mankind in the West.

Heart disease has been, and remains at the time of writing, the NUMBER ONE KILLER - WHY???

It is very simple really. The Word of God tells us that; **The heart is deceitful above all things and desperately wicked!" (Jer. 17:9)** as we will see in chapter five. It follows that if the human heart is born with such a horrible SPIRITUAL disease, eventually that spiritual disease will translate into a PHYSICAL disease.

We know that **the physical human heart suffers from the spiritual diseases of sin and death** (Rom. 5:12), so it is not difficult to accept that sin and death will gradually take their toll within the physical heart organ in due time. Men and women may diet or exercise or do any number of things to reduce the risk of heart disease (and there may be nothing wrong and everything right in what they do) but the fact remains that most of these attempts do not address the REAL problem (which is spiritual) and so the best result that can be achieved is a few extra years of life.

However this scenario can be turned upside down when we accept Christ as Saviour and Lord of our lives. We are then what the Bible calls *"born again"* or *"born anew"* (John 3:3-5) and we get a NEW spiritual heart (ruling spirit, i.e. the Holy Spirit). The prophet Ezekiel describes it as having a heart of **stone** replaced with a heart of **flesh** (Ezek. 36: 24-29), but in the New Testament it is described as a NEW creation (2 Cor. 5:17) or birth, or enlightenment (Eph. 1:18, Rom. 5:5).

It is the old story of cause and effect, where the real cause is SPIRITUAL and the effect is manifested in PHYSICAL flesh, in God's good time.

Perhaps even more important is the subject of **cancer,** and again we should apply the law of cause and effect.

We are being told today, in the year 2000 A.D., **cancer** is the second biggest killer, and the areas of the human body most affected are the **prostate** in men (with **testicular** cancer increasing rapidly), and for the ladies, **breast** and **cervical** cancer.

WHY? Why are those areas involved with our sexuality and the reproduction of the human race so prominent in these destructive attacks?

Do you REALLY need me to tell you? Just think back to the heart disease scenario where our spiritual condition manifests itself by physically destroying the heart organ. Then turn on your television (dramas, sitcoms and advertisements) and note how our sexual natures are being bombarded!

The spiritual state of rampant immorality and rebellion against the God of the Bible is bearing its own evil fruit (Num. 32:23).

Colon cancer is not far behind, being a manifestation or reflection of our gluttonous eating habits. The lusts of the flesh (Gal. 5:16-21) are very costly.

If the medical profession is correct in describing cancer cells as WILD or REBELLIOUS cells which have broken out of the normal laws of nature and have thus rebelled against God's order and design for His creatures with wild, chaotic growth rather than orderly growth, then what do you think would be the SPIRITUAL cause of such destructive disorder?

Yes, you are right. **Rebellious cell growth is inspired by a spirit of rebellion.** There may be physical causes for cancer, such as smoking cigarettes or the sun's ultra violet rays etc. etc., but I am suggesting that these are only catalysts or triggers that feed the spirit of rebellion and assist it to create rebellion in the flesh.

In any event smoking cigarettes is an act of rebellion in the majority of cases. Not too many parents encourage their children to smoke but rather the opposite. My oldest son smoked deceitfully and against his parent's wishes from the age of fourteen. He rebelled - and continues to pay the price.

An interesting report appeared in the Sydney Sun newspaper[1] as follows:

---

1. Sept. 14, 1976

BEAT CANCER
LIFE-STYLE "LINK IN CANCER"

Beat cancer by joining an austere religion - that's the advice from visiting expert **Professor John Higginson.** Professor Higginson, from the **International Agency for Research on Cancer,** said in Brisbane that the cancer rate was closely related to life style.

He said:

"I'm not trying to take all the pleasure out of life but people should be aware that over-drinking, over-eating, too much cigarette smoking and exposure to sunlight are primary causes of cancer. These people should at least moderately reduce their over-indulgences to reduce the risk of cancer". Professor Higginson said the general life style of the western industrial societies had established their cancer rates.

He said members of societies such as the Seventh Day Adventists in the United States had lower rates of cancer because they did not smoke or drink and were semi-vegetarians.

There is a 50% less cancer in men and 70% in women in relation to other American citizens", he added.

I suggest that although Professor Higginson's advice is good, the main reason an austere religion is a bulwark against cancer is that membership involves **discipleship (discipline) based upon obedience and submission to religious authorities.** It is true that basic human weaknesses are cut down to the minimum, and therefore manifestations through the flesh are hindered and weakened, *but the main principle is that OBEDIENCE DEFEATS REBELLION!*

This is not meant to imply that people who develop cancers are to be considered more rebellious against God than others - it simply means that because we are ALL born in sin, with an old nature which is or was rebellious (Eph. 2:1-3) natural, earthy, devilish, etc. (James 3:15), we are ALL susceptible to cancers. The way to destroy satan's grounds for putting cancers upon us is to fully submit FIRST to Christ as the Son of God, and SECOND to all divinely constituted authorities (church, civil and family) according to God's revealed will in the New Testament.[2]

---

2. We must be very careful here NOT to allow UNCLEAN authority over us that wants us to obey principles NOT supported by the New Testament.

In a phrase, forgiveness of sins through the blood of Christ and obedience to the New Testament break down satan's claims upon us, for **where our rebellion is utterly defeated, the physical symptoms of rebellion are unlikely.** Can a good tree show forth evil fruit? Certainly any ministry to the afflicted must bear these principles in mind.

Rebellion can be seen today in the almost total disregard the human race has for God's guidelines to life - indeed for the Godhead! Some historic church denominations are experiencing a falling away which only a genuine revival by God's Spirit can reverse. Such falling away is, as we will see in chapter 7, prophesied by Paul in his second letter to the Thessalonians.

Other Spirits

Is there anything more than a spirit of REBELLION inspiring cancer? Well, let us think about that. Remembering the law of cause and effect, what do you think?

Is cancer a terminal illness? Yes it is, so what spirit causes death? **Death!** And we were all born with that one too! That is why we normally all die.

Is it an **infirmity?** It certainly is, so there are many strong spirits of those around also (cf. Luke 13:11-12). There is no one living who has not been born with hereditary infirmity spirits in them, and in this present wicked world of adultery, fornication, homosexuality, drugs, rebellion and unbelief etc., it should not surprise us that the evil one has so much scope to defile, deform and destroy us, even before we are born. Plainly, **to break the Law of Christ** by rebelling against the teaching of the New Testament **is in reality to submit to the authority of the evil one** and become his targets.

There may be other unclean spirits in "fellowship" with those mentioned above, which you will have to seek out with the Lord's help, and obviously a person's life-style will tell you a lot about what has enslaved them (2 Peter 2:19). However I think I only need to mention one more as being highly likely to be present in cancer victims - **Destruction.**

So I suggest that in ministering to cancer sufferers you will usually need to do battle with **REBELLION,** plus also **death, infirmity, cancer** - and **destruction.**

Warning!

Because rebellion is the root cause of cancer, many sufferers will find it difficult to follow your counsel, such as attend Deliverance and Restoration meetings, read the Word, (fast and) pray, exercise and revolutionize their eating habits (i.e. crucify their flesh, 1 Cor. 9:26-27, Gal. 5:24) etc. The rebellion may have almost totally overtaken them, so it is very difficult for them - and you.

A number of people known to me have been shocked to discover they have cancer, but few have ever submitted themselves to our Deliverance and Restoration program.

Doug stopped me on the golf course to tell me of his recently discovered stomach cancer, and imminent operation. Doug is a decent man, brought up in a strict Methodist home which was caught up in puritanical legalism - no fun on Sundays, it is the sabbath (Rest)!

As a result of the poor theology behind such religious restrictions Doug can now only find fault with the Christian faith, not realizing that such man-made traditions are quit contrary to true Christianity. His rebellion is so set in that even if he were to listen and discover EVERY day now belongs to the Lord (Rom. 14:5-6, Gal. 4:9-11), that such O.T. legalism is a thing of the past (Gal. 4:8-11, Col. 2:14-17), and that we now enter God's Rest because we have BELIEVED, and will one day fully enter it (Heb. 3:18-4:6), it is doubtful if he could break the chains of his mind-set, humanly speaking. He is full of excuses (rebellion) and will need grace from above.

However cancer certainly makes people stop and think - and re-think! When diagnosed, it gets everyone's attention!

So many people with cancer are looking for an instant healing - a miracle! It doesn't occur to them that God wants the REBELLION in them dealt with before the healing is granted, in the vast majority of cases. **Bill Banks,** president of **Impact Christian Books Inc.** and a highly effective deliverance and healing minister in the USA, tells the story of his healing from cancer in his testimony book **"Alive Again"**. He was declared healed by his doctors seven months to the day after he received the ministry of healing and was anointed with oil in the Name of the Lord according to James 5:16-18.

It took Bill seven months to get his healing after the prayer of faith had been made, because as Bill says, he had so much to learn back then (1970).

People learn very little from a miraculous healing except that God is God and He heals, and most of us know that anyway. Cancer victims need to see that their rebellion has to be broken and their lives cleaned up in His sight, spiritually AND physically.

All you who minister can do is your part in Christ Jesus, and hope and pray they WILL do their part. By God's grace you will see many saved and healed that would otherwise have experienced an early death. Hallelujah!

2.2 REBELLION IS WITCHCRAFT

Most of us will know the Bible says that witchcraft is rebellion, that is obvious (Deut. 18:10, Gal. 5:20 etc.), but does it really say that (all) rebellion is witchcraft? The Bible does just that, through the prophet Samuel **"For rebellion IS the sin of divination (witchcraft)"** (1 Sam. 15:23). The Greek translation of the Old Testament (the Septuagint) translates even more emphatically - **"Because sin is divination"**.

Let us get that right into our mind and heart and spirit right now. **It is one of the most revelational statements in the whole of the Bible.**

REBELLION (against God) = SIN = WITCHCRAFT
or if you prefer the shortened form:
REBELLION = WITCHCRAFT

Rebellion is not "AS or LIKE the sin of witchcraft". It is not SIMILAR to witchcraft, it is IDENTICAL TO or the SAME as witchcraft [3].

That is why it is so important to train our children to be obedient, from the cradle to adulthood, because *"rebellion"* or its euphemism *"independence"* is a terrible curse.

In the translations above I don't think the difference in choice of words between "rebellion" and "sin" will worry any Bible student, because we all know that **"sin is lawlessness"** (1 John 3:4) and that sin entered into the world through the rebellion of Adam and Eve.

When I went to school I can vaguely remember being taught that if A=B and B=C, A must also equal C. If this holds true in the spiritual realm, and we are given that:

(all) rebellion	**= witchcraft**	**(1 Sam. 15:23 - literal Hebrew)**
(all) sin	**= witchcraft**	**(1 Sam. 15:23 - literal Greek)**
(all) sin	**= lawlessness**	**(1 John 3:4 - literal Greek)**

it follows that   :

   (all) sin = (all) rebellion = lawlessness = witchcraft

---

3. Don't take any notice of translations which weaken the equation made here by the Holy Spirit, that rebellion IS witchcraft. Translators in past years could not be expected to understand the vital importance of this equation for the End-time.

Bible students will know that every move of the human race, collectively and individually, which breaks or ignores the New Covenant (sealed for man's salvation by the precious blood of our Lord Jesus Christ) flows from rebellion and sin against God out of the heart of man (Mark 7:21). The heart is lawless towards God because it is **embedded in witchcraft by nature, since the fall of Adam and Eve and that first occult meeting with the serpent. This basic spiritual disease of the human heart, namely Sin, Rebellion, Lawlessness and Witchcraft will henceforth be shortened to S.R.L.W..**

Here we will have a moments pause, while you recover.

This is why natural-heart religions are always hopelessly out of touch with true (Christian) religion. It explains why **friendship with the world is enmity with God** (Jas. 4:4) and why **the mind set on the flesh is (1) death (2) hostile to God (3) does not submit to God's law** and **(4) cannot please God** (Rom. 8:6-8). It explains why the **soulish (natural) man** does not receive the gifts of the Spirit of God. They are foolishness to him and he does not understand them (1 Cor. 2:14) and why bitter jealousy and selfish ambition in our hearts are considered **earthy, soulish (natural), devilish or demonic** (Jas. 3:14-15).

Do you want another pause?

You now know the answers to three VERY IMPORTANT questions:

1. *Why does the practice of witchcraft and spiritism come so easily and naturally to people in tribal cultures, and indeed, to people everywhere in the world?*

2. *Why is it that eastern mystic religions and meditational practices from nations that have suffered terribly under the curses of poverty, sickness and death have caught on so quickly in the once prosperous "Christian" nations?*

3. *Why is it that a people whose Christian religion has brought them so much blessing will turn to other religions which rob them of those blessings they once had? (We touched on spirits of rebellion and stupidity in chapter one).*

    THE ANSWER TO ALL OF THEM IS S.R.L.W.. in the human soul.

2.3 THE DRAMA OF DYING

We have already discussed the spirit of death (1.12) and now I would like to express some opinions drawn from human experience of dying.

My oldest son works in the nursing profession and cares for the aging in a nursing home. He daily experiences the drama associated with mental confusion, forgetfulness and all the symptoms of Alzeimer's disease believed to be caused by deterioration of the brain cells through aging.

However the aging process not only produces forgetfulness (especially short term memory lapses) but also manifests a whole range of obsessive behaviour patterns AND, most importantly, PERSONALITY CHANGES!

(i)   THE AGING

Only yesterday **Tim** told me of a little old lady, normally refined and appreciative, who experienced a personality switch and called him a "f...ing pig", amongst other things. What caused the change? Because he was cleaning her up. She had defecated into her clothes and he not only had to deal with the excrement from her bowels but also the excrement from her mouth, at the other end. Unfortunately this is "normal" in care for the elderly.

Two minutes later she was back to her normal self and this is also a normal every day occurrence - ask any nursing home or hospital worker.

You don't have to be brilliant to understand that as we get older and our minds lose their ability to control the way we express our soulish feelings, control spirits within the soulish area manifest themselves with all their ugliness. A society's standards of conduct and speech between human beings, those which have been practised throughout a lifetime, are of no interest to the unclean control spirit. It thinks to itself that now it can express itself and really take charge whenever it wants to. It can hurt family members, and curse and blaspheme and spit and punch whenever it feels like it, especially against the nursing staff who have duties to perform.

(ii)   THE DAMAGED

Likewise any kind of injury involving brain damage, whether caused by a road accident, sport or violence etc., can cause immediate personality changes of the ugly kind. There is no doubt in my mind that where skin is broken and skeletal damage experienced, spirits of infirmity and destruction etc. seek to take possession of the human being. The lines of defence have been broken down and entry into the soul is easily achieved.

Please remember, the SOUL is in the BLOOD (Levit. 17:11, 14; Deut. 12:23; cf. Gen. 4:10), and where there is bloodshed, the body's natural defences are broken down to some degree, both physically and spiritually.

Personality changes can also be caused by alcohol, drugs (including medical) and medical conditions such as changes to our blood sugar level (diabetes) etc.

(iii) THE DYING

My wife **Verlie** has spent a lifetime in nursing and has many anecdotes concerning experience of dying. To record just one, a woman vomited a black syrupy, sticky liquid, like molasses, many times before leaving this world.

I remember being in hospital as a little kid, with double pneumonia, and seeing a man in a bed at the end of the ward coughing continuously. He was so bad the staff moved him to a private room. I later found out he died before morning.

Again, this kind of suffering is not unusual before death. Unclean spirits usually know when the spirit of death is going to be allowed to bring our PHYSICAL functioning and existence to an end, and so they leave in great numbers. They cannot (normally) exist in a dead body because, we remind you, their area of activity is the soul and the soul's physical area of location is in the blood. When we die, rigour mortis sets in and our blood disintegrates into lifelessness (cf. John 19:34).

So they have to leave and find a new home to dwell in, if not just before death takes over, then very soon after[4]. This may well explain the noise nursing staff hear just before death, known as "Cheyne-Stokes" breathing, and the expulsion of "gases(?)" soon after death. It is as well to note here that the original word used in the New Testament for **"breath"** or **"wind"** can also be translated **"spirit"**, so perhaps the "gases" being expelled are really spirits?

Likewise the human spirit has to leave when death shuts down the body, sometimes with an audible sign or a gasp and its departure is very often heard by those nearby (cf. Mark 15:37, Matt. 27:50, Luke 23:46, John 19:30).

(iv) THE NEAR-DEATH EXPERIENCE

All of us store up thousands of memories from our childhood, our teenage, our young adulthood, and our middle and old age. Should we face the prospect of IMMINENT DEATH, many testimonies tell us that countless old, hidden and forgotten events would be raised up and flash before our "eyes".

Why?

What earthly good is it having our life flash visibly before us like some movie camera running film at high speed?

---

4. See discussion in Book 2 **"Engaging the Enemy"**, chapter 5.5 (ii).

When we visited **Peter** and **Fiona Horrobin's** work, **Ellel Ministries**, Lancashire in 1989, he shared with Verlie and myself the importance of identifying **Entry Points**[5], that is, times in our lives when demons have been able to gain access into our souls. Identification of such key incidents and entry points then enables the minister to lead the sufferer in a renouncing prayer, thus taking back the lost "ground" in Jesus' Mighty Name. This is the basis of much mental and emotional healing, removing from the unclean spirit any last vestige of legal right it is holding onto in order to stay put. If our authority in Christ is exercised resolutely, it must loose the sufferer.

So what does the prospect of imminent death produce? It produces a rush of unclean spirits from deep within the soul and into the mind, and as they come up they visibly reproduce the scenario of the incident through which they entered, usually many years before.

They are shocked at the thought of having to leave when death takes place and as they exit they bring those memories of their entry experience up with them. This explains why the imminent threat of death brings a rush of old dramas and traumas before our "eyes", that is, the eyes of our hearts (Eph. 1:18). They seek to find a new home for the future prior to their present home dropping dead!

If death does not eventuate or the "signals" prove to be a false alarm, these spirits have no trouble in re-entering their previous home, unless the person involved takes specific steps involving spiritual warfare to prevent it.

(v)   THE EXPERIENCE OF DEATH

Our most senior brother-in Christ, **Richard Coleman** (81), was promoted to Glory on Thursday November 16, 2000, and the funeral held at Northern Suburbs Crematorium chapel on Friday 24th.

On the Sunday morning that our Northern Travellers' bus normally picked up Richard, the drivers were instructed not to call for him, but without explanation.

"Is Richard okay?" someone asked. "He's in very good shape" I replied. Another asked "Is Richard away?" I replied "Yes". "Is Richard all right?" "He is fine" I said. (No one can say I wasn't telling the truth).

---

5. **"Healing through Deliverance"** pp. 193-194, Peter Horrobin.

THE NON CHRISTIAN'S FATE
(BUT NOT THE CHRISTIAN'S - JOHN 14:1-3)

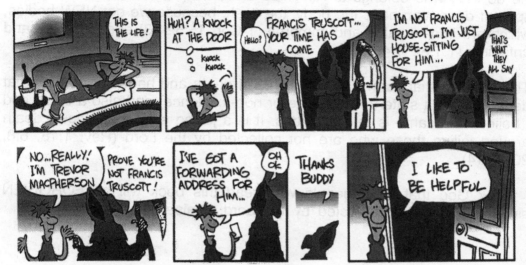

Reproduced by kind permission of Planet Media
email:piperlee@ozemail.com.au

I wanted to tell the WHOLE truth to the Committee as a group, rather than have some being informed and others left out. After the initial shock they were all able to genuinely rejoice FOR Richard's promotion.

What happens when we die? If the testimony of many people can be accepted[6] our human spirit slips out of our body frame-work and is able to look down at our body. Some have even watched as other humans have tried to save or revive them.

If they are successful we wake up back in our body again. If not, we (our human spirit, the part of us that really matters) begins a journey into realms unknown.

So our human spirit, the real us, does not stop living, we just leave our house of flesh. It is like going out the front door of our house to go and visit.

Death is not a problem for the Christian who has fully put their trust in the Lord Jesus although, of course, it is normally a great loss to the remaining family.

---

6. E.g. **"Voices from the Edge of Eternity"**, John Myers.

Very simply the Lord personally comes and collects everyone (how does He do it??) who belongs to Him, true disciples (John 8:31-32, 14:3). The spirit of death can have the body, the flesh, because we get NEW bodies, which are imperishable and immortal (1 Cor. 15:52-53) and undefiled and unfading (1 Pet. 1:4).

The non-Christian is met by the spirits of death and hades. We know that death is both a state (of existence or non-existence) and also a spirit, and I believe the same is true of hades. It is a jailing spirit that follows death around jailing those who are not collected by the Lord (Rev. 1:18, 6:8, 20:13-14).

I thank God that most people who read this book will be FORGIVEN sinners and will be collected by the Lord. Praise His Holy Name!

CHAPTER 3

RELIGIOUS SPIRITS

INTRODUCTION

"I could scarcely reconcile myself at first to this strange way of preaching in the fields, of which he (Whitefield) set me an example on Sunday; I had been all my life (till very lately) so tenacious of every point relating to decency and order that I should have thought the saving of souls almost a sin if it had not been done in a church".
John Wesley 29 March 1739

-confessing his RELIGIOUS churchianity. No wonder the good Lord forced him into the open air to preach!

When I read this entry in Wesley's Journal it reminded me very much of my astonishment when as a young man (teen-ager?) I read that **Pat Boone,** the sales record-breaking recording artist and film star, had baptized someone in a Hollywood swimming pool (the ultimate luxury symbol at that time).

How could he do that, I wondered? Don't baptisms have to be carried out by an ordained minister and in a church (building)? Such were the religious, cultural limitations imposed on many of us at that time.

Have you ever been on holidays and wondered where you would go to worship when Sunday came around? For **Orthodox** and **Roman Catholic** Christians, this usually poses little problem, but for **Protestants** who are aware of the main themes of the Bible's teaching, especially Christians into **Renewal** (Charismatics), it can be a major headache. From the **Anglo-Catholic (Anglican)** tradition to **Toronto**-style experiences it's so hard to find a church today to "suit" an informed, born-again, Bible-believing worshipper who wants to worship "in spirit/Spirit and in truth" (John 4:24).

If you are not careful you could find yourself surrounded by idols (graven images) and crucifixes, ministers who call themselves "priests" and dress in glorious apparel, right down to the "beat" generation who put on a rock concert with its noise and drum beat hypnosis. It seems to me that whenever I go to other churches to meet with the Lord I have to suffer something unclean as well, as part of the "package".

Through most church assemblies there runs a stream of the truth of God's Word but often it is surrounded by so much spiritual pollution I personally can't always face it and prefer to stay home for private devotions - and then I feel guilty (Heb. 10:25).

I wonder how many Christians out there in "Western" nations instinctively feel the same way, perhaps without being able to put it into words?

How can you tell if you have a religious spirit? Well, the truth is most people have - especially if they have been TAUGHT religious practices and habits as a little child.

We are all born with a significant religious need and capacity which forces mankind to inquire, to search for truth and answers to questions regarding the meaning of life. Why were we born? Why do we die? What "gods" can help me? What are the "laws" of life, the universe (creation) etc. ???

The Lord has created this spiritual area within us *(the Holy of Holies in each human temple/house created by Him and for Him to dwell within),* and even if we let the **Man of Sin**[1] enter where he ought not (2 Thess. 2:3-4) he can only partially "satisfy" our religious needs.

I'm all for people going to church but simply going and learning to do religious forms physically (kneeling etc.) WITHOUT meeting with Jesus personally and spiritually, tends to make us ritualistic, and therefore "religious". Also **religious spirits** tend to belong to a grouping which includes **legalistic, critical, condemnatory** and **accusing spirits**. They can be mixed up with a lot of Holy Spirit too (hence the two-souled[2] Christian), so sometimes it is very difficult to discern the mixture that comes out of our mouths (James 3:8-10). (One has only to think of the mixture that sometimes comes forth from the mouth of a modern prophet in the assembly). If it is any consolation, the Apostle Paul testifies to his old religiosity (e.g. Acts 22:3-5) before he met with Jesus, was broken in spirit by physical blindness, and set free to SEE, physically AND spiritually, by the fullness of the Spirit of God (Acts 9:1-9).

3.1 RELIGION AND CHRISTIANITY

I am sure many of you readers have heard people say **"I'm sick of religion"**, especially if you have a ministry of personal evangelism which you seek to use in the market place.

---

1   The application of this personality dwelling in a human being rather than in a Temple built in Jerusalem is discussed in Chapter 7.

2   "Two-souled", usually translated "double-minded" - James 1:8, 4:8.

I can remember a recent occasion when three strangers who I engaged in conversation, all within a period of only two days, said the same thing,

"I'm sick of religion!"

It may be they were referring to rituals and forms of services, or boring messages, or lack-lustre ministers, or stifling religious rules, or sexual abuse, or any number of ugly practices carried out by demonised sinners, under the banner of "Christianity".

The churches have always had the problem similar to that of wordly societies, that is, they are full of sinners. But as one sage put it, *"If you find the perfect church, don't join it, because it won't be perfect any more!"*

Today, Renewal churches have a significant number of damaged people in their meetings, many of whom are on their way to recovery. They are receiving **healing and deliverance, inner cleansing and RESTORATION-** praise the Name of the Lord!

And so today there is a BIG DIFFERENCE between *Religion* and all its man-made showy practices, and *Christianity*. Just read the Gospels of our Lord Jesus Christ and learn of HIS true Christianity. True Christianity is vastly different from religious practice (Jas. 1:27), that is why we need RENEWAL and Renewed churches.

Why, even the Old Testament religious Laws and practices of Israel are, since the Victory of the Cross of Christ, seen as being inspired by the *stoicheia,* that is, *the elemental spirits of the world,* and not the Holy Spirit.

The apostle Paul put it this way:

"... when we were children we were slaves to the elemental spirits of the world. But when the fullness of time came, God sent forth His Son .. born under the Law so that He might redeem those under the Law.

... now that you have come to know God ... **how can you turn again to the weak and poor elemental spirits,** *which you again wish to serve anew?*

You observe days and months and seasons and years.

I am afraid for you, that I have laboured among you in vain".
(Gal. 4:3-11, cf.Col. 2:8,16,20).

Can you imagine that? The enemy (the elemental spirits) used the Old Testament Law so they could CONDEMN the Israelites and, indeed, the whole world (Rom. 2:12,3:19,4:15,5:12-13,20-21).

Praise the Lord, we Christians are no longer under the condemnation of the Law but under God's grace! (Rom. 5:1-2, 20; 6:14) - but if we go back to observing the religious laws[3] of Moses we put ourselves back under the authority and control of the elemental spirits again! God forbid! Many church traditions (Col. 2:8) are a brick wall, instead of being a doorway to our Creator God.

There have been many attempts to explain the difference between Christianity and all other religions in the world. Christians rightly emphasise that **Christ offers the forgiveness of our sins** - a pardon - to those who become His followers and this seems to be unique to the Christian faith. Another enormous difference lies in the definition of Christianity which is described as **God reaching out to man"** (through Jesus Christ) whereas all other religions are based on the gropings of **"man reaching out to God"**. God has succeeded where man has failed.

The Word of God indicates it is impossible for man to find God with His own efforts alone (John 15:5b) hence man-made religions always fall far short of the truth and often end up in spiritism, ancestor-worship and witchcraft.

CHRISTIAN CELEBRATIONS

Have you noticed how happy the western world is to recognise "Easter" and Christmas? However the recognition is becoming more and more heathen and less and less Christian, which is not surprising.

Most of you have no problem with honouring the birth of Christ on Dec. 25th. So it's the wrong date - so what? At least its name honours the Christ and His becoming flesh amongst us. Not so with "Easter". Many Christians have been telling us that the word "Easter" is a direct reference to a pagan goddess of creation and fertility, and has no Christian meaning at all, hence easter bunnies and eggs. Together with this information we should also note that before and after God told the Hebrews to destroy the shrines and idols of the gods of the nations around them He also instructed them to **not even speak the names of their gods, ever again.** (Exod. 23:13, Josh. 23:7, Psalm 16:4). Apparently to even use the word

---

3. As distinct from the MORAL laws, which are carried through to the NEW Testament.

E....r is to honour this pagan goddess, and as a consequence the emphasis that the New Testament gives the **Resurrection** of our Lord Jesus Christ is almost completely lost.

The foolishness of applying the name of a pagan goddess to a vital and holy Christian celebration is quite repugnant to informed Christians, but not at all repugnant to the secular and pagan society around us. I urge all true disciples of the Lord to not only put Christ back into Christmas, but also re-establish the day we celebrate for the Resurrection as **"Resurrection Sunday"**. Let us completely eliminate the alternative pagan word. If you feel you have to use the word E....r, I suggest you put a Y in front of it and make it **Yeaster.** As most Christians know, yeast represents **sin** in the Bible, hence Holy Communion is, or should be, celebrated with **unleavened** bread, that is, bread without yeast. Yeaster is a time when our sins were paid for.

If all this is too much, just stick with **"Good Friday"** and **"Resurrection Sunday"**.

VIOLENCE AND MURDER

Australian Christians were shocked at the incineration of **Pastor Graham Staines** with his two children in the family car while on mission in Orissa State, India, during January 1999. The crime was allegedly committed by extreme Hindu radicals, while the whole world knows that sections of Islamic fundamentalism have been butchering Christian communities whenever they think their religion is losing ground.

Religious unclean spirits are among the strongest and most dangerous in existence. This can be seen from the well-known clashes between the Lord Jesus Christ and the Pharisees. Jesus accused them of killing the prophets of old (Matt. 23:29-31,37) and warned His disciples that sincere religious people would want to kill them also (John 16:2).

There has always been a life-threatening tension between "religious" people and God's true Christian servants. The Church of the day has even executed saintly great men like **John Hus**, the Bohemian Reformer (1415 A.D.), **Savonarola,** the Italian Reformer (1498 A.D.) - a host of **English** and **French Reformers**, while others like **Martin Luther** escaped plots against their lives. **John Wesley** and his band of preachers suffered violence during the eighteenth century Wesleyan Revival in England, but all this is simply following in the tradition of John the Baptist and, most importantly, our Lord Jesus Christ Himself.

With the revelation of Jesus of Nazareth we have God sending His only Son who declares that **He (alone) is the Way, the Truth and the Life. No one can come to the Father God except through Him (John 14:6). This is Christianity** - God reaching out to a lost and helpless mankind through His Son (John 3:16-19) However, in many places the Church has not been built on the foundation of Jesus Christ ALONE, but also on the PAGANISM of resident religions, making a very unhappy mixture indeed.

3.2 NON-CHRISTIAN RELIGIOUS SPIRITS

Spirits that seek to set up gods other than the Christian Godhead are, according to the apostle Paul, idolatrous and religious (Acts 17:16,22). **Unclean spirits, of course, love an audience.** They are not concerned with worshipping God through Jesus Christ, but they are interested in mockery, deception and self-advertising, **parading their "spirituality" for the applause of men, and seeking the pre-eminence.** There are, of course, religious spirits controlling every non-Christian religion in the world and I suppose every Christian evangelist and personal-worker has been confronted with the opinion that *"all roads lead to the top of the hill"*. According to this universalist theory, **Buddhists** find God their way and **Shintoists** their way, **Christians** their way and **Hindus** their way. Well, other religions may say that all (religious) roads lead to God but the Christian faith does not, because Jesus Christ, the founder of Christianity, made it absolutely clear that He was and is the ONLY way, and this is how Paul presented Him in his message on the subject of "the Unknown God" at Athens (Acts 17:23). This direct and only Way to God is to continue until the Day of Judgement (Psalm 96:13, Matt. 28:20, Acts 17:30-31).

The Deliverance Ministry brings spectacular confirmation of Jesus' claims. At commands issued in Jesus' Name spirits or demons of any and every non-Christian religion you can name have come spitting, whining and wailing out of people. *Hindu spirits, Buddhist spirits, Qabbala spirits* - out they come - all of them - at the Name of **Jesus.** They are no match for His Name or the power of His Holy Spirit. Praise the Lord!

In referring to non-Christian religions and the unclean spirits that inspire them we ought not to leave out a religion that has destroyed the lives of probably **one billion people** this century. That is 1000 x 1000 x 1000 people, consisting of two generations of people belonging to the old **Union of Soviet Socialist Republics**, and one generation of their satellites such as **Bulgaria, Romania**, etc., since World War 2.

The **USSR** consisted of fifteen republics controlled from Moscow, with a daily population of around 250 million, but that has all changed now, thank

God. However we are not just referring to Communism, that section of the Labour Movement dedicated to violence "whenever necessary", but the **Labour Movement** as a whole. Many people have made the Labour Movement their religion and are perfectly open and honest about it. They think of it as a religion that changes things for the better - gets things done and not just talk.

The Unity of Labor is the Hope of the World? So says this political publication of 1907. It is a classic example of how good intentions and visions of future hope can quite unconsciously produce an anti-Christ (alternative Christ).

The Word of God declares that Christ (and Christianity) is the Hope of the World (John 4:42, 1 Peter 1:20-21). Alternatives are deceptions, no matter how sincere, good and noble the intentions may be. We cannot serve God and mammon (Luke 16:10-13).

In the beginning (around the eighteenth century) it was a Christian movement inspired by influential men such as **William Wilberforce** who attempted to address the terrible injustices suffered by the poor and slaves alike. Such injustice bred an equally terrible fury and hatred amongst the working poor, and soon God was left out. New gods such as **Marx, Lenin,** and **Engels** replaced the Creator and a new religion was born, inspired by an anti-Christ spirit, which preached a gospel of hate. Today we can look back and say that although members (true believers) of this religion have seen socialism fail horrendously with enormous cost in death and poverty to many peoples, many are still controlled by the religious spirit responsible, because it is a SPIRITUAL BONDAGE. It therefore lives on today (albeit under different labels such as humanism, fabianism, internationalism, social democracy etc.) as a theory (fantasy) of prosperity which its adherents (slaves) are determined to foist on all of us and make work somehow, over our dead bodies if necessary.

When casting out this religious spirit you may need to include **anger, violence, unbelief, idolatry, hatred** and **murder** in your ministering, and perhaps **insanity** as well. The Labour Movement has only ever been united by force (tyranny) and fear.

The Labour Movement continues to use the blasphemous banner **"The Unity of Labour is the Hope of the World"** at its conferences, and has done so at least since 1907. Christians who have any understanding of the Word of God in the New Testament will know that **the Lord Jesus Christ is THE HOPE of the World!**

3.3 RELIGIOUS SPIRITS IN THE CHURCHES

It is obvious that the activities of religious spirits in the Christian church are often manifested together with the use of the Name of the Lord Jesus Christ. In fact one could say that not only does the use of the Lord's Name NOT guarantee that only the HOLY Spirit is involved but on the contrary, continuous involving of the Name of the Lord Jesus at every opportunity so as to create the impression of holiness, may well be unclean and counter-productive for the Glory of God. It may be serving the glory of men and therefore by definition, and by its fruit, be seen to be unclean. Also spirits of self-righteousness, mockery and ridicule may be involved.

Christian Hebrew prophet and teacher, **Arthur Katz**, reminds us His Name, Jesus, is to be HALLOWED, not thrown around loosely. This should not surprise us because Jesus warned us so strongly about the religiosity of the Pharisees, who **"for a pretence make long prayers"** and **"like to**

go about in long (religious) robes and have the best seats in the synagogues (churches)" (Mark 12:38-40, cf. Matt. 23). This religiosity was not simply a problem confined to non-believers, because the Lord specifically **warned His disciples** to **"beware of the leaven of the Pharisees"** (Matt.16:6). Such a warning would not be necessary if there was no real danger His followers could be infected by the disease of pharisaism. Likewise the apostle **Paul** discovered himself in deadly conflict with a **"circumcision party"** in the early church, so that he had to issue the strongest possible warning to the Galatian church to reject their influence (Gal. chapters 2,5).

More recently in our own day the American prophet **J. Leland Earl** published a revelation he received from the Lord:

> *...After this experience the Lord began to deal with me concerning other spirits which are especially troubling the Body of Christ at this time. He showed me two other groups of three each. In the second group are PROUD SPIRITS, **RELIGIOUS SPIRITS,** AND DECEIVING SPIRITS. In the third group are COVETOUS SPIRITS, LUST SPIRITS and LYING SPIRITS.*

> *These six, plus the three "bitter" spirits (Jealousy, Criticism, Resentment), are the nine kinds of spirits which are especially defiling the Body of Christ and ARE HINDERING THE SAINTS FROM MOVING INTO THEIR FULL INHERITANCE IN CHRIST. Beloved hear me! **The present move of the Spirit of God is primarily to bring cleansing and deliverance from these spirits of the enemy that the saints be no longer hindered.***

> *I cannot go into all that the Lord has shown me concerning this subject and the relation of His present move to it. But I do know that HE IS RAISING UP AND ANOINTING VESSELS OF HIS CHOOSING TO BE USED IN THIS MINISTRY.*

> *He has also promised KEEN DISCERNMENT, and I know that along with this gift will go the GIFTS OF KNOWLEDGE AND WISDOM, and also MUCH LOVE AND COMPASSION. FOR THIS IS A MINISTRY OF HELP AND DELIVERANCE, NOT OF CONDEMNATION.*

> *There are many saints who are vexed and oppressed by one or more of these spirits and THEY ARE NOT FULLY AWARE OF IT. THEY MAY SENSE THAT SOMETHING IS WRONG, BUT THEY DON'T KNOW WHAT TO DO, OR HOW TO GET DELIVERANCE.*

> *The Lord has shown me that the nine spirits mentioned are the very antithesis of the nine fruits of the Spirit mentioned in Gal. 5:22-23.*

*How can the Lord impart love, joy and peace when many saints are experiencing the bitterness of jealousy, criticism and resentment. It is impossible for saints to express genuine long-suffering, gentleness and goodness towards others if there are PROUD, **RELIGIOUS**, AND DECEIVING SPIRITS AT WORK IN THEIR LIVES.*

There can be very little real fidelity, meekness and self-control evidenced in those who have succumbed to covetous, lust and lying spirits.

Brother Leland has done us a great service in bringing these revelations before us. Please notice that **RELIGIOUS** spirits are grouped with PROUD and DECEIVING spirits, as one would expect.

(i)   OBVIOUS RELIGIOUS SPIRITS

Did you know that the **traditions of men are inspired by demons?**

Beware lest anyone rob you through philosophy and empty deceit, ***according to the tradition of men, according to the elemental spirits[4] of the world****, and not according to Christ. (Col. 2:8).*

Did you know that **religious legalism** is **inspired by demons?**

*If you died with Christ from **the elemental spirits of the world** why do you live as if subject to the world's decrees? Do not touch nor taste nor handle **...according to the injunctions and teachings of men...** (Col. 2:20-22).*

These spirits in "Christians" will ALWAYS oppose genuine Holy Spirit Renewal (Acts 7:51), and finally, did you know that much **human wisdom** is earthy, soulish and **demonic?** (James 3:15). Please keep these vital spiritual truths alive in your mind as we now look at obvious religious activity.

Some people are so obviously bound up and active with religious spirits that almost anyone in the Renewal movement can discern them. Some sections of the Church are so totally taken over and controlled by them that it is a miracle and a demonstration of the grace of God that anything inspired by the Holy Spirit ever happens! However, as Paul said, **"the Word of God is not bound!"** (1 Tim. 2:9), and **"the Spirit blows where He wills"** (John 3:8).

---

4. Elemental spirits is translated from the original "stoicheia" which we explain more fully along the way in 3.3 (iv).

Some of the more obvious areas that we can see the operation of religious spirits are as follows:

(a) CLOTHING FOR SERVICES

"...holding the FORM of religion but denying the POWER of it. Avoid these people." (2 Tim. 3:5)

That is, long, "priestly", colourful robes full of symbolism (dare I say superstitious symbolism). Anything that accentuates a priestly, mediatorial class over and above **the priesthood of ALL believers** (1 Peter 2:5, Rev. 1:6, 20:6), and focuses attention on the ministers rather than the Lord is a potential disaster area.

Men who have a hidden need to be the centre of attention and who do not have the ability to get into **"show biz"** may well find themselves attracted to a form of priesthood. Is it any wonder **transvestite spirits** love to get their houses (captives) into a priesthood. They can then prance around the "altar" with great showmanship, in front of a stupefied audience, dressed in glorious apparel (cf. Luke 7:25) and wearing skirts at that! (Deut. 22:5).

Yet others may have sexual problems and hope that drawing near to God as a priest will help them, by means of a life of holiness empowering them to overcome their dark urges.

All of these situations greatly hinder and taint the genuine servants of the Lord who wear skirts only because their training and traditions require it. They find themselves surrounded by those who are in the "priesthood" for all the wrong reasons. It is probably unnecessary for me to add that those with genuine motives (even though theologically flawed) are seriously compromised by the actors around them.

(b) CHURCH ORNAMENTS AND IMAGES

Back in 1989 Verlie and I visited **Israel** and **the U.K.**. Two things happened relating to images. In **Jerusalem** we used a Moslem tour guide who led us into one of the churches. Up until that time he had shown us various images and icons without emotion, but when we came to a statue (three dimensional image) of the virgin Mary with a sad face, he passionately implored us to gaze upon her (its) countenance.

Later in London we visited **St. Paul's Cathedral** and again our guide became emotional. "Look what they did!" he cried out, pointing to many figurettes with damaged faces and bodies.

He was referring to the **iconoclasts (image breakers)** who went around smashing idols and icons during the biblical **Reformation** of the **16th Century**. I looked (as he requested) and quietly rejoiced!

Most of us know about the **1st and 2nd Commandments** from the **Law of Moses**. They read:

> *You shall have no other gods before me. You shall not make any graven image, or any likeness of anything that is in heaven above, or in the earth beneath, or in the water under the earth: You shall not bow down to them, nor serve them: for I the Lord your God am a jealous God, visiting the iniquity of the fathers upon the children to the third and fourth generation of those who hate me; and showing mercy to thousands of those who love me, and keep my commandments.*

One might ask why the Lord is concerned about the MAKING of images when He also commands us not to bow down and worship them? Is it not sufficient to instruct us not to worship them? Can we not make images for purposes other than worship? For decoration perhaps, or to satisfy our creative skills or to enjoy?

Quite obviously the good Lord knows how vulnerable we are and how superstitious *(religious, demon-fearing - Acts 17:22)* we can get. It is so easy to "cross the line" in spiritual things and find ourselves chained to something. For example, some men can grow long and luxuriant hair which gets a lot of attention. To suggest that it be cut short (cf. 1 Cor. 11:14) for any reason can be tantamount to starting World War III.

Clearly if we are forbidden to MAKE graven images (no matter what the reason) in the first place, we cannot then be deceived into giving them undue attention or affection (*follow, serve, worship* - Deut. 8:19) and get ourselves into BIG trouble!

It may surprise many Christians to learn that this matter of images in the Church has been a tumultuous one throughout early church history, with different leaders (Emperor Leo III and Pope Gregory II) contradicting each other, and much bloodshed.

Clever excuses[5] for present day images such as fabricated by the eighth century church cannot justify such rebellion.

The Media is not particularly known for its support of Christianity, but they are often "kindred spirits" with **religiosity** and **churchianity.**

When they came to "my" church, **St. Michael's Surry Hills (Sydney),** to cover the outbreak of deliverance many years ago, on what did they want to focus their cameras? You've guessed it! Stone walls, gloomy interior, stained glass windows, (two dimensional images) and me sitting in the choir stalls with the old organ behind me.

That is how people see the historic church, largely because the Media often present Christianity today as (unclean) religion, dead as a dodo! To be fair, they don't know how else to present Christian matters visually.

Mournful, old, decrepit, anachronistic, dark, musty, reeking of death and the religious (spirit). Although there may be plenty of numinous[6] from familiar and ancestral spirits, there is not much hint of the **HOLY** Spirit in some historic church buildings, except the presence of a sparrow or a church mouse created by God (Psalm 84:3), There is plenty to indicate "religion".

Artwork: Tim Field- used by permission

Don't be surprised when earthquakes and earth tremors demolish these churches!

(c) CONDUCT OF SERVICES[7]

What value is **bowing** to other robed figures - and the Cross, **turning** to the east, **chanting** and **genuflecting? Processions** may possibly be free of religious activity, depending on the hearts of those involved. I have usually found them a great temptation to indulge in pomp and self-importance but **sometimes** have succeeded in keeping a pure heart, I think! However there can be a temporary closeness and warmth in praise while passing through a worshipping assembly.

---

5. See Appendix C
6. Feelings of spiritual presence
7 We say much more about this in our booklet **"Religious Spirits"**

(d) CHRISTIAN SYMBOLISM

Almost all contrived ritual and symbolism in Church service springs from the activity of religious spirits, not the Holy Spirit. You will find nothing to support many of these activities in the New Testament of our Lord Jesus Christ. They are distractions and diversions which focus human attention on themselves, rather than the object/person they are supposed to symbolise.

So much Church symbolism is attention-seeking showmanship! In the New Testament I see only four key symbols for Christians to use

   (i)   **Unleavened Bread** represents the Lord's Body in Holy Communion.

   (ii)   **The fruit of the vine** (not necessarily wine) *represents* the Lord's Blood. (Mark 14:25)

   (iii)   **Water** represents the Holy Spirit in Baptism. (Acts 2:38)

   (iv)   **Oil** represents the Holy Spirit in Healing (James 5:14).

There is nothing gaudy, flashy or colourful about any of these symbols. In New Testament times they were everyday items easily available to all and probably found in every Hebrew home, yet these common items *represent* the Lord Jesus and His Spirit! Do you perceive the wisdom of the Lord in this?

If you have been taught that the bread/wafer and wine used in the Mass or Holy Communion **LITERALLY** become The Body and Blood of our Lord, this contradicts the figurative, representative and memorial nature of **the Bread of Affliction** as presented in the **Jewish Passover**, which is the origin and basis of our **Christian Passover**, often known today as the Mass or Holy Communion.

Please note also the memorial and representative nature of the Cup:

> *"This Cup is the New Covenant in/with/by My blood."*
> *(Luke 22:20, 1Cor. 11:25)*

There is no way the Cup Jesus used was/is LITERALLY the New Covenant. "Covenant" means a binding legal document or agreement, not a drinking vessel, so He is speaking figuratively:

"This Cup (its contents) represents the New Covenant (sealed/obtained) in/with/by My blood."

I believe a religious spirit is at work encouraging many Christians to feed on Christ in their **stomachs** and not their **hearts.** Jesus' words are SPIRITUAL and not intended to be taken literally (John 6:51-56,63).

(e) SICKNESS

Getting all this wrong can have disastrous consequences.

The apostle Paul warns us that to profane the Body and Blood of the Lord is a doorway to sickness, and even (early) death.

"For anyone who eats and drinks without discerning (spiritually) the body eats and drinks judgment to himself. Therefore many among you are weak (sick) and feeble, and some sleep (have died)."
(1 Cor. 11:29-30).

Many ministers have tried to exercise a healing ministry but have become disheartened when their prayers for a sufferer have not been answered. They have expected instant, or at least, speedy healings and when neither of those things happen, they give up, thinking they do not have the necessary gifting from the Holy Spirit.

In fact *"failures"* should teach us much. If we REALLY believe the Word of God is true for today we need to search in every way possible for the reason(s) why we "fail". For example, do you know of anyone who has led a sufferer in repentant prayer for wrong, false, flippant, fleshly, idolatrous, thoughtless, careless and even profane participation in Holy Communion??? No? Neither do I, outside of our own ministry.

Now, back to Christian symbolism.

Unleavened bread and the **fruit of the vine** *represent* His body and His blood - given and shed for us upon Calvary's Cross - not gold crosses and ornate crucifixes. Neither do we need long robes in the market places, or even in Church, **IF** our hearts are filled with the Holy Spirit. Christianity is not about visible externals. Man looks on the outward appearance, but God looks on the heart (1 Sam. 16:7). When we emphasise visible, external symbols it robs us from focussing on the Holy Spirit within us. They will know us by our love (John 13:35) and the FRUIT of the indwelling Spirit in our lives (Matt. 7:15-20). These fruit are SPIRITUAL, not physical.

LIFE, NOT DEATH

I am not suggesting there should be no preparation for services or meetings. Nor am I suggesting there should be no format or order, or earlier choosing and **preparation of worship songs, prayers and messages.**

However any such prepared material must be held together gently and sensitively, so that the Holy Spirit can FLOW in - without having to BREAK in! Those who lead meetings must be spiritually fluid enough to change the program, to allow the expected (a word of prophecy?) or the unexpected (a demonised man creating some drama down the back?) to happen, and respond to that happening as the Holy Spirit leads (cf. Mark 1:21-28).

Having read prayers in historic church situations for many years, doing "my best" by the grace of God to make them alive and meaningful, I can say that, beautiful as many of them are, they miss the mark more often than not, because **the Kingdom of God consists not in word (talk) but in Power** (1 Cor. 4:20), and the Holy Spirit is inhibited from LEADING the prayers.

Prayer MUST come from the human heart and born again spirit, or it is just a religious exercise, as bad as saying prayers by numbers (1,2,3....). I don't need to tell you who or what inspires such religiosity.

With services that are strictly read from a prayer book, the best one can hope for is that parts of the service will be inspired for the participants, but we should not expect the Holy Spirit to take control, except in very unusual situations.. **"The letter kills, the Spirit gives LIFE!"** (2 Cor. 3:6). The choice is READ prayers or LEAD prayers! DEAD prayers or LIVING prayers!

RELIGIOUS CONVERSATION

It is probably obvious to most Christians that the clearest exposure of a "hidden" unclean religious spirit, outside of church building services and meetings is - ordinary conversation. I once had a very keen, Bible-trained Deaconess on my staff at **St. Michael's, Sydney,** but-oh the vocabulary!

Every conversation was couched in the most syrupy, gooey, pious, religious language. It was rather like the script of a slow-moving Hollywood religious epic (not, I hasten to add, on the life of Jesus, which have generally been done as well as one could expect).

Some people pray like that. They produce a different language from the normal with plenty of *thees*, *thys* and *thous*. They even produce a different voice, especially when they prophesy. In very severe cases the language is always couched in such a way as to make sure you know you are talking to a full-on, mature, spiritual giant. Such Christians do not often manifest the genuine joy of the Lord. How can they? The religious spirit has them in chains and they are more likely to carry associated problems of legalism, and perhaps mournfulness. Their personalities are NOT a good witness which will attract people to the Lord Jesus, but rather the opposite.

SUPERSTITION

Superstition can sometimes be demonstrated by the sign of the Cross being made by someone across their shoulders with the right or left hand. I normally have mixed feelings when I see a small cross hung around someone's neck, if only because it reveals that person to have an awareness of spiritual things and probably God-fearing.

Even if a cross or crucifix is worn as an act of superstition, hoping for Godly protection, it gives me the opportunity to speak about faith and Christ. When I ask "Are you a Christian?" they usually respond "Catholic"- but at least we are TALKING!

You may remember the apostle Paul was deeply offended by the idolatry in Athens, but used one altar inscribed "To An Unknown God" to launch his message:

> *"What therefore you worship as unknown,*
> *This I proclaim to you......!!!"*

People wear a cross for many reasons, and I would suspect the larger and more obvious it is, the more "religious" they are, depending on gadgets and visible symbols rather than the invisible blood of the Passover Lamb (Exod. 12:12-14, 1 Cor. 5:7) which should be prayed (and sprayed) over us (believers) at the beginning of each day.

Although there was **once** a mystery about God He has now revealed Himself through His only begotten Son (John 14:7-11, Eph. 3:8-11, Heb. 1:1-3). He has now revealed to us His character, attributes and power. He has made Himself known through His Word and by His Spirit. Indeed - wonder of wonders! - He has even made us temples of His Holy Spirit and dwells WITHIN EVERY BORN AGAIN CHRISTIAN. We are in Him and He is in us! (John 3:3-8, 1 Cor. 3:16-17, 6:19, John 14:7, 20,23).

Thus He has revealed Himself to us in a very personal way. He has revealed His person, His salvation and His will. He has even revealed the enemy, and how He has legally defeated him (Col. 2:15, 1 John 3:8). He has dispelled darkness with light (John 1:4-5), and shares an intimate friendship (confides) in those who fear Him (Psalm 25:14). Therefore **superstition** can only thrive amongst Christians where there is false teaching (doctrines of demons - 1 Tim. 4:1) and ignorance of the Word of God. (cf 2 Cor. 2:10-11).

During his preaching at the Areopagus in Athens **Paul** began tactfully but truthfully, declaring that he perceived the Athenians were very **superstitious** or **religious** (Acts 17:22). The word means literally **"demon-fearing",** and understood to mean **"gods-fearing",** as indeed demons and gods often mean the same things in Bible passages and in tribal societies today. So when a person says they are superstitious it usually means they are very sensitive to the activities of the spirit world, especially the unclean spirit world and its rule of fear over mankind. The bottom line is that **superstitious behaviour within the Christian church is a very clear and obvious indication of the activity of religious (and other) spirits.**

ANGER

I have often been amazed at the manifestation of anger that springs out of the most unlikely people at times.

At a Rural Deanery meeting in 1974 I was asked to speak on the Deliverance Ministry. After 15 minutes one usually quiet and highly respected minister could not contain himself any longer. *"Where do you get the term deliverance from anyway?"* He snarled, his eyes popping with anger.

When I calmly told him it came from the Lord's prayer, he just glared at me, speechless. We could easily have enjoyed an effective deliverance session right there in the middle of the Deanery.

We know that many of the wars that have erupted in the latter half of this twentieth century have been over religious matters, especially when we understand that Communism and Socialism are religions. Things can get to a place where hate just takes over and human rights are "forgotten", but I believe we are going to find that, more and more, people's religious differences are going to cause divisions and bloodshed all over the world, and the deception known as **multi-culturalism** (in reality idolatrous POLYTHEISM, and therefore inspired by the anti-Christ spirit -1 John 4:1-6) lead to civil wars within nations.

As a theological student I belonged to a group of Christians that was very confident they had most of the answers, and at least twice as many answers as any other Christians. Then came the **Charismatic** or **Renewal movement** and evangelicals suddenly found themselves on the defensive. On three separate occasions my evangelical friends became very angry with me when I parted from the traditional line of thinking. I found that very interesting, because normally when an evangelical finds himself in a theological dispute, he welcomes debate, confident he has the truth. He will debate long and lovingly to win the day because he believes he is in a winning position and cannot be shaken.

However when HIS traditions are also exposed by the Spirit of God and he is put on the defensive, watch out for the anger of the religious spirit!

SELF-MUTILATION

There is so much of this destructive activity of cutting one's own body with knives and razors going on today but, to my knowledge, no one has yet identified it as being inspired by a **religious spirit.**

The prophets and priests of BAAL did this as part of their religious rites (1 Kings 18:26-28). Likewise today, throughout the world primitive cultures that are based on a witchcraft religion continue to practice self-mutilation. Our own Aboriginal people, those who are still locked into their tribal rites, allegedly continue this practice today.[8]

The problem is not unknown in our psychiatric hospitals indicating possible transference from primitive cultures to western cultures. This should not surprise us, because for every indigenous person who becomes a Christian there are probably two westernised people who sink back into occultism (BAAL worship). In addition *ancestral (hereditary) pollution* can go back many generations.

However, what is becoming noticeable is that this condition is being linked with **Multiple Personality Disorder (M.P.D.),** more recently re-named **Dissociate Identity Disorder (D.I.D.).**[9]

Radio legend John Laws, on his morning **2UE Radio** talk-back program (7 March '99) interviewed a **Cameron West** who had written a book about the many "personalities" that controlled his life and for which he blamed child sexual abuse. At least one of these personalities caused him to inflict blows and/or cuts to himself. I first came across this condition in 1969 when, as a young Anglican curate I listened to a shocked housewife recount her horror at finding her soldier husband standing in front of the bathroom mirror and bleeding from self-inflicted cuts from his razor.

This peculiar behaviour is well attested to in the Word of God. We have the father of all multiple personality cases in the man with **the Legion** (of demons) whom the Lord Jesus Christ delivered (by casting out all the

---

8. " Man, Myth and Magic" p.180
9. I have to say I am not impressed with the new label D.I.D.. You can call a serious "mental" problem what you like and play with words forever but that doesn't help the sufferer. M.P.D. IS adequate and ACCURATE. See chapter 8.3.

invaders) and restored to his right mind. (Mark 5:1-20). While he was ill he repeatedly cut himself with stones, among other things (v.5), apparently because his ancestors had worshipped the false god **BAAL**, and their religious spirits had been passed down the blood line[10] to him.

He didn't know why he performed such stupid, self-destructive actions on himself, but **religious control spirits** simply took over in their turn, with the rest of the Legion of spirits, and he couldn't help himself (Compulsive Self Mutilation Disorder ???).[11]

Why did the prophets of BAAL cut themselves? When their prayers to their false god were not answered (after a full morning's concerted effort) they offered BAAL a BLOOD sacrifice. Not the blood of bulls and goats. Not the blood of their children (this time - cf. 2 Chron. 28:3. Psa. 106:37-38 etc.), but their OWN blood! It was their "best" effort, but it still didn't work (1 Kings 18:20-40) because they were opposing the Lord God and His prophet Elijah.

There are several Old Testament references forbidding self mutilation (Lev. 19:28, 21:5, Deut. 14:1, Jer. 16:6 etc.) but it is the story of "Legion" which inspires us because we learn about M.P.D., self mutilation and the demons inspiring and controlling all such unclean activity. Most importantly we learn of God's solution to the evil slavery. Unclean control spirits CAN be removed, and replaced by **God's Control Spirit - the Holy Spirit!** (Eph. 5:18 etc.) - in Jesus' Name!

We no longer have to sacrifice birds, animals and children like the pagans did (and do). We no longer have to shed OUR blood to please or appease pagan gods which are no gods, in reality (1 Cor. 8:5). Even our indigenous Aboriginal people have a tradition of shedding their blood during some of their tribal dances. It is part of their culture that has to be crucified (Rom. 6:3-7) if they are to enter the blessings of Almighty God. The **Lord Jesus Christ has shed HIS blood** in order to give us TOTAL victory, recorded in a LEGAL COVENANT (the New Testament) over ALL OUR ENEMIES. The apostle Paul's letter to the Colossians tells us that through the Cross of Christ, God has:

(a) *made us alive together with Christ*
(b) *forgiven us all our trespasses*
(c) *cancelled the written laws (of God) against us*

---

10. The soul is in the blood - Lev. 17:11,14 lit. Heb.
11. My best choice for Self Mutilation would be I.B.S.D. (Idolatrous, Blood sacrifice disorder), blunt but true!

(d) ***dropped His charges against us***
(e) ***nailed them to the Cross***
(f) ***thereby stripped the powers of darkness of their weapons against us***
(g) ***therefore shamefully exposed our enemies, and***
(h) ***triumphed over them by the Cross of Christ (Col. 2:13-15).***

What a victory! **It is a legal, spiritual victory that can be ours IF:**

(i) *we are, or become, true disciples (John 8:31-32)*
(ii) *understand this legal victory (above)*
(iii) *know, or learn how to appropriate this victory into our lives*
(iv) *live in the light of it*

It's time for us all to move into it.

A SURPRISING MIXTURE

Even more obvious as the activity of religious spirits is the hypocritical behaviour of some people who claim to be Christians. I remember an acquaintance expressing horror at the conduct of a business "friend". My acquaintance was owed quite a lot of money by his "friend", who had also cheated him in another business deal. So when this "friend" asked him to make a donation to his Church charity, he said to me "How is that for a two-faced hypocrite? He cheats me and then wants me to help his church!"

Did you know that the Word of God says that this will be normal in the last days (of this Age)? Men will be:

> ***lovers of themselves, lovers of money,***
> ***boasters, proud, blasphemers,***
> ***disobedient to parents,***
> ***ungrateful, unholy, unloving, unforgiving,***
> ***slanderers, without self-control, brutal,***
> ***despisers of good, traitors, headstrong,***
> ***haughty, lovers of pleasure rather than God,***
> ***HAVING A FORM OF GODLINESS, BUT DENYING ITS POWER,***
> ***.... always learning and never able to come to the knowledge of the truth (2 Tim. 3:1-7).***

What an incredible mixture of religiosity and evil!

Here is the largest list of **the works of the flesh** recorded in the New Testament, even larger than the well-known list in Galatians 5:19-21, and one of its longest phrases tells us that **holding to religious forms as a kind of counterfeit, powerless Christianity will be a feature of the End Time!**

The Word of God encourages us to avoid altogether the kind of people who hold the FORM of religion but deny the POWER of it (2 Tim. 3:2-5). Note carefully. The Word doesn't say that we should fellowship with the FORMAL religionists and avoid the effective ministries with God's POWER, but just the opposite! You will realise that, generally speaking, today's situation is that the FORMAL religionists of the traditional church denominations are busy warning the people of God NOT to be drawn into the Renewal movement of God's POWER and so they expressly contradict the Word, that they may keep their tradition and (hopefully) their people (Mark 7:9).

So much for **obvious manifestations** of religious spirits.

However in this book I want to focus attention on the more **subtle, hidden religious spirits** that have infested the Christian Church, home and society for centuries. It is the Lord's time to expose them in order that the Church might be cleansed!

SOME MAJOR PROBLEMS

Religious spirits **must** be exposed in the Church of God for the Church to be purified. Here are some areas against which we need to be on our guard.

SELF-RIGHTEOUS DOGMATISM

Many people with religious spirits, and that is most people, Christians included, truly believe they have a quality of holiness or godliness in the right way. They are like **Job's three friends** who meant well but ended up having to apologise to Job because they got it WRONG! (Job 42:7-10).

All their religious counsel (29 chapters of it) was not the mind of God in this case (cf. Isa. 55:8-11). Without realising it **some have replaced the righteousness of God with a righteousness of their own** (Rom. 10:3); they believe they are righteous and "holier than thou" (Isa. 65:5), because **"religious" people are hyper-religious and self-righteous.** They naturally and genuinely believe that their attitude and approach is right, and others are WRONG or less spiritual. Therefore they enjoy this form of uncleanness. It is not like beastly lust or violence or treachery for which it is easy to feel guilt, shame and condemnation. Religiosity carries a very strong sense of righteousness and *it is therefore most difficult for people with this form of problem to:*

(i)   **recognise that it IS unclean, not holy, and**

(ii) **WANT to change**

Self-righteousness gives people a sense of **self-esteem** and **worth,** and also **power** and **superiority** over other "lesser" mortals and not everyone wants to lose these "advantages".

It is very often a spirit which enters after earlier experiences of rejection and inferiority by way of compensation for the lack of human love and attention. When a child or person fails to obtain sufficient attention and acceptance to meet their emotional needs, they may turn to the Lord as the One who is always there, always supportive and comforting and who fills the needs not met by the human family. Thus it becomes so easy to create a set of religious exercises by means of which one is supported and sustained, while rejection and inadequacy are overruled with a new sense of self-esteem founded on spirituality. Hence the people likely to have religious spirits in the normal Christian assembly will often be found amongst those who truly love the Lord and are generally considered mature in the faith. However this love of the Lord is mixed with a desire to be recognised and accepted by other Christians, similar to **Diotrephes'** problem of seeking pre-eminence (3 John 9).

WORLDLY NOTIONS OF RIGHTEOUSNESS

Religious spirits may also enter during "brain-washing" by educational facilities such as High School or University. In studying the Humanities old historic injustices are regurgitated, provoking anger at man's inhumanity to man. This anger creates a receptive and fertile hot-bed for socialistic notions[12] of "equality" and "justice" to find root. So much of this historical information is inaccurate or at the very least warped, fragmented and biased presentations of what really happened because, very simply, historians were not present at the events they describe. They piece together fragments of information from documents and diaries etc., and then weave their "histories" together with a lot of imagination based on probabilities. The "flesh" they put on the "bones" is not always (seldom?) right (cf. 1 Cor. 15:39?).

---

12. The socialist's view of equality is a totally non-discriminatory world where everyone eats the same, dresses the same, lives in the same style house, drives the same make of car. Factors such as integrity, industry, study, intelligence, laziness, immorality, blessings and curses do not count for much in their systems. They even label you "sexist" or "chauvinist" if you distinguish between men and women!

"History is bunk!"
        Henry Ford (July 1919)

"All our ancient history... is no more than accepted fiction".
        Voltaire (in Jeannot et Colin)

"(Read to me) anything but history, for history must be false!"
        Sir Robert Walpole to his son.

Historians are required to INTERPRET facts; which is why they so often differ from each other. They are like three preachers who present three different messages from the same Bible passage, according to their individual bias and interpretation. Consequently religious spirits inspiring Marxist, Communist or Socialist notions find easy access into the hearts of angry and idealistic young men and women students, especially during tertiary education. So it should not surprise us to discover that such political movements become religions, and even Communism, which has decimated nations and millions of people for nearly a century, as we have already said, still holds sway deep in the hearts of many.

Why? It is a heart/soul thing. It is spiritual. **It is a spiritual bondage that is religious** (as so many of them freely admit), and therefore it is one of the most difficult chains to break. **Usually it is only death or Jesus who can help us change our religion.** Even atheists (those who believe there is no God) are religious. In denying the existence of gods or a supreme God they elevate themselves into that position. They recognise no being higher than man, and therefore they view man (themselves) as God. They set themselves up in His place and serve themselves in a man-centred religion.

WE LIKE BEING RELIGIOUS

The major difficulty remains. We know and like our religion. Most of us would rather die than change this part of us. Verlie and I have been in Deliverance work for more than twenty five years and during that time people have cried out for help and removal of a huge variety of unclean spirits of fear, infirmity etc. etc., but **no one has ever come to us and requested deliverance from their religious spirits!!**

We do not perceive our religious spirits as being a problem to us. Indeed Christians think they are being led by the Spirit of God, and so gain a sense of security from them (e.g. revering statues, paintings of Jesus, crucifixes). Such spirits make one feel important and right (dogmatic) and enable us to "correct" other lesser mortals.

They make us formidable opponents, so why would we want to lose them? If we are self-centred we will NOT want to lose them, but if we are truly disciples of the Lord, seeking the fullness of GOD'S Spirit and HIS Will for our lives, we have no choice.

Verlie and I have lost at least two very dear friends through religious spirits. Verlie prayed and fasted three weeks for one sister, but she didn't want to lose them and so they stayed put. Many other victories were obtained during those three weeks - by people who WANTED to be set free, but NOT the Christian who would not listen. It can be very difficult to tell a brother or sister in Christ that the spirit leading them is NOT the Holy Spirit, but unclean. Then it becomes a battle of trust. Will they continue to trust their OWN judgement, or will they trust (accept) ours?

The battle for their cleansing is won or lost right here!

BE CAREFUL WHAT YOU SAY!

I used to think that the closer I got to God the more successful I would be in my ministry. I thought that all true Christian people would see how close I was to God and they would be attracted to the Christ in me (i.e. in my work or church or whatever) because they would respond to the REALITY of God in Christ, in me, But I had not fully understood what Jesus meant when He said that He repelled many men because He was the Light and when men saw Him as the Light they would WITHDRAW from Him because their deeds were evil. (John 2:23-25, 3:19-21). Now that may be understandable regarding the men of the world, who have not known God the Father or His Son, Jesus Christ, but why would CHRISTIAN men and women be repelled by meetings or services where the presence and power of God was very strong, or where His REALITY was powerfully confirmed through miracles of healings and deliverances? I remember one woman who came up to me after a *Deliverance and Restoration* meeting and said *"I've been to a lot of Renewal meetings, but that was the most powerful meeting I have ever attended!"* It disappointed us that we never saw her again, or others who have said the same.

Another deeply committed Christian wept with joy after his first visit with us. *"It's what I've been looking for!"* We didn't see him again either!

Another woman told us *"I'm full-on for the Lord"*. Our hearts went clunk! - when we heard that, because we knew the Accuser would take her words before the Throne of God and get permission to test her spiritual condition (Rev. 12:10). She barely lasted one meeting. Another young man said the same thing. He lasted a record two meetings.

The truth is that many Christians are more RELIGIOUS than they are Christian and the same principles of attraction and repulsion apply, that is, unclean spirits of religiosity which have been passing themselves off as the HOLY Spirit are equally appalled at the REAL PRESENCE[13] of Christ as any other unclean spirit. These religious spirits love playing games and masquerading as the Holy spirit, parading their religiosity for the admiration of the undiscerning, but when the HOLY spirit is present in burning power to cleanse and deliver, it becomes all rather too dangerous even for them, and so both non-Christians and Christians who have an appearance and measure of Godliness may be discomforted and repelled by powerful, searching ministries that expose pollution; deep, hidden, inner pollution, without really knowing why in their conscious minds.

THEN AND NOW

I remember a joke Dr. Billy Graham told an audience many years ago (1968?) regarding a new convert. The man was a bit of a misfit but experienced a wonderful conversion. For three months he went along to his local church and tried to fit in.

Nobody was interested. They didn't believe in evangelism or sudden conversions. They thought Billy was a salesman and were suspicious of any "fruit" from his ministry. The new man felt shut out and rejected. As he desperately prayed one night, he said *"Lord I've tried and tried. Sorry, but I can't seem to get into that church." "That's okay",* replied the Lord. *"I can't get in there either!"*

There is no doubt that some churches have organised the Holy Spirit right out of their system. The meetings, the activities, the forms continue but the Spirit of God has long since gone. The saddest part is no one has noticed!

Just how "religious" the historic Church has become, and continues to be is easily demonstrated from history. **John Hus** was a livewire early reformer of the Church who was ex-communicated and burnt at the stake on 6th July, 1415, a hundred years before **John Calvin** and **Martin Luther** set Europe alight with the **Reformation.** Less than 300 years later **John Wesley** and his preachers were thrown out of British churches and forced to preach in the fields. Just as well, for the church buildings could not have contained the huge crowds who wanted to hear them, and so sparked

---

13. Not to be confused with the Anglo-Catholic doctrine concerning the bread and the wine in Holy Communion.

the Christian revival of England in the eighteenth century. In this twentieth century we have seen the traditional churches' inability to cope with the Pentecostal movement to the extent that Christians who spoke in tongues, prophesied, and ministered deliverance and healing were forced out of their churches and obliged to form their own assemblies under the broad banner of **Pentecostalism.**

Now we have a new surge forward in what has become known as the **Renewal Movement,** incorporating Christians from every historic church denomination who are prepared to move forward with the Holy Spirit wherever He leads, regardless of any earlier Church tradition.

Let us ask ourselves the question *"Why is it that, down through 2000 years of history, the Church denominations of the day ALWAYS RESIST a fresh move of the Holy Spirit (Acts 7:51)?"* One answer is obviously that they are not guided by the Holy Spirit. The next obvious question, *"Then with what spirit are they controlled?"* you can answer for yourself. It is interesting to note that most Christian denominations which have clung to their traditions and resisted the Renewal move of God's Spirit today are in decline, perhaps because they did not know the time of their visitation from above (cf. Luke 19:41-48).

(ii) DEFINITION OF "RELIGIOUS SPIRITS"

I think it is now time to attempt a definition of "religious spirit".

This may not be the greatest definition in the world, but to my knowledge no one has ever defined or described the function of an unclean religious spirit before, so here goes:

A religious spirit is an unclean spirit seeking to achieve one or more of the following:

(a) **Replace the effective worship of The Creator** (Almighty God, through the Lord Jesus Christ) throughout the Creation, with the worship of the demonic gods of this world by means of idolatry and alternative religions.

(b) Hinder, pull down, replace, mock and destroy the genuine, spiritual worship and communion of Christians with their Lord.

(c) **Parade its own religiosity** with a view to:

  (i) advertising its "spirituality" (holier than thou!)[14]
  (ii) establishing a spiritual "superiority" over "lesser" Christians.
  (iii) establishing its own false "righteousness"

---

14. See Isaiah 65:2-5 (Note v5)-Authorised (K.J.) or Revised Version.

(d) Express religious lies, deception and/or fantasy.

This includes *spiritualising* the natural, for example, seeing God's *supernatural* power at work when He has used his *natural* power (nature – e.g. rain) to answer prayer.

Rain may be answered prayer, but it is not a miracle. A miracle is the manifestation of a remarkable or marvellous event, *usually contrary to nature!*

I offer this definition as a combination of the Word of God and experience in the deliverance ministry.

(iii) RELIGIOUS EXHIBITIONISM

Attending a medium-sized charismatic church in Sydney I was amazed to find myself seated behind a lady who, during each worship song, arose and performed a wriggly dance in the style of a Baghdad belly dancer. There may be a place for holy dancing in worship, based on the precedent set by **King David** (2 Sam. 6:14). I'm not into it myself, and the jury is still out on the matter, as far as I'm concerned, but we would not want to make the mistake of **Michal**, David's wife. However the incident above was blatant exhibitionism.

The wriggly arms and body movements were so snaky it did not surprise me when the Pastor commented *"Sometimes I worry about you, sister"*. Neither did it surprise when she signalled to go on stage so she could share a vision she had just been given. It was some religious, useless thing I can't even remember today, about as valuable as a fifty cent watch. No wonder the apostle Paul warned us NOT to take our stand on visions (Col. 2:18).

Later in the program I was invited to say a few words as a visiting minister, and could not resist warning the assembly about religious behaviour inspired by deceiving spirits. My comments were well received but there are no prizes for guessing which person was nodding most vigorously in agreement!!

She just couldn't keep out of the action!

Some time ago I wrote the following in one of our **Full Salvation Fellowship** Newsletters:

> *"Some churches prefer to run a drama (creative arts) program rather than a deliverance (cleansing) program. I wonder why?"*

I have always had a wariness towards Church Creative Arts programs and schools because it is so obviously an area in our lives in which it is so easy to fulfil **the lusts of the flesh, the lust of the eyes and the pride of life** (1 John 2:16).

And even if ALL comes under the control of the Holy Spirit (and that can be a big **IF!**), we then have to challenge its level of PRIORITY in a church or ministry. There are questions that need to be asked:

1. How much TIME does it take out of the pastoral week?

2. What is the price tag for all the tuition and equipment?

3. What scriptural support is there for any particular art?

4. (How) Is it bearing fruit for the Kingdom of God?

These are not necessarily NEGATIVE questions designed to pour cold water on ALL art skills.

For example question 3 can produce much scriptural support for musicians - no problem, and there is some support for dancing, but I have always been concerned it is so easy for a stage presentation to degenerate into entertainment for the audience on earth, rather than worship for the Audience on the Throne in Heaven.

However I must add that although the lusts of the flesh etc. are an ever present danger in many types of ministry (e.g. *preaching to impress PEOPLE with self* rather than presenting the Christ) the few segments of worship dancing I have seen have been beautifully done unto the Lord!

Question 4 presents us with the bottom line and the acid test. Is the Lord, the everlasting and almighty God magnified and glorified through an activity, and the Kingdom of God extended? (cf. Matt. 12:28). The good news is that MANY people have (to my limited knowledge) been saved through dramatic presentations of the sinful, hopeless state of mankind and the grace of God in providing a Saviour, Who is Christ the Lord!

Perhaps we could add to the old saying "It's not what you do but the **way** that you do it", the words "… and the reason **WHY** you do it!" The final question to be answered is:

5. What are our MOTIVES?

Lying and religious spirits may bring forth a false prophetic Word if they feel that it will give them the pre-eminence in the Assembly, and there is no one sufficiently experienced present to detect them. Such "prophecies" are not always doctrinally inaccurate but may be simply insipid - having no real message or value at all.

For example, some prophets will continuously tell you *"Thus says the Lord, I love you ..."* There may be times when you need to hear that, but you know it from the Holy Spirit in you, and you can read it in the Word, so you don't really need a prophet to tell you that God loves you almost every meeting.

Another very common revelation is that God has got big plans for you. If you will just make a couple of minor adjustments to your life then God will mightily use you and make you into a great vessel of honour.

*   **You are going to be rich!**

*   **You are going to be great!**

       Praise the Lord!

Such revelations rarely happen, but by the time the "guidance" has fallen apart nobody else remembers it anyway (if it is not recorded) and it is conveniently buried in the past.

(a) COUNTERFEIT GIFTS

A classic example of a counterfeit gift seeking to mislead and obstruct a Christian ministry is presented to us in the Acts of the Apostles. **Paul** is preaching the gospel of Jesus to **Macedonians** in the city of **Philippi.**

> *"As we went to the place of prayer a certain maid with **a spirit of a python** met us, who brought much gain to her masters by practising soothsaying (divination). (17) She followed after Paul and us, crying out **'These men are bond slaves of the Most High God, who proclaim to you the way of salvation'**. (18) And this she did over many days. But Paul became greatly troubled and turned to the spirit and said, **'I charge you in the Name of Jesus Christ to come out from her'**. And it came out the same hour".* (Acts 16:16-18).

Clearly the enemy has counterfeit gifts to at least match the nine gifts of the Holy Spirit listed in 1 Cor. 12:7-10, and they are not always easy to discern. Even the apostle Paul had to wait many days before getting the discernment he needed. After all, the girl was telling the truth in describing Paul and Silas as bond-servants to God who preached the way of salvation.

This is what confounds so many Christians today, as it nearly did Paul. Religious spirits can and will present a good deal of truth in order to achieve their unclean mission, but of course, this **python spirit** was saying **the right thing at the wrong time**. It is equivalent to a member of your church standing up and reading the Word of God out loud while your Pastor is trying to preach a message. The result would be disastrous. She (it) must have driven Paul nearly out of his mind with her constant harassment and interruptions. He needed a few days to check things with the Lord, and then - **POW!** The snaky deception was over!

Christians who have genuine gifts of the Holy Spirit, such as prophecy, should know that there can be occasions when an unclean spirit will seek to break in and take over the message, or whatever is happening.

The activity of religious spirits infiltrating other genuine vocal gifts such as tongues[15] and prophecy is a very subtle attack upon the Holy Spirit inspired proclamation of the pure Word of God and is designed to nullify the power of the Word, and to confuse and mislead. "But", you say, "Surely the Lord would not allow that?" Well, the truth is that it happens all the time (1 Tim. 4:1-3), because Christians generally are so unaware of the kind of spirit with which they speak. But, praise the Lord, He is giving the Renewal Church more and more perception with which to discern the truth.

It is not that the speakers are aware of their spirit so much as the hearers. The speakers are usually quite sincere and genuine but are themselves deceived. They usually give words of knowledge or describe vision upon vision in technicolour which never seem to come to fruition. Prophecies inspired **totally by religious spirits** seem to be less common, perhaps because *it is easier to remain undetected from the weighing of other prophets if the misguidance can be threaded into a genuine prophecy.* This "mixture" may then achieve the result of bringing a genuine Word into disrepute, because of a measure of distortion, so that it is rendered ineffective or even destructive.

(iv) EXAMINE YOURSELF!

Genuinely gifted vessels should be careful to tune into the Lord and check the spirit/Spirit before they actually speak. I remember an Anglican Renewal Conference held in Port Macquarie in 1992, with Bishops, Clergy and lay people present in which the Lord "forced" me to prophesy, after six promptings by the Spirit. Towards the end of the prophecy the Lord told the assembly (through me) to *"come before Me in repentance and renewal..."*

---

15. We acknowledge here the existence of false tongues

I balked at telling this mature gathering to repent. I remember a shock-wave hitting my spirit, and in that thousandth of a second I asked *"Surely you don't want me to tell **these people** to repent Lord? That can't be right, can it? They repented when they became Christians and then they experienced major repentance again when they came into renewal. Do you really want me to tell them to repent some more?" "Yes", said the Lord, "Tell them again to repent!"* So I did (speaking for the Lord) and so did **Bishop Hamish** of **Bunbury Diocese** when he preached that evening, confirming the prophetic word.

What I hedged about saying in a few seconds, the Bishop hammered for more than an hour! The Lord really wanted to get His point across then, and the point I am making now is that we all will experience the enemy seeking to break into genuine gifts and pollute them, either totally or in part, and there needs to be a constant checking (weighing, judging - 1 Cor. 14:29) moment to moment, during the operation of ANY gift.

Experienced preachers who want to preach Jesus but fall into the snare of preaching or teaching intellectualism are a classic example. The pride in them overrules their spirit and the Holy Spirit has no free course in their hearts. They unconsciously preach to impress men with SELF and not to lift up Jesus, so they give their flocks dry stones instead of living bread. It's so very easy to do - I know - and such religiosity is not of the Lord.

A clergyman friend of mine (yes, I still have a few!) resigned from his denomination and I asked him why he had done so. He had not been viewed with anything like the suspicion I had been subjected to since moving into Deliverance ministry. He was in Renewal with an emphasis on prayer and intercession, drawing closer to God, so why did he resign?

"The Church (organisation) is controlled by a religious spirit", he told me simply.

Even though I have not resigned from my own denominational Orders and links, and am still an accredited minister of the Anglican Church of Australia (although not under a Bishop's oversight), I could not disagree with him.

3.4 RELIGIOUS SPIRITS IN THE HOME

I suppose the most obvious example of the activity of a religious spirit in the home is demonstrated when a Christian spouse seeks to bring his or her unsaved spouse into the knowledge of the Lord.

Let us assume, for the purpose of illustration, it is the wife that is converted and the husband is resisting the invitation of the Lord. The root cause may be that the husband's soul is in a mess and when the Holy Spirit comes into the wife's soul, all the sin and uncleanness in the husband's soul takes fright, knowing that the one-flesh situation means an unbelieving spouse is sanctified by the believing spouse (1 Cor. 7:14) and therefore **every unclean kingdom in his heart is threatened by the arrival of the Holy Spirit into his wife's heart.**

However, on many occasions the root cause of continuing division between the man and wife after her conversion is that not only does the wife have the HOLY Spirit but she also has religious spirits in her soul which raise their ugly heads at every opportunity.

Husbands of Godly women with a mixture of religious spirits in their soul can receive a very hard time. If it was truly the Holy Spirit speaking to them consistently, through their wives, many, many more of them would be converted, because there is such a fresh, cleansing, uplifting, liberating beauty with the Spirit of Christ. But if the wife "comes on strong" with a "pious", sickly, revolting, suffocating, super-spiritual act with all its religious, legalistic criticism and self-righteous rules and regulations, and constantly removes herself from under her husband's headship by prefacing everything SHE wants with **"The Lord said",** thus effectively reducing her husband's considerations to ZERO in value, it is no wonder that he digs his toes in and rejects such an unclean lordship over his life. He doesn't know why and he can't put it into words, but he is just not going to submit to that kind of domination, and who can blame him? Deep within himself he thinks if that kind of syrupy religiosity is the hallmark or characteristic of Christianity he is better off as he is. Thanks, but no thanks!

The good news is that it is not, in this case, the Lord he is rejecting but a religious spirit. When someone gets around to showing him the truth of the beauty of Jesus, unclouded by the uncleanness he sees in Jesus' disciples (followers) THEN he has every chance of being born again by the will of God (John 1:13). In the meantime however, the sad consequence is that in rejecting the unclean religious domination of his wife he also blocks himself off from the Lord Jesus - the Saviour he needs so much! It hardly needs to be added that this husband and wife situation can be reversed with the husband having the self-righteous problem.

Dear Christian spouse - "What can you do?"

Well the first thing to do (by the wife in this illustration) is to turn to the Scriptures for wisdom, and do what it says:

> *"Wives, be in subjection to your own husbands so that even if any do not obey the Word, **they will be gained by the behaviour of their wives**, without the Word, observing your reverent and pure behaviour.*   (1 Peter 3:1-2)

So the key to a wife's (spouse's) campaign to win the heart of an unbelieving spouse for Christ Jesus in NOT to try to badger or control THEM, but (first of all) control YOURSELF!! They may still fail but, if they do, you will not be at all to blame.

> *Do not let your outward appearance be of the World, with plaiting of hair and putting on ornaments of gold and clothing of (wealthy or fashion) garments but (rather be clothed with) the hidden man of the heart (Jesus) with* **the incorruptibility of the meek and quiet (human) spirit** *which is of great value before God". (1 Peter 3:1-4, literal translation with bracketed words inserted by me).*

Obviously **it is not the Word alone**[16] **but the Spirit which is important in communicating God's truth to unbelieving spouses.** And not only is it what we say but the WAY we say it, i.e. **the spirit by which you say it** that is important. Especially our own conduct says more than a thousand words.

Cut out the religiosity. Cut out "The Lord said ..." attitude, He probably didn't say it at all and you are promoting a lie that has deceived YOU! Test the spirits. Examine the results you are getting from your guidance. Every time you say "The Lord said ..." record it in a book (with the date) and watch for its fruit. Remember that in the vast majority of cases the voice of the Lord is a still small voice and the message He gives you in your spirit is usually confirmed by two or three witnesses independently of yourself. That is, get confirmation from the Lord before you start putting His Name to your ideas which involve other people, at least until you have had proven success in **knowing** the leading of the Spirit.

He will confirm His guidance to you from totally unexpected sources - one of them may even be your husband or wife, if you care to listen ... Even then, train yourself to take responsibility for what you say, e.g. **"I believe the Lord is saying ..."**

3.5 RELIGIOUS SPIRITS IN THE PSYCHIATRIC WARD

There is a fairly high percentage of people suffering from mental disorders and receiving psychiatric counselling who ritualistically go through

---

16. There are two Greek words translated WORD in English: (i) **Logos**, which means a legal, positional, covenantal word and (ii) **rhema** which means a LIVING, experiential word which is alive and applies NOW! It is the Holy Spirit that makes the LEGAL word alive for us and turns the **Logos** into a **Rhema** or, alternatively, brings a prophecy or a word of knowledge compatible with the **Logos** word.

questionable religious activities - some may be genuinely Christian activities - others certainly are not. The psychiatrist can be faced with any one of the following situations:

(i) **The genuine Christian** who not only has the Holy Spirit and wants to exercise valid Christian worship, but nevertheless has **other demonic or physical problems** for which the psychiatrist would seem to be God's answer to their needs. In this case genuine Christian activity can be mistaken for a "religious problem."

Back in 1975(?) I remember one young lady who was obviously a born-again Christian, but who had a dramatic background of lack of care and broken relationships. She was one of those people who you would think of as a victim, a prey rather than a predator. She loved the Lord but lacked stability in her early life.

One day I received a 'phone call from her asking me to visit her in a psychiatric hospital. When I arrived she was in tears. Apparently she had been badgering the psychiatrists to let her go, saying she was fine and that Jesus would heal her if she needed any healing.

The more she claimed divine help the more the hospital staff thought she needed THEM! What really convinced them she should be kept in hospital was the regular tears, the praying out loud in the Ward, even to the point where she would drop to her knees in the middle of the Ward and cry out to the Lord to get her out of there!

Cries of desperation perhaps, but not wise! She was not all right. She was saying the right words but her behaviour was decidedly bizarre and unstable, and there was no way she was going to get out until her behaviour became "normal," according to the doctors.

I think this was my first experience of perceiving the dilemma of the medical profession. No wonder so many of those involved in psychiatric work believe that religion, any religion, is a problem that needs curing.

Even I could not always discern when the Holy Spirit or when the religious spirit was operating, so what hope would a psychiatrist - even a Christian psychiatrist - have? We are totally dependent upon discernment from the Lord in this!

(ii) **The genuine Christian** who is overtaken by unclean religious spirits and exercises ***worship in a way that is hypocritical, fleshly,***

counterfeit and "showy", and brings the Christian faith into grave disrepute. ***Religious display for the purpose of getting attention*** is repulsive to Christian and non-Christian observers alike and is often responsible for the charge "hypocrites" being unfairly levelled at all church-going Christians.

(iii) The non-Christian who has not been born again and who has the same problems as (ii) and practices a mockery of Christian worship. There is no redeeming quality here whatsoever and the true faith is again brought into disrepute. There is no Holy Spirit present, only the unclean counterfeit.

(iv) The non-Christian religious practitioner who wants to exercise the faith of his choice and thus draws strength from the demonic powers which (unbeknown to him) made him sick in the first place and therefore can never be substantially helped, e.g. a transcendental meditation advocate who hallucinates during or after meditation.

CONCLUSION

From the non-Christian psychiatrist's point of view it would appear that the patient's religion is a major factor contributing to their mental illness and therefore the less religious activity the better. While this may be true in some cases, it is unfortunate that a genuine work of God's grace tends to be confused with or viewed as something from which the patient should be cured. Unless the psychiatrist is an informed Christian he or she is most unlikely to be able to make the necessary distinctions, which are spiritually discerned.

3.6 THE FALSE JESUS SPIRIT

One of the more difficult things to do in discerning of spirits is distinguishing between the false or counterfeit Jesus spirit and the real Spirit of Christ. The apostle Paul links preaching a false Jesus with a false or different spirit and a different gospel (2 Cor. 11:4).

In my early days as a curate and in the Holy Spirit Renewal movement an Emu Plains housewife was converted by the Lord, but during my follow-up visits I began to feel troubled in spirit. This lady was always saying ***"The Lord told me to ...." "Jesus said to ......".***

I had been a Christian for nine years (9) and the Lord had only spoken audibly to me twice in all that time!

When people do this, what can you say? They have effectively "pulled rank" on you, because **IF** the Lord has spoken, it is time for everyone else to shut up.

In the very act of someone promoting their spirituality by claiming to get loud and clear direct guidance from the Throne of God, in reality they effectively cut themselves off from the wisdom of God's ministers. They are not open to a different view and can become impossible to pastor.

What is left but to speak the truth in love (Eph. 4:15) and pray the good Lord will give them the grace to examine their guidance.

I didn't know what to make of it then, and it is still a problem needing discernment today. Looking back, I suspect she was a closet (undiagnosed) schizophrenic and an unclean control spirit was desperately trying to undo her conversion to Christ; perhaps seed on stony ground (Mark 4:5-6).

As we discuss in chapter 8 it is a fairly common occurrence today for people who hear voices in their head to be told by a voice to attack people, commit crimes and even murder. These voices sometimes identify themselves as Jesus. The following media report is an example:

> *"The Manly (Sydney) Court was told that one of the women was attacked as she walked along Tower Street, Manly. She was punched in the mouth, knocked to the ground and had her handbag stolen.*
>
> *A second woman was also punched and knocked to the ground in Raglan Street, Manly.*
>
> *A young man is alleged to have signed statements admitting all offences, having told police he acted in such a way "because Jesus wanted him to seek retribution from the bad ladies of Manly".*
>
> *In one instance he had punched one woman in the face, knocked her to the ground, kicked her in the lower back and said: "Jesus wants this".*[17]

(i)   THE NAME JESUS - ITS USE, MISUSE AND ABUSE

The famous English bard **William Shakespeare** unintentionally misled us when he wrote:

---

17. Manly Daily, Jan. 15, 1988.

"What's in a name? That which we call a rose by any other name would smell as sweet". (Romeo and Juliet)

Shakespeare was speaking of names for IDENTIFICATION only.

It is true the names men entitle or call anything may be pure romanticism and quite uninformative as regards the character or substance of any particular object. However in the Bible names have specific MEANINGS which reveal the nature of the thing named as well as identify the personality.

For example, prophecies of the Lord Jesus Christ's first coming say:

"His Name shall be called Wonderful Counsellor, Mighty God, Everlasting Father, Prince of Peace".   **(Isaiah 9:6)**

".…. you shall call His Name Jesus, for He will save His people from their sins."   **(Matt. 1:21)**

We also know from a literal translation of John chapter 17 that the Father has given Jesus His own (the Father's) Name, just as men today pass on their own names to their children.

*"Holy Father,[18] keep them in your Name, **which (Name) you have given to me** ...* (v.11).

*"While I was with them I kept them in your Name, **which you have given me**....* (v.12).

"I have made known to them your Name...." (v.26).

The name Jesus actually comes from two Hebrew words, **JAH** and **Hosea**, which means combined, **JAH (God) (is) Saviour**.

So you can see that the Name of Jesus is not just for identification only but carries the most powerful message for the human race!

What do you make of the Name of Jesus? The full identification is **"Lord Jesus Christ"** and there is no mistaking the identity of the One you are

---

18. It is not a good idea to call the Pope "Holy Father". (John 17:11)

addressing when you use the three-fold titles and Name. **"Jesus Christ of Nazareth"** is also an accurate identification. Although there may have been others named Jesus over the centuries who came from Nazareth, there is only one Jesus of Nazareth who is the Christ!

In the English speaking nations almost no-one names their son Jesus, but in some Latin/Spanish speaking parts of the world it is quite common. It seems that the Name itself carries no authority or power from God **unless the IDENTITY of the Son of God is invoked intentionally for God's purposes.** I am treading dangerous ground here but let us examine the evidence; it is just so important that we understand and use the Name of Jesus correctly:

a)   The words **"Lord"** and **"Christ"** (Acts 2:36) are not names but titles surrounding the Name of **Jesus.**

b)   The name of Jesus was fairly common in New Testament times, for example the robber **Barabbas** was himself known as **Jesus Barabbas,** according to some ancient manuscripts of Matt. 27:16-17. Likewise **Elymas** the sorcerer was also known as **Bar Jesus** (Acts 13:6) which means son of Jesus. Also in Paul's letter to the Colossians a Christian named Jesus had apparently been renamed **Justus** (Col. 4:11). Jesus is a translation of the Hebrew name of **Joshua.**

c)   The name Jesus has been bestowed upon many children in the poorer nations of the earth and in itself (dissociated from the **PERSON** of the Lord Jesus Christ) certainly carries no power to transform lives or lift people out of the curses of poverty and sickness.

d)   The name of Jesus used in open or mindless blasphemy brings no blessing to the user, but rather the wrath of God. It brings the kind of response we can do without, sooner or later! (Exod. 20:7).

e)   It should not surprise us that many unclean spirits appropriate the name of Jesus for themselves, and as counterfeit spirits they answer to that name - Jesus.

(ii) EXPOSING FALSE JESUS SPIRITS

It is absolutely essential that ANY spirit being which appears to a human being must be questioned as to its identity and allegiance. You must not be afraid. You must question it (test the spirits - 1 John 4:1).

(a) If it claims to be Jesus it should be asked if Jesus Christ came in the flesh (1 John 4:2-3), and flowing from that, if Jesus Christ:

(ii)   is the ONLY begotten Son of God (John 3:16)?

(iii)   ROSE again from the dead (Mark 16;6, 1 Cor. 15:12-20)?

(iv)   is now seated in Glory at the right Hand of our Almighty Father God (Heb. 1:3, 13, 12:2)?

(v)   is now LORD of Lords and KING of Kings (Matt. 28:18, Rev. 17:14)? And

(vi)   is our Lord and our God (John 20:28)?

I think you will find that any spirit/angelic being that confronts you will either be able to answer positively all the above questions, OR be unable to affirm ANY of them. Likewise if the supposed *christophany* (appearance of Christ) cannot acknowledge these truths, it is obviously an enemy deception and not the REAL Jesus at all.

(b) If it claims to be an angel of God (e.g. Michael or Gabriel etc.) it must be asked the same questions and affirm the same truths as above. If it fails or refuses to do so, or gives you some smart, evasive "doubletalk" you know it is *a false angel of "light"* (2 Cor. 11:14).

Beware of the spirit of the False Prophet which one day will be cast into the Lake of Fire after it has deceived millions and caused much bloodshed (Rev. 16:13-14, 19:20, 20:10).

How important it is then, to be absolutely "focussed" or specific in calling on the One who is not only named **Jesus,** but who is also **Lord** and **Christ** (Acts 2:36), and who is from Nazareth. My own favourite address to the un-clean spirits which are to be cast out during a **Deliverance and Restoration meeting** has been **"In the Name of Jesus Christ of Nazareth ..."**

By Oliphant for the Denver Post

" In a manner of speaking, what we lose on the
merry-go-round we pick up on the swings!"

By kind permission of the Denver Post

The tragedy is that the churches have not yet grasped the truth in this cartoon, that is, the HUGE NEED for the inner cleansing of the human soul from all its spiritual pollution

CHAPTER 4

WE ALL HAVE OUR DEMONS!

"We constantly deny the darkness in ourselves and others but our minds are so thoroughly drawn to it".

Gabrielle Lord - Author of "Feeding the Demons"

I can remember back in 1973 finding myself in an accelerating ministry, a "new" ministry of deliverance with fresh discoveries every day of how satan had bound the people of God, but now they were beginning to experience all kinds of releases.

As I mused over the exciting events of each day while shaving early one morning, I became aware of how blessed I was in the Lord, being of sound mind and not, as I thought at the time, at all demonised. As I looked at my face in the mirror, half covered with shaving soap, I sent up an earnest prayer to the Lord, something like this:

"Lord, it's great seeing your people set free but I am relying on you to protect me. Please, please, please don't allow any of the ugly spirits we are seeing cast out each day to transfer into me. I would hate to be demonised Lord….and this gracious work would be brought to an end… Please don't let this happen!"

I had in mind King Nebuchadnezzar's madness (Dan. 4:33-34). Little did I know at the time that I was already demonised. It was just that being in most respects a "normal" Christian minister, I did not think I was in need of any help that normal christian growth and maturity could not supply.

Later when the Lord showed me something of the true state of my soulish nature, I was only too happy to RECEIVE ministry as well as give it. By that time my fears of demons overtaking me had been overcome through many battles and victories, a more specialised study of the Word of God and understanding of Holy Spirit weaponry.

In one of the lowest periods of my ministry and walk with the Lord, when I was desperately hanging onto Him with both hands, a slogan bookmark from **Basilea Schlink** arrived on my desk and strengthened my spirit immeasurably:

"You are a true servant of God under whose feet all the powers of the enemy shall be trodden down if you confront them by calling on the Name of Jesus whom you serve."

I hope it strengthens you and your resolve to be a true servant of the Lord, as it did me.

4.1 THE WORLD

I happen to think that, not withstanding the many fine Christians who live in Hollywood and work in the film industry, the world-wide industry itself is one of the wickedest activities on the face of the earth, spewing out rampant *fornication* and *adultery, witchcraft* and *violence, profanity* and *blasphemy* etc., throughout the nations, all for the box office dollar. Many films continuously appeal to and strengthen the dark side of human nature, and it will be no surprise to me when the San Andreas earth fault produces an enormous earthquake to demolish the area. The same warning applies to the Australian film industry, and others.

However the film industry's involvement with evil and fantasy has made them much more aware of SPIRITUAL forces than many church-going Christians, and indeed, many church leaders.

Way back in the 1980s **Warner Bros**. In Hollywood produced a terrifying television mini series entitled **V** about aliens who came to earth in peace and negotiated for a small share of the earth's natural resources, in exchange for their advanced technology and science.

They were believed - until entire cities began to vanish from the earth. As the heroes in this story wake up to the truth they discover the aliens, who are in the form of human beings, are actually **reptiles,** similar to the biblical expression of false prophets (Matt. 7:15) and false brethren (Acts 20:29), being described as *wolves appearing as God's sheep* (in sheep's clothing).

The heroine **Juliet** rips the human mask at the side of the **Supreme Commander's** face to reveal **shining blackish green SCALES and his reptilian features** through the hole (page 262 of the novel written by **A.C. Crispin**).

This fictional Sci-Fi adventure may cause serious Bible students to reflect on **the serpent** which deceived Eve and then Adam and took them over with his own sinful personality, and also the young girl who exercised divination and had the **spirit of a python** (lit. Greek) cast out of her by the apostle Paul (Acts 16:16-18).

Could it be that the human race which, through Adam and Eve's rebellion has fallen from God's favour and been invaded by spiritual forces of sin and death (Rom. 5:12), is really made up of spiritual snakes clothed in human flesh? What a terrible result and condition for man, originally made in the image of God! By the end of this chapter you may be surprised at the snaky behaviour flowing from the least expected sources (cf. Matt. 3:7, 12:34, 23:33 and Luke 3:7 where the charge of **viper's brood** is applied to EVERYONE, not just the Pharisees and Sadducees).

In the **Chuck Norris** film *"HERO AND THE TERROR"* (copyright 1988) the policeman hero (O'Brien) is talking to a **police psychiatrist** and asks how to overcome fear. Dr. Highwater replies very perceptively *"Don't even try! WE ALL GOT OUR DEMONS - just live with it!"*. "Hey Doc", responds O'Brien as the psychiatrist walks away, "What if you can't?" The psychiatrist makes his parting comment, "What other choice we got?"

Thank God we Christians don't have to "just live with it!" We have another choice because of our Deliverer, the Lord Jesus Christ!

Four years after this film was completed, reporter Michelangelo Rucci filed the following story about actor **Tony Curtis**:

> *Curtis, 67 yesterday told of his 'heartbreaking secret' - the life of his brother Robert Schwartz - in the hope "my painful story might help relatives cope with their torment.*
>
> *"Bobby was 15 years younger than I; he was a schizophrenic and a manic depressive", said Curtis. "His life was always sad and painful. His illness overwhelmed him. It devoured his life. **Demons drove his mind,** but he was my brother and I loved him.*
>
> *"It's my secret tragedy. I never talked about it."*
>
> *Curtis said he had spent thousands of dollars on doctors as he sought a cure for a brother who started hearing mysterious voices as a child.[1]*

More recently the television series **"The Twilight Zone"** has been echoing Dr. Highwater's comment, only in better English, with its advertising. The spiel goes **"We all have our demons...."**

Not only Hollywood film-makers but also Rock singers are acknowledging this truth. British pop star **Sir Cliff Richard** had this to say about his part in a musical adaptation of **Emily Bronte's "Wuthering Heights"**:

---

1. Daily Telegraph 29 Nov '92.

"They think I'm just the goody two-shoes who sings Living Doll. **There is a demon in all of us***. Just because I'm a Christian doesn't mean the demon isn't there.[2]"*

I couldn't have put it better myself!

The same kind of expression recognising the activity of demons is occurring more and more amongst sportsmen and sportswomen. **Liz Smylie**, an Australian tennis star who was voted **Comeback Player of the Year** by the international tennis media in 1990 is quoted as saying:

"Tennis to me is 90 per cent mental. I have slammed balls, and I have bounced racquets. I have even gone mad at umpires and line judges. **The battle is really to conquer the demons inside yourself".** [3]

The same can be said about the Australian judiciary. Case after case sees a judge sentencing a murderer or a child molester after the gruesome details have been presented in court, with acknowledgment that the guilty party was led by his or her demons. I record one example:

Justice Frank Vincent *told the killer he had "forfeited your right ever to walk among us again".*
"You are sentenced to imprisonment for life on each count without the possibility of release on parole", he said.
Camilleri, 29 and his companion Lindsay Beckett, 25, abducted, repeatedly raped and murdered the Bega teenagers for 10 hours on the night of Saturday, October 5, 1997.
"Once their ordeal started Beckett and you abandoned all pretence of any human decency", Justice Vincent said.
"Upon 'the demon' within you being let loose it was not to be controlled until its lust and anger were exhausted.
"Whether or not Beckett saw 'the demon' as you later enquired of him ... I have no doubt that you did."[4]

In later years we've had reports and talk about demons causing problems in motor cars and various technological and mechanical areas. In fact it has become quite fashionable for the media to ascribe a whole variety of problems to demons.

---

2. Daily Telegraph, 5 March '96
3. Woman's Day, 8 Jan. '91.
4. Daily Telegraph 28 April '99.

What is **important** truth is being trivialised by humour and over-use. We need only to look at the way the term "Born Again" has been trivialised. You pick up a newspaper and see an article headed **"Jack Spratt has been born again!"** When you read the article (half hoping that Mr. Spratt has received the Spirit of Jesus) you discover that he is a successful man who went bankrupt, but due to special circumstances is now back on the road to success again. It could be a sportsman, a politician, an actor or anyone who is making a successful fresh beginning. In nine cases out of ten it has nothing to do with being born of the Spirit of God (John 3:3-8).

Likewise with someone or something having its demons. The enemy has given up on hiding the truth, so now he's hoping that over-use and wrong use will neutralise the damage that the truth can do to his kingdom.

We need to remind ourselves that demons are the enemy of ALL mankind. They are the front line of the enemy, the robber, who seeks to steal, to kill and to destroy (John 10:10). Thank God that *the reason the Son of God appeared was to LOOSE (DESTROY) the works of the devil* (1 John 3:8).

Well now, so far we have shown that Hollywood film makers, a British pop star, sports people and the judiciary ALL recognise the activity of demons in themselves or in western society. (Eastern cultures have no problem with recognising spiritual activity either, only they may not think of the spirits they recognise as demons or unclean).

Apart from **Sir Cliff Richard**, they all represent the world. What does the Church say?

4.2 THE CHURCH

(i)   **Corrie ten Boom** is a well known Dutch Christian lady who spent much of World War II in a German concentration camp for assisting Jewish people and others escape capture by the Gestapo. She has written many books about her experiences and *"Tramp For The Lord"* records her efforts to speak to Christian gatherings in Communist nations. In one large Cathedral she repeatedly found her listeners *"chained like animals, dying of hunger, but unable to reach the food ... their hearts were shackled so they could not taste the food I was offering them."*

'Could it be that demons keep them in bondage?' I wondered. I opened my Bible and read, 'In my name shall they cast out devils.'

'Lord, what must I do?' I cried out.

'Obey Me!' came the answer.

'But how, Lord? There are so many who are bound by demon powers and I cannot meet with each of them individually'.

'Where did I say that you can deal only with individuals?' He asked ...

...That night was the final night of the meetings. The great cathedral was crowded with people, but it was the same as on all the other nights ...

I knew God was calling on me to act. I trembled, but I had no choice. 'I must interrupt my message for a moment, friends,' I said. 'Many of you cannot grasp the richness the Lord offers us this evening. The servants of Satan are keeping you in bondage.'

Then I obeyed. Taking a deep breath and offering one last quick prayer I said in a loud voice, **'In the Name of Jesus I command all dark powers keeping people from the blessings of God to disappear.** Go away! Get out of the hearts of these people. Get out of this church. Go to the place where God sends you' ...

I was afraid but I felt secure. I knew God had told me to do it. Then, as I opened my eyes and looked out over the huge congregation, I saw a miracle happen. The people who had been in bondage came alive. They began to rejoice and as I continued my message I could sense their eager hearts drinking in the living water as I poured it out before them.

After the service I was scheduled to meet with a large group of local pastors who had attended the meeting.

'How could you do that?' one pastor asked as soon as I entered the room. 'Communists do not allow people to speak about demons!'

'I had to obey God,' was my only answer ...

There was a long, uncomfortable silence. **When the Bible interferes with man's theology, it always causes a strain ...**

That was the end of the pastors' meeting, but, oh, what a lesson I learned that night. It is tragic to be around people, especially men of God, who do not recognize the fact that we are surrounded, not only by angels, but also by the powers of darkness ...

In **"War on the Saints,"** Mrs. Jessie Penn-Lewis wrote, '... when the existence of evil spirits is recognized by the heathen, it is generally looked upon by the missionary as "superstition" and ignorance; whereas the ignorance *is often on the part of the missionary, who is blinded by the prince of the power of the air to the revelation given in the Scriptures, concerning the satanic powers.' ...*

We have a good safeguard and guide - the Bible - God's Word. Here we find not only the necessary information about Satan and demons, but also the weapons and the armour that we need for this battle ...

*I remember in **Ravensbruck (Concentration Camp)** for instance, when we had very little to eat, my sister **Betsie** said, 'Let us dedicate this involuntary fast to the Lord that it may become a blessing.' Almost immediately we found we had power over the demons that were tormenting us and were able to exercise that power to cast them out of our barracks.*

It is interesting to note that **Mrs. Penn-Lewis**' book, considered her most important, and written in collaboration with the famous **Welsh revivalist Evan Roberts**, was ABRIDGED for many years because church leaders and the editors could not handle the truth about demonic influence in and on Christians. It wasn't until 1973 that the first printing of the UNabridged edition found the light of day.

According to the foreword of her book, this mighty saint's discovery **"was misunderstood and her teaching misinterpreted"** *Does that sound familiar?*

Corrie represents people of simple Bible-loving faith who believe the Word of God says what it means and means what it says. They correspond to the tax collectors and fishermen of Jesus' walk on earth.

(ii) ANGLICAN DIOCESE OF SYDNEY

(a) CHURCH OPPOSITION

So what do many church leaders of today say? Pretty much what they said in Jesus' day!

I quote to you from my Archbishop of yesteryear:

Letter 21 March '75

> *"It is not for me to argue that you may claim some warrant for what you are doing but your emphasis and the extent to which you have allowed yourself to concentrate on this field of activity goes beyond the perimeters of the Ordination Service.*

*"I think I ought to be more explicit. I ordained you to the Priesthood without the full support of the Examining Chaplains because of the way in which you replied to their questions. I did so only on the clear assurance which you gave me that you were willing to exercise your ministry **within the limits of our Anglican formularies** and that you would not use your ministry to promote charismatic interests.*

*"It is true that at the time it was glossolalia which I had especially in mind and I believe that you have remained loyal to the undertaking which you gave me. However, I can hardly be content with **another form of charismatic ministry** which is even more open to question than the practice of glossolalia."*

Letter 21 May '75.

*"I am now writing further to my correspondence to you on this subject to advise you that such meetings ought not to be held in a licensed church building without the Archbishop's consent for which you should have applied, as the Sydney Church Ordinance requires. **I regret that I cannot consent to St. Michael's Church being used for this purpose** and I must ask you to discontinue this practice forthwith. **I would further advise you against continuing these meetings on other church property.***

Letter 30 June '75

*"My first serious objection is simply this. When our Lord delivered a man or woman from demon possession it was by a single word of command. **This was equally true in such cases as may be traced in the Acts of the Apostles**. Nothing could be further removed from this than the way in which you and your counsellors deal with those who come to you. (Anyone would think we **wanted** drawn out deliverance battles!!!)*

"Secondly, there is nothing in the New Testament records which allows anyone to identify demons in the way in which you do. They are called unclean spirits; but even that does not necessarily mean that the person who was possessed was impure in life. No other definition of their character is given and I think it is quite fantastic to classify the demons which you say you exorcise."

The Archbishop obviously overlooked several references to the identification of demons or unclean spirits as follows: **dumb** (Mark 9:17), **epileptic**

(Matt. 17:15 with Mark 9:20), **blind** (Matt. 12:22-24), **infirmity** (Luke 13:11), **python** (Acts 16:16, normally translated divination), **bondage to fear** (Rom. 8:15), **fear/timidity** (2 Tim. 1:7), **stupor** (Rom. 11:8), **antichrist** (1 John 4:3), **error** (1 John 4:6). With so many sick people in the world and the church, how could one miss the spirits of infirmity and fear?

The identification of the ruler **"Legion"** was also obviously quite important or it would not have been recorded for us. We will say more about this soon.

We have also found **jealousy** (Num. 5:4), **pride** (Eccles. 7:8) and **harlotry** (Hosea 4:12, 5:4) in the Old Testament. You may find more.

> *"I may add that many of those things which you describe as demons are nothing more nor less than sins; **lust, envy, hatred, and a score of other things to which you refer are not demons at all; they are sins of the mind or the flesh** and they should be dealt with as sins, not as demons."*

He is obviously unaware of the meaning of Genesis 4:7, see next chapter!

The Archbishop's next letter responds to my understanding that NOT ALL deliverances and healings are IMMEDIATE or can be obtained on a single word of command. In this letter he does admit that the **Legion** spirit "argues" with the Lord Jesus AFTER having been commanded out. Is it any wonder they often argue with us mere mortals?!

Letter 8 September '75

> *"In St. Mark's account (Chapter 5:1-13) the command appears to be in two parts. **The controversy appears to have been after the first command to come out of the man.** There was no resistance; the words spoken were words of fear. The deliverance was complete when the Lord gave them leave to enter the swine."*

> *"In St. Luke's account (Chapter 8:26-33), the command is again in two parts. **The controversy occurred after the initial command;** the demons left when He gave them leave."*

This whole matter of the passage of TIME is fully discussed in our **"End-Time Deliverance and the Holy Spirit Revival"** publication. Chapter 5 is entitled "TIME" IN THE NEW TESTAMENT. It is a great mistake to think that ALL the healings and deliverances took place immediately.

The difference between our views was that of a notable Bible scholar interpreting New Testament incidents from the brief details given us by the Holy Spirit, but without any practical front-line experience, opposing an ordinary Parish shepherd who had been thrust into the front-line of the battle for human souls when the good Lord forced him (me) to "accidentally" cast out an unclean spirit from a Bible-trained, born-again Deaconess. This very quickly led to hundreds of Christians wanting to be set free of a HUGE range of (spiritual) problems. The learning curve was large - and fast!

Letter 16 March '76

*"I must repeat that I think your present emphasis on exorcism is exaggerated and mistaken; that the guidelines should be strictly observed; that the "lee-way" of **emergency uses should mark the exception and not become the rule**; and that if this is not an acceptable way forward for you within the Church of England then you should give serious consideration to the exercise of a ministry outside the Church of England.[5]"*

I'll confine my comment to saying that the emphasis on "exorcism" (as it was then known) was not mine at all! I needed more work like a hole in the head. It was ALL the Lord's doing, bringing people in from all over Australia, begging to be set free from unclean spiritual chains, and teaching us HOW!

I was supposed to say *"Get lost. The Archbishop says we are all wrong. Forget the New Testament. Forget the Great Commission with which the Lord Jesus has charged His Church. You are imagining things. You need drugs or something! See your Doctor (again!)".*

And that is supposed to be in accord with the Ordinal (Prayer Book). God help us!.

The Archbishop by then had some unworkable regulations drawn up for the ministry which gave the appearance of approving the ministry of "exorcism" in theory, but with many "wise" safeguards.

To be fair, various wild reports were being circulated about our methods which would have affected any leader with a fetish for "respectability" and good report. Thank God **the apostle Paul** (2 Cor. 6:8) and **the early Church** didn't let that stop them (Acts 28:22)! A Bishop visited one of our meetings and his report, at least that part of it made known to me, made no adverse comment on its conduct. If there was adverse comment I should have been informed.

---

5. Now the Anglican Church of Australia.

If indeed there was anything "wrong" with the **conduct** of the ministry, all that was needed was some scriptural counsel and Godly correction from the leadership.

(b)   RENEWAL EXPOSES PHARISAISM

As most Christians know, the Lord rarely seems to choose to bring RE-FORM and REVIVAL through church scholars these days. In centuries past He used scholars like **Luther, Calvin** and **Wesley** because people were illiterate and certainly had no access to the Word of God, let alone the original **Hebrew** and **Greek** texts of the Bible. However revivals of the twentieth century have usually been brought through gifted but fairly "normal" people such as **Kathryn Kuhlman, Billy Graham, T.L. Osborn,** etc.

Even **the Lord Jesus** by-passed the **Sadducees** and **Pharisees**, selecting ordinary men to usher in the **Age of the Holy Spirit** at Pentecost. He could do that because He knew the Word of God better than they did; indeed He was/is the Word (John 1:1-3). Eventually however, the early Church needed the scholarly pharisee **Saul** to steer it through the transition from Old Testament regulations to a new and living way (Heb. 10:20). Saul became a new creation (2 Cor. 5:17) named **Paul**, who became God's instrument to provide us with much of the New Testament and the **law of Christ** (Rom. 8:2, Gal. 6:2). Thank God for **Dr. Derek Prince** who has been given a similar role for the latter part of the twentieth century.

However, it has now become necessary to reveal damaging information about the leadership's handling of this Holy Spirit breakthrough for deliverance ministry in the Diocese, but for the right reasons. I have had to forgive all the leaders involved, known and unknown. Having forgiven them, I have no desire to publicly shame those who remain alive. Those who have already died and appeared before the Lord know their errors, as we ALL shall in due time, and they will want their damage to cease, so I feel free to now reveal those errors. However some damaging information is particularly relevant to the aims of this book. For example:

(1) the initial threat of jail contained in a draft of a new proposed Church Ordinance prepared by a Church lawyer. To their credit the leadership did not proceed with this proposal.

(2) the anger manifested by a member of the Standing Committee (which runs the Diocese) towards this ministry, which shocked a new member, who asked me what I had done to merit this.

(3) the Archbishop confided to a friend (someone who could call him by his [first] Christian name without all the formal titles) the primary reason

for setting up the *"Enquiry into the Occult"*. It certainly was not to get my contribution, because although I was appointed to the commit-tee[6] as an "exorcist", it was pure window-dressing for the media and the wider church, deceiving them into thinking there was to be genuine and open discussion about the place of deliverance ministry in com-bating the occult threat.

I think there were only two of us on the Committee who were not asked to make a contribution. When the discussion turned to deliverance, the committee secretary, editor and the chairman's right hand man, turned to the chairman, **Dean Lance Shilton**, and asked *"Why don't we get Dr Alan Cole* (scholar and missionary) *to write something. He met a demon-possessed man in Asia once!"* So they did. It needed an incident like that to get through to my tiny, simple, naive, trusting mind to realise I was wasting my time on the Committee. (In fact Alan Cole had received some requests for "exorcism" while on the mission field and only the Lord and he knows what he did about them).

There was never any intention that I should be allowed to contribute what the good Lord had taught me through spending up to thirty hours a week for more than two years in deliverance work.

Anyway, the Archbishop's friend in whom he confided was also an acquaintance of mine and chose to be a part of God's truth instead of the deception. He later informed me the primary reason for setting up the Enquiry was to put a stop to our ministry, that is, have the Committee's Report received in Synod (the Diocesan Parliament) with a view to imposing the regulations referred to earlier. I was far too naive and innocent in matters of church politics, believing everyone was acting in good faith and wanting the best for the people of God. It was like a lamb being led to the slaughter, but when I think back on it now it comforts me to reflect I was walking in Jesus' footsteps, even though I didn't know it.

Notwithstanding his unfortunate opposition in all of this historic and long-awaited thrust by the Holy Spirit, it should be recognised that my Arch-bishop was an outstanding Christian leader in many respects. He was a highly respected Bible scholar, author and lecturer, an inspiring preacher and described by media legend and author **Malcolm Muggeridge** as **"The Godliest man I ever met"**.

---

6. See my letter of resignation - *Appendix D.*

That such an intellectual and spiritual giant could err so seriously regarding a salvation ministry made available through the blood (bruise-Isa. 53:5 lit., 1 Peter 2:24 lit.) of Christ Jesus his Lord should surely cause EVERY Christian leader to examine themselves afresh.

I personally held him in great affection but am constrained by the Holy Spirit to reveal the truth, so the Church of God EVERYWHERE can benefit. He was a great man in many ways, but he was fallible and locked into his own set of traditions, so what does that say about the rest of us?

We know that unclean spirits are responsible for false teaching (Acts 13:8-10, 2 Cor. 11:3-4, 1 Tim. 4:1-2, James 3:14-16, 1 John 4:1-3) and the traditions of men (Col. 2:8-20), and we also know the Bible says that all we Bible teachers make many mistakes (James 3:1-2). Yes, we ALL got our demons! What happens is that as we learn more and more truth (John 8;31-32) and put to death all our earlier errors in understanding so we increase in the knowledge of God (Col. 1:9-14) and become even more controlled by the **HOLY** Spirit, instead of the remaining unclean spirits! Praise the Lord!

So, the real problem was that *traditionalism* (Mark 7:8-9), *intellectualism* (1 Cor. 1:27) and *legalism* (2 Cor. 3:6) were being threatened by the Holy Spirit. Hence those crafty, stifling regulations referred to earlier were imposed upon the whole Diocese, probably to the relief of most of the clergy who were thus provided a "legitimate" excuse for their disobedience of the Great Commission (Matt. 10:1,8, with 28:20).

It might surprise you to learn that the exercise of a bright intellect can be an unclean bondage. Having a clear, undamaged and retentive mind is obviously a great blessing, but what is even more important is having the RIGHT (HOLY) Spirit using, guiding and controlling your mind. The Apostle Paul not only exhorts us to be transformed by the renewing of our minds (Rom. 12:2) but we should be renewed in the SPIRIT of our minds (Eph. 4:23) by the HOLY Spirit (Titus 3:5) so as to have the mind of Christ (1 Cor. 2:16).

So, then, the bottom line is that *the Spirit/spirit which uses and controls our mind is far more important than our intellectual ability.* If we Christians allow ourselves to get puffed up with intellectual knowledge and pride (1 Cor. 4:6, 18-19, 5:2) then the good Lord is going to deal with that, sooner or later (Prov. 8:13, 11:2, 16:18, 29:23). In my view, my Church leaders were now in the firing line.

(c) THE SPIRIT IS MOVING
HELP!

It seems history is always repeating itself! Here we had a situation where the Faithful of a Church Diocese had been praying over many years for a spiritual revival and/or renewal, and for their churches to be filled to overflowing again.

So what happens when the Lord answers their prayers? They fight it!

What they should have prayed was:

> *"Dear Lord, please bring revival/renewal to our Church, but when you do, please don't make me change my traditions or make me change my theology too much.*
>
> *I want you to move powerfully amongst us, according to my terms, conditions and comfort. I want success MY way.*
>
> *Thanks very much Lord!*

It is tough enough engaging the demons in lay Christians in Spiritual Warfare on a regular basis, but when you get no support from your Church leadership as well, but rather opposition, things can get very difficult.

And the work load ......! Up to thirty hours a week doing one-on-one deliverance on top of everything else. We were so overworked throughout the early learning period I would have welcomed ANY leadership interest, any guidance, help, support or back up. But, except for one visit by my Bishop to our Deliverance and Restoration meeting, no one in leadership came near.

WARNINGS

I want to add a friendly warning to those who would seek to justify their opposition to what was happening at St. Michael's by saying - *"I'm not against the deliverance ministry, but I don't approve the way you do it".*

Christians who make that sort of comment while trumpeting their belief in the Word of God fit comfortably into the **"Gerasene condition",** which we explain very soon.

Deliverance being a key New Testament ministry "Gerasenes" cannot question its validity, which leaves them only one excuse for their non-support, that is, they question the method(s) practised.

The obvious answer is to invite these doubters to show us how it should be done. Not just talk but demonstrate, leading by example.

Frankly I view such a comment above as blatant hypocrisy, usually made by people who have never knowingly cast out a demon in their lives, and neither have they read our books. Anyone who reads our publications[7] will know that our methods are based on the Word of God and executed in the Name of the Lord Jesus Christ. Our books have drawn glowing praise[8] from biblical Christians around the world - glory only to the Lord Who inspired them! The only reason we tackle Deliverance and Restoration (D. and R.) in groups instead of individually is because we (the team) are so small and the need is so great. Remember Corrie ten Boom's huge meeting in the Cathedral?

If every evangelical pastor or minister reviewed their priorities and established a D. and R. program we may not need to process large groups all the time. It's a matter of taking care of one's own "sheep", instead of forcing them to go elsewhere to a so-called "specialist". In the meantime the Lord is not bound and can deal with groups just as easily as individuals. If we call out the spirit of fear in Jesus' Name, does it matter that twenty people get deliverance from fear instead of only one???

Another friendly warning. Anyone who opposes a genuinely Christian deliverance ministry is despising the victory of the Cross (Col. 2:13-15). **Sickness,** whether mental, emotional, spiritual or physical **is a curse** (Deut. 28:58-61) and **Jesus has borne and carried that curse for us** (Matt. 8:16-17, Gal. 3:13-14). Hence **we can be loosed from the works of the devil** (1 John 3:8b) and **by His bruise[9] we were healed** (1 Peter. 2:24) **and are healed** (Isa. 53:5b).

If you oppose a salvation ministry won through the blood of Christ, do not expect His blessing upon your work. It would be wiser to heed the VERY strong warning not to speak against the PERSON or the WORK of the Holy Spirit.

You may remember the Lord had just healed a blind and dumb demonised sufferer and the Pharisees who had come all the way down from Jerusalem to stop this young rabbi in his tracks fell into the trap of accusing Jesus

---

7. See list inside back cover.
8. See Website http://skyfamily.com/fsf/
9. Most people know that a BRUISE is caused by **internal** bleeding - shedding blood internally.

of using the power of Beelzebub, the ruler of demons and a Philistine deity, because He had an unclean spirit, they said.

Today's leaders sometimes get very close to the dangerous position of the scribes and Pharisees in the New Testament when they speak against the WORK of the Holy Spirit. From Jesus' warning it seems that to speak against the WORK is getting very close to speaking against the PERSON of the Holy Spirit (Matt. 12:22-32, Mark 3:22-30).

About thirty five years ago I thought I had committed this unforgivable sin because of some stupid joke I had uttered. I went through emotional and spiritual agony for some 24 hours before the Lord took the burden away. It was a lesson I have never forgotten.

So how can Christians who oppose God's cleansing and deliverance program expect the Lord to bless and prosper their ministries when the Bible implies they are wolves, wolves who scatter the sheep (Matt. 12:30)?

To use a modern expression, "In your dreams!" - it is not going to happen. *If you ignore the warning, the best you'll get is crumbs* (Matt. 15:26-27). *Observe Sydney Diocese in the 1970s and 1980s and learn the lesson.*

(d) CHURCH POLITICS

SYNOD 1975

The politicking continued into the Synod debate held 13th October 1975 over the Occult Report. To make sure I could not influence the Synod against the preparing of his regulations the Archbishop's assistant and chairman **(Bishop Dain)**[10] ruled that a time limit of **FIVE MINUTES** would apply to each speaker. I spoke, pleading that a salvation ministry should not be regulated by church law because it was part of the gospel of Grace. **The Sydney Morning Herald** (national newspaper) quoted me as saying *"How can you legalise grace? How can you legalise the Holy Spirit? The whole host of angels is listening to us. It will be a day of shame if this Synod restricts the gospel of grace".*

ANGLICAN MEDIA IN THE 70s

Soon after the then editor of the **Australian Church Record** (the recognised Diocesan newspaper) stood up and attacked my method of using a tape

---

10. I do not doubt for a moment that **Bishop Dain,** like **Bishop Reid,** did not like following the Archbishop's battle plan. I believe he was a reluctant pawn-er-bishop.

recording to maintain the ministry to a sufferer while I spoke to him for a few moments during a visit by him. I often used a tape player to save my voice, but engaging in conversation during ministry was very unusual. My motive was to impress him with demonstrating how simple and sometimes easy it was for people to be helped/delivered, and there was no need to fear. BIG MISTAKE!

I need not have bothered. His motives we can only guess because his mind was set in theological cement before he arrived. He told me plainly that "we" (the newspaper and the hidden faces behind it) would ignore our ministry. This still seemed to be the policy in 1999 A.D. when the editor of the current Diocesan print media declined to review our latest publication **"Sex, Demons and Morality"**.

The A.C.R. editor also questioned (in Synod) in a critical way why I sent demons only 50 miles away (as an appointed place). He revealed no understanding of the biblical guidelines of where to send them[11], nor the grounds necessary for demons to re-enter humans again. I wonder what he would have said to the Lord for allowing them to enter a herd of swine? Obedience to the law of Christ (Gal. 6:2; Jas. 2:8, 12; Rom. 8:2) and being covered with Christ's blood (Rom. 3:25 lit., 1 Pet. 1:2) are ALWAYS going to be necessary to prevent an increase in someone's level of demonisation, no matter where we are, or live, or who we are!

The most alarming thing of all is that he never at any stage enquired about the progress of the sufferer he had seen receiving deliverance ministry. Less important was that he (a newspaper editor) somehow thought using technology was wrong. (I was converted to Christ through a **Billy Graham** radio broadcast in May 1959, so I had no such limitations).

As the editor spoke AFTER me and I had already spoken for almost five whole minutes, I had no chance to reply - until now.

Five minutes to present my case for a salvation ministry obtained through the Blood of the Lamb of God!!! The Synod decided to trust the Archbishop to handle it, passing Dean Shilton's motion (and the buck!) to that effect. That was **their** big mistake, but with some speakers sounding so reasonable and responsible, the Synod simply made the mistake I had been making for years - they trusted **men** (John 2:24-25) and worldly wisdom (James 3:15).

---

11. See **Book 2 "Engaging the Enemy"** chapter 5.4.

THE GERASENE RESPONSE

We need also to remember that the traditional churches are full of Gerasenes, who were responsible for one of the saddest verses in the Bible:

> *"And those who had seen it told what had happened to the demonised man and to the swine. And they began to beg Jesus to depart from their neighbourhood." (Mark 5:16-17).*

Imagine it! A violent madman - one who could not be controlled or contained and who had been terrorising the neighbourhood is delivered in one afternoon, and instead of rejoicing and praising God, THEY COULD NOT WAIT TO GET RID OF JESUS. It was not the monetary loss of the swine that upset them primarily, because Luke's Gospel tell us *"they were seized with great fear"* (Luke 8:37).

Their fear was obviously building up (v. 34-35) - Why? The Lord had just performed a wonderful deliverance work on an unfortunate man who had been a constant threat to them all. You think they would have celebrated - held a feast - or at least a party - and honoured Him greatly? He was offered nothing - zilch!! Not even a cup of tea - or cold water (Matt. 10:42). No. They were seized with great fear and couldn't wait to get rid of the Lord (Matt. 5:34, Mark 5:17). - Why?

Even the disciple Peter experienced a similar desire to get rid of Jesus, or to put it more acceptably, the one who recognised he was sinful (full of sin?) wanted to distance himself from the Holy One and begged Jesus to leave:

> **"Depart from me for I am a sinful man, O Lord"** (Luke 5:8).

Perhaps his fear, confusion and sense of unworthiness was similar to that of the Gerasenes, and both these incidents bear thinking about for a moment. In the light of all that our books have been saying about the widespread nature of demonisation (and its relationship to sin, the spiritual disease of the human heart) and how this consists of kingdoms of the powers of darkness, is it any wonder that, seeing the man who had the Legion was freed, all the unclean kingdoms and their ruling spirits were at panic stations **within the souls of the Gerasenes?**

Obviously the unclean pollution in their own hearts and minds was panicking (Jer. 17:9-10). Why, at any moment Jesus might have turned on THEIR kingdoms and cast them out! Their demons were not to know the Lord was only dealing with obvious and abnormal human problems at this particular time in history. The big, total clean-up, when He would remove deep-seated, hidden, ancestral problems, would come at the END of the Church Age, not at the beginning of it! (1 Peter 1:5).

REJECTION IS NORMAL

Every unclean thing in the souls of the Gerasenes was afraid. *"He's got rid of all our mates in 'Legion'. What's he going to do with us when He finds us in this house (heart, soul, body)? If He gets onto us and commands us out, even though we are strong we won't be able to stay. Is He going to cast me out next?"* And so it is today. We are surrounded by Gerasenes in the Body of Christ who have enemies within them with a great fear of exposure and removal. It does not matter whether they are anointed leaders who are filled (topped up) with the Spirit or rank beginners.

At the very least we can expect many people, even people who call themselves Christians to, like Peter, **distance themselves from exposure to the truth** and from Him who is the Truth. Jesus said many that are first will be last, and the last first (Mark 10:31) and so we can expect many surprises as the Lord's "sorting out" gets under way.

One thing that should NOT surprise deliverance ministers is an earnest request to depart from the assembly, parish or denomination to which they have belonged. **They are a threat to the hidden kingdoms and agencies of satan in EVERY place** (John 3:19-21). However the Word of God encourages us. Let us pray that the WISE MAIDENS will come forth and make themselves ready by getting their salvation cleansing (Matt. 25:1-11) NOW!

Let it not be said of YOU,

> *Well did Isaiah prophesy of you hypocrites .... All too well you reject the commandment of God, that you may keep your tradition ... making the Word of God of no effect ... (Mark 7:6,9,13).*

Yes, deliverance is COMMANDED! (Matt. 10:8, 28:20). Choosing between obeying Christ or pleasing the Archbishop was burdensome but not difficult.

(e)   CHARISMATIC RENEWAL

Scholars can be babies in the things that really matter - those areas of ministry battles which have been won for us legally through the Blood of Christ Jesus. They seem to sink their teeth into all kinds of complicated and peripheral issues and can't see the wood for the trees. They are often babies in *evangelism,* babies in *healing the sick* and still only in embryo form where **deliverance** and **inner cleansing** are concerned. The few ministers that put loyalty to the Lord Jesus before their fear of the Pharisees and have embraced Renewal were often treated like outcasts.

As one minister put it *"My hopes (for advancement) are finished. I'm on the outer!"* This dear brother had received the gift of tongues a few hours after discovering that Christ's healing power flows from His blood sacrifice on the Cross. Reflecting on these things while driving, the Holy Spirit fell upon him and he had to pull into the side of the road. As he did so he found himself praising God in an unknown language (Acts 2:4,11; 10:46; 19:6, 1 Cor 14:4-19)

Another minister who had the enormous privilege of introducing **tongues** and **prophecy** to the Diocese in 1962 was told that he would be left stuck in his country parish outpost because any attempt to transfer to another parish would not be approved.

The **Rev. Allan Alcock** resigned as a priest and a member of the Anglican Church on 25th November 1986, recording three basic reasons in an open letter of resignation to all his associates. He listed reason no. 2 as:

> **RENEWAL.** *Whilst I used to think God wanted to renew the Anglican Church (and did as much I could to bring that about) I now see He is only interested in renewing people and local assemblies. The problem arises that parish renewal can be stifled by the hierarchy and, perhaps with some exceptions, in general has been. There are some bishops, some clergy, some people and a small number of parishes that have experienced Holy spirit renewal but the denomination has hardly been touched. My conclusion is that the Anglican Church has missed any opportunity of meaningful experience of renewal.*

In pastoral matters the lay saints (God's sheep) have to come first, before the leaders. I have wonderful memories of the saints in Narrabeen, Eastwood, Penrith, Cambridge Park and Kingswood, and all the folk who came to us for deliverance ministry in Surry Hills.

They came first in our order of care. Leaders are important but we are not charged with the responsibility of pastoring them; they have that responsibility towards US! So they come second, and **the Religious System within which we work comes a big, fat LAST! None of them can keep up with what the Holy Spirit is doing today.**

I want to make it quite clear that I consider the Diocesan leaders who have consistently and ruthlessly quenched the Renewal movement over the past 35 years to be responsible for the potentially terminal "illness" now being experienced, both spiritually and influentially.

They have not known the time of their visitation (cf. Luke 19:44) and have resisted the Holy Spirit, as usual (Acts 7:51). As a consequence thousands of faithful Anglicans have experienced prolonged emotional and mental illness without rescue. Thousands of others have suffered physical illnesses without the Saviour's ministry, and many have died preventable early deaths, (I speak in human terms - Rom. 3:5b, 6:19a, cf. 1 Cor. 12:28-32), all because their spiritual leaders were riddled with unbelief. (Luke 23:34)

In our publication **"TORONTO and the Truths You Need to Know"** we discuss four (4) areas of major failure within some Bible-based churches. They are:

1. **Failure to obey the Great Commission** - ALL OF IT.
2. **The intellectualisation of the Faith.**
3. Failure to distinguish between the **human SOUL and human SPIRIT**
4. **Failure to understand SIN** - the spiritual disease of the human heart.

To my knowledge these failures have not been addressed except by a handful of Bible-believing ministers. This has resulted in perhaps the biggest failure of all, the failure to give Godly leadership to the Renewal Movement today. But, to be fair, the contemporary Church has NEVER been able to cope with RENEWAL in ANY age!

I write this material in the year 2000AD about the Diocese of Sydney[12] in the seventies, conscious that in due time I will appear before the Judgement Seat of Christ (Rom. 14:10, 2 Cor. 5:10) to answer for it all. The Lord knows my heart, that I only wish to see Revival, Renewal, Cleansing, Full Salvation, truth and Christ's glory manifested upon Christians EVERYWHERE; and bondage to legalism, covering up, politicising and selfish ambition brought to an end.

Think SHEEP! SHEEP! SHEEP! - and their needs. Not self or systems.

---

12. If you think I have been too critical of the Diocesan leadership, the opposite is true. See our booklet *"We All Got Our Demons"* which gives a wider account of events for ALL leaders to note and avoid. Countless ministers have been bullied in the past but kept silent so as not to hurt the Church, and so the Pharisees continued unchallenged. Not any more.

Only when we see the Full Salvation ministries of **evangelism, deliverance** and **healing** given priority in theological and other training colleges should we consider trusting leadership again.

Meanwhile, praise the Lord for the Renewal churches!

All this is necessary for the preparation of the Bride of Christ and before the Coming of the Bridegroom! I remind you the good Lord is not coming to wed the Harlot Church (Rev. 17-19:9).

Yes, *we all got our demons.*[13] You were never going to learn this vital truth from traditional Church leadership, so the good Lord chose to do the unthinkable, the unbelievable, the utterly incredible. Even as I write this it stops me in my tracks. *He chose to use Hollywood and the entertainment industry.* Sinners they may be, but not religious hypocrites. *"The Lord works in mysterious ways, His wonders to perform!"*

I ask ALL churches to look to themselves, to examine themselves, especially those of Christ's servants who are in the role of powerbroking and political maneuvering within a denomination's administration.

I beseech you to never be afraid to CAREFULLY, HONESTLY and THOROUGHLY examine something "new." Remember, amateurs built the Ark, professionals built the Titanic.[14] The Ark was built for the purposes of God. The Titanic was built for the glory of man. And while you are at it, please look afresh at YOURSELF, before the Lord! (1 Cor. 11:28)

The next sections should give you enough evidence from the Word of God, dating back to the beginning of Creation, to blow you away (mentally!). Stick with it!

"It is no good setting a tepid Christianity against a scorching paganism."
Prof. James Stewart
Scripure Union Centenary - LONDON

4.3 WIDESPREAD BIBLICAL DEMONISATION

We have some strange expressions in the English language which we may often say without giving them a second thought. But when we stop to think, we could well be amazed at how revealing they are about our innermost nature, for example:

> *"It lifted my spirits....!"*
> *or*
> *"You are in good spirits today"!*
> *"What on earth has got into him?"*
> *"God bless you!" (after your friend sneezes)*

---

13. Offended? I am only saying what the Bible says - see next chapter.
14. The huge ocean liner (ship) sunk by an iceberg in 1912.

A sneeze is an expulsion of bodily enemies, and really is a blessing, so long as it is not onto or into YOU! We have to keep in mind that, before our human spirit was born again it was *"dead in trespasses and sins"*, that is, powerless as far as running its/your life is concerned (Eph. 2:1). We manifested different characteristics as various spirits influenced us, as the expressions above indicate.

We had a quick look in the previous section (4.2 (ii)(a)) at a list of unclean spirits or demons actually NAMED in the Word of God, so let us now try to consider this list with an attitude of believing that the Bible says what it means and means what it says.

If we try to "de-mythologise" the Bible or spiritualise sections which should be taken literally, or even naturalise others which are plainly miraculous[15] or spiritual, then we won't even get to first base.

This is the list of demons we have been able to find:

VARIETY OF SPIRITS

1.	JEALOUSY	Num. 5:14	
2.	PRIDE	Eccl. 7:8	
3.	HARLOTRY	Hosea 4:12, 5:4	
4.	LEGION	Mark 5:1-20	MIND
5.	EPILEPTIC	Mark 9:17-25	MIND
	DEAF, DUMB, BLIND	(Matt. 12:22)	
6.	INFIRMITY	Luke 13:11	
7.	PYTHON (OCCULT)	Acts 16:16	
8.	BONDAGE TO FEAR	Rom. 8:15	
9.	FEAR/TIMIDITY	2 Tim. 1:7	
10.	STUPOR	Rom. 11:8	MIND
11.	ANTICHRIST	John 4:3	
12.	ERROR	1 John 4:6	MIND
13.	DISOBEDIENCE	Eph. 2:2	
14.	LYING	1 Kings 22:19-23	MIND

These are all called *a spirit*, obviously unclean, and all the intellectual wriggling in the world will not be able to deny that fact. There are a number of other spirits hinted at fairly strongly without actually being named as such. For example there are the problems King Saul experienced when his armour bearer David became more popular with Israelites than himself -

---

15. Some "teachers" have suggested Jesus was walking on a sandbank thinly covered with water when He walked on water (The boat must have been six inches deep!).

15.	**PARANOIA ?**	*1 Sam. 16:14 - 23:18*	**MIND**
also			
16.	**BITTERNESS**	*Heb. 12:15*	
17.	**WORLDLY WISDOM**	*James 3:15*	**MIND**

In our publication *"End-Time Deliverance and the Holy Spirit Revival"* we tried to illustrate the widespread need for deliverance ministry throughout the Body of Christ by discussing in chapter 3:

(i)   Large **Numbers of spirits** can inhabit humans

(ii)   Huge **Numbers of people** need deliverance

(iii)   The HUGE complexity and **variety of TYPES** of spirits.

Of course, the modern, traditional pharisee would say we are exaggerating, or scaremongering or mad. They read the apostle Paul as writing (Eph. 6:12). **"We do not fight against (spiritual) rulers and authorities ... but against blood and flesh ..."**

You know he did NOT write that, so who is being deceived?

Now please take a look again at the spirits listed:

3.   HARLOTRY

The spirit of Harlotry is a key which opens the door to us understanding the SPIRITUAL inspiration behind sexual lusts. We touched on this in the introduction and sections 1.5 and 1.11 (iii)

This area of demonic activity is so huge it required the publication of a separate book **"Sex, Demons and Morality"**, our largest book prior to this one, the size of which I am constantly trying to reduce!

6.   **INFIRMITY.** As we explained in 1.13 the word *"infirmity"* covers every human weakness of the spirit, soul and body and, because we are less than perfect we ALL have weakness(es) and, to that degree, we can be described as *infirm.* Bones (Luke 13:10-16), sense organs (Mark 9:25, Matt. 12:22-24) etc.

This area of demonic activity is HUGE!

If we can grasp this mind-blowing truth that ALL our imperfections are caused by the devil and his spiritual agencies then the remainder of this section - and indeed, this book - will be an enormous source of WISDOM for you, as you serve the Lord and His people.

7. PYTHON (OCCULT)

"An Australian Python"

If you have read some of our other publications (see inside back cover) you will know the unclean spirit which the apostle Paul cast out of the clairvoyant girl (Acts 16:16-18) was actually the spirit of a python (original text).

All over the world various religions are based on honouring a serpent or snake spirit, including our Aborigines who (used to) honour the serpent spirit as the Creator of life. To informed Christians the use of a snake or serpent in religion shows the great deception which we are warned against in the creation account:

"Now the serpent was more cunning than any beast of the field which the LORD God had made......" (Gen. 3:1).

The serpent spirit is a replacement, false (anti) Christ which deals in deception, poverty, sickness and death, as many nations in this grip of paganism amply demonstrate to us today.

This area of demonic activity is HUGE!

8-9 FEAR. We discussed this in 1.2.

This area of demonic activity is HUGE!

10. **STUPOR.** Just take a look around you. How many people are aware they are on the Broad Road to destruction? (Matt. 7:13-14). They are too busy partying and making millions and absorbed in fashion, rock music, lust, various addictions and television. See chapter 1.3.

It is as the apostle Peter wrote:

"They promise ... freedom but they themselves are slaves of corruption, for whoever overcomes another makes him his slave"
(2 Peter 2:19).

How do we measure the level of stupor throughout a nation? One way would be to observe it's loss of the fear of God. The measure of social and cultural sin would be an accurate indicator of both the level of stupor and a resultant loss of the fear of God.

".... concerning the transgression of the wicked: There is no fear of God before his eyes." (Psa.36:1, Rom. 3:18, cf. Gen. 20:11)

This area of demonic activity is HUGE!

11. **ANTI-CHRIST.** As has been explained many times, the word **ANTI** in its original and biblical meaning means **"alternative"** or **"substitute"**. The enemy has been able to cover this by imposing a more modern meaning of **"against"** or **"opposed to"**.

The Latin equivalent of the Greek word **ANTI** is **VICAR** and so some ministers are called Vicar (unfortunately) because they are considered to be Christ's substitute.

It gets a bit tricky when the Pope is called the "Vicar of Christ" because his Office is really being promoted as an Anti-Christ. Such is the devious work of the devil that he has hidden this from tens of millions of professing Christians by changing the meaning of the word *anti* in modern times.

What it comes down to is ANYTHING that takes the place of Christ's rule in and over our lives is a substitute for Christ, that is, an ANTI-CHRIST.

This does not simply refer to leaders of other religions such as **Buddhism** or **Hinduism**, although they obviously qualify, but it also refers to, for example, our idolatrous political support for **Marx, Lenin, Engels,** or our pursuit of money, sexual lusts etc.

Also the Apostle John, inspired by the Holy Spirit, revealed as an anti-christ anyone who denies our Father God and that Jesus Christ is the Son of God.

> *"... **He is antichrist who denies** the Father and **the Son.***
> *whoever denies the Son does not have the Father either;*
> *he who acknowledges the Son has the Father also."*
> (1 John 2:22b-23)

If something or someone else other than the Spirit of the Christ of God controls our life then that something or someone is an antichrist and is SPIRITUALLY inspired. This not only applies to non-christians but also to Christians who are double-minded (James 1:8, 4:8), that is, most of us!

This area of demonic activity is HUGE!

12. ERROR. What can I say? Every area in our lives where we are ACTING in error or BELIEVING error (because of the STUPOR?) is inspired by a spirit of error (see also 4.2 (ii)(b)).

The Bible warns us against false teachers, false prophets and false apostles and the apostle **James** humbles every teacher by saying that **we all make many mistakes** (James 3:1-2).

This area of demonic activity is HUGE!

13. DISOBEDIENCE / REBELLION

I repeat again the staggering statement the Bible makes about the WHOLE human race being born with a spirit of disobedience (to God) controlling them (Eph. 2:1-3 - see chapter 1.4, 2.1 and 2.2).

This control changes, of course, when we become born again Christians and receive the HOLY SPIRIT in to us to be our Spirit guide. We then have the power to obey God, and make right choices.

To say the demonic activity of Rebellion is huge, when it has influenced ALL mankind, seems quite inadequate.

14. LYING

We only have to watch a Hollywood television sit-com (situation comedy) which are so very perceptive and expert in presenting human weaknesses, especially self-preservation and deception. They cause us to laugh at human foibles as the characters presented to us get into all sorts of problems and then make matters worse by trying to extricate themselves with lie after lie.

The character **George** in "Seinfeld" is probably the worst liar of all because his role is that of a walking disaster. There are plenty of others - **Hogan** in "Hogans Heroes" (but then, he is lying to the "enemy"), and even the psychiatrist of great integrity, **Frasier,** makes so many mistakes in human relationships through lying he is usually forced to eat "humble pie" before the segment finishes. Also **The Nanny** is not averse to telling some whoppers.

If we are to believe Hollywood (and I think we can in this matter) sit-coms represent human beings as being quite comfortable about lying when it is (i) to our personal advantage, (ii) for our self preservation, (iii) to cover up our mistakes.

But, as Hollywood depicts, lies usually take us deeper and deeper into problems until we end up exposed, shamed and punished mentally and emotionally, and forced to "come clean" with the truth.

The more we practice lying, the more these spirits take over and control us so that some folk get to the place where they not only lie all the time, but they themselves are not even aware of the truth or otherwise of their speech. The fate of unrepentant liars etc. can be found in the book of Revelation, chapter 21 v 8.

Do you still think it is an exaggeration to say **"We ALL Got Our Demons"**?

May I just mention three (3) more areas of demonic activity which are HUGE. We discussed WITCHCRAFT (2.2) and **SIN**, which has chapter 5 all to itself.

WORLDLY WISDOM is earthly, soulish and *Demonic,* according to James (3:15) and, of course, the world operates on worldly wisdom all the time, that is why we have wars, and life is full of struggle. Related to No. 12 ERROR.

James says it springs from the human soul so we again have confirmed that *"we all got our demons"* and they operate from the soulish area, which includes the mind and the emotions. I think it is true to say that worldly wisdom, with all its lies and deceit, cunning and shrewdness, planning and pursuits, politics and power struggles has the spirit of STUPOR laughing its head off at nearly all of us.

All this can be summarised with a word of humour. Do you know what makes God laugh? No? When we tell Him OUR plans! It is wiser and better to flow with His!

When we add the spirits of JEALOUSY and PRIDE the diagnosis and extent of human pollution becomes almost beyond our comprehension. No wonder the apostle John wrote *"The whole world lies in (the power of) the evil one"* (1 John 5:19).

How has the good Lord put up with the human race for so long? His love and His grace are beyond measure. I thank God for the mercy that is extended to each one of us through Christ's bearing of **OUR** sins on the Cross and the offer of His pardon if we repent!

THE MIND.

Please note there are at least SEVEN (7) spirits that could be labelled under the broad title of MIND-CONTROL so it should not surprise us when young students come out of University or T.A.F.E. Colleges with their minds filled with the religions of the Labour Movement, paganism and witchcraft. They have had to study, and study, and study, and write assignments with stupor, worldly wisdom, lies and deceit abounding to overflowing in their minds and souls (see also chapter 8).

Are you getting the picture? If so, can you also understand that the WEATHER we are experiencing on this planet reflects the SPIRITUAL WARFARE taking place in the Heavenlies.

The war in the Heavenlies is hotting up (Exod. 9:16-26, Josh. 10:11-14, Job. 38:22-25, Psa. 18:12-14, 78:42-49, 148:8, Luke 21:25-26), and that is why things are hotting up on earth. Many nations are experiencing foul and severe weather, with the prospect of much more to come.

But take heart and be of good courage. This book is not only an expose on human nature but also an offer of hope, because we repeat that Christ is THE HOPE of the World (Psa. 42:5, 146:5, 1 Tim. 1:1, 4:10, 6:17, cf. Prov. 10:28)! If you are unsure about your relationship with Him, you can make sure by using the **Sinner's Prayer** (Appendix B). When you can say this from your heart, it will give you a FRESH START!

THE WAY FORWARD

Now that you know how the Lord sees your polluted state, even though you are supposed to be a temple of God in which only the Holy Spirit dwells (1 Cor. 3:16, cf. John 2:13-22), are you content to leave things as they are?

Or are you going to heed the counsel of the Holy Spirit when He caused the apostle **Paul** to write:

"Let us cleanse ourselves from ALL pollution of flesh and of spirit, perfecting holiness in the fear of God". (2 Cor. 7:1).

... and the apostle **Peter** when he wrote: *"So then, dear friends, ... **make every effort to be found spotless**, blameless and at peace with Him". (2 Peter 3:14).*

Can you now understand something of the mind of Christ (1 Cor. 2:16) when **WHOLE assemblies** of church meetings, including pastors and ministers, experience the so-called Toronto Blessing (c 1993), and what a tragedy it is that ignorance by both those FOR and AGAINST the movement has allowed it to come almost to a standstill (for the moment).

WHOLE ASSEMBLIES need the Lord's cleansing Deliverance, from the least to the greatest. Very soon we are going to find out which Christians are stupid and which are wise (Matt. 25:1-13), those who can put their life (discipleship) where their mouth is.

The Lord is sick of talk, He wants the WALK! He wants His children to move into His cleansing Renewal!

PROPHECY (CLAY W. ENGLAND)

DO YOU RECOGNIZE YOUR NEED?

My holy servants must admit that there IS a problem. This is one of the hardest things for My leaders and servants to do. Spiritual pride prevents many from reaching their intended goal, which I have sought to encourage them to reach. Sometimes I have to work a lifetime to get even My fully dedicated ones to realize that THEY have a spiritual need.

When at last they discover how great their need is, they too cry to Me for deliverance. Then I send them forth, allied with My angels, to go against the demons who seek to oppress them, and also to go against the demons who oppress others.

My believers see that they have only begun to live more fully after I have delivered them. And I am daily in this process throughout the earth.

Believers in Me are the chief targets of the devil and his demons. And the demons are so cleverly deceptive that no man, woman, or child on earth is able to clearly detect them without My help. Satanic spirits go about to convince Christians that their vile carnality (the sinful remains of their fleshly nature) is "only natural."

By this means they rob some of My sweetest saints of reaching their very best for Me. True, they have been converted and they escape the fires of hell, and they have a few rewards in their spiritual heavenly account. But they never reach the utmost heights of usefulness for Me.

*...... You must turn over to Me what you cannot do for yourself. You are to listen closely to Me. You are to follow My directions AND **ADMIT** your need of help as you work together with Me for your complete deliverance. I deliver you only AT YOUR REQUEST and with your full cooperation to command demonic forces to **go** in My name Jesus, by My blood, and by My Word.*

*...... You must accept the facts as they are and THEN call on Me actively **for deliverance.** I told My disciples, "Behold, I give you power (authority) to tread on serpents and scorpions, and over ALL the power of the enemy; and NOTHING shall by any means hurt you." (Luke 10:19)*

Will YOU admit YOUR NEED? Will YOU call on Me for help? Will YOU put on the whole armour of God So that YOU may be able to withstand in the evil day?" (See Ephesians 6:13). Will YOU let Me fill YOU with My fullness so that My fruit of the Spirit (Galatians 5:22-23) and My power gifts of My Spirit (1 Corinthians 12:8-10) are evident in Your lives ......?

Extracts from the book **"Jesus Says Come Higher"** as given to **Clay W. England.** 521 East Olive Street, RICH HILL. Missouri 64779 United States of America.

We must move on in the presentation of the biblical evidence.

HAGAR THE HORRIBLE

"By kind permission of King Features Syndicate"

ICEBERG OF THE KINGDOM OF SIN

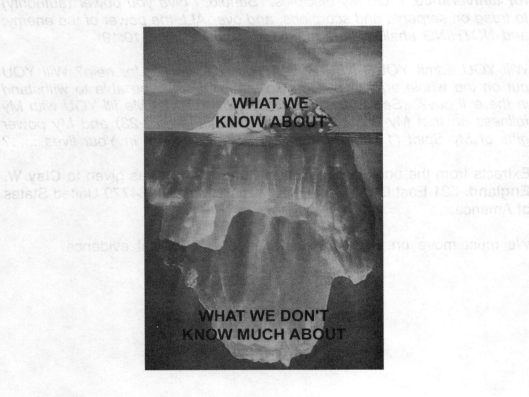

CHAPTER 5

SIN IS DEMONIC

Therefore having these promises, beloved, let us cleanse our-
selves from all pollution of flesh and of spirit, perfecting holiness
in the fear of God. (2 Cor. 7:1)

INTRODUCTION

"If you continue in my Word, you are truly my disciples, and you
will know the truth, and the truth will free you.
(John 8:31-32).

I realise that many readers will know these words of Jesus very well and
some will even have preached this Scripture, but we should never tire of
this message, or even let it get filed away in the back of our heads.

In the film **"A Few Good Men"** a **military prosecutor (Tom Cruise)** has a
marine Colonel (Jack Nicholson) in court and in the witness box. The
prosecutor cries out *"I want the truth!"* and the Colonel snarls back, *"You
can't handle the truth!"* Regrettably both statements can apply to many
of us today.

We don't mind learning the truth when it supports us or is to our advantage,
but it can also be very challenging, hurtful and even devastating. For
example, one of the ladies in our early Deliverance and Restoration team
discovered that not only did her husband have a previous wife, BUT there
had never been a death or divorce, and so her "marriage" had been a
bigamous sham! And her four children …???

It was truth exposed. It was necessary the deceiver be revealed by the
Holy Spirit, but it really hurt. In these end-times when so much is being
opened and revealed by the Holy Spirit can we handle the truth today,
notwithstanding the demands it may make on us, by the grace of God?

This chapter will NOT be an easy read for most people. It will be solid Bible
study for most of the way, yet it contains one of the great and vital revelations for this century of Renewal and preparation for the end of the Church
Age.

WILLIAM E. GLADSTONE: There is but one question of the hour: how to bring the truth of God's
Word into vital contact with the minds and hearts of all classes of people.

May I suggest you take it slowly and steadily, checking everything as you proceed. For some people it may be better not to let any unclear section block your study progress, but slip over that section and come back to it later.

5.1 SIN IS SPIRITUAL

Oscar-winning Director, **Sir Richard Attenborough** has recited in public on a number of occasions how his admiration grew for **Gandhi,** the famous Indian Hindu leader. Apparently Gandhi was walking on the same side of the pavement as a number of white people, who obliged him to step off the pavement making way for them to pass. The perceptive Gandhi asked himself the question what was it in mankind that derived pleasure, self-esteem, pride and honour from the humiliation of another human being?

It seems to have escaped Sir Richard (and Gandhi) that while Gandhi only posed the QUESTION, the Lord Jesus supplies the ANSWER throughout the New Testament. It is simply the sinful heart of mankind inspired by the powers of darkness, playing their all-too-familiar power "game"!

Most Bible students have been trained to understand that the most basic problem human beings face in this life is the problem of SIN, and we are referring here to the deposit of sin in the human heart/soul, the disease itself, not the sins of omission or commission performed by our flesh. The apostle Paul goes to a lot of trouble to explain the indwelling problem of SIN which caused him to commit sins, in Romans 7.

There can be no doubt that the rediscovering of the Deliverance Ministry during the twentieth century, by the grace of God, has raised the vital question of the relationship between indwelling SIN and indwelling DEMONS, and also the FLESH.

(i) FACING THE CHALLENGE

I wrote to my area Bishop[1] way back in April 1976, seeking to encourage theological discussion and investigation as under:

---

1. My reading of the Diocesan situation was that Bishop Reid was caught in a conflict of loyalties and felt he had to carry out the instructions of the Archbishop against our ministry. I think they troubled him deeply.

"SIN AND DEMONS

I believe this to be an area where theological research could be very enlightening. I would think one could hold one of a variety of views here... ...One group may categorise everything as sin, another as demons and yet another see this problem not in "either-or" terms but "both-and".

In any event we should recognise that the gift of discerning of spirits is bound to cause some theological shocks when applied, but what does it matter if we get at the truth? We need to be girded with truth in this spiritual warfare. Spirits can be tested without difficulty, and again, if the ministry is indeed genuine it will bear fruit in the life of the Christian....

If we have put off the old man with his practices (Col. 3:9) we are supposed to have died to the elemental spirits of the universe (Col. 2:20) because we have been crucified with Christ (Gal. 2:20). It appears that in dying to sin (Rom. 6:10-11) we have died to THEM. This relationship between the powers of darkness and sin(s) is an area in which I believe this generation of Christians can examine with great profit."

By the time you have completed this chapter you should be in no **doubt that the human heart disease of SIN is spiritual and DEMONIC.**

The main revelation of this book is that EVERYONE needs deliverance, and true Christians should set about obeying the Lord's command to be cleansed (2 Cor. 7:1, James 4:8, 1 John 3:2-3) before the Trumpet of the Lord blows (1 Thess. 4:16-17) and it's too late (Matt. 25:10-13).

I believe I can show that the Word of God says everyone, **Everyone, EVERYONE** needs deliverance from unclean spirits in their soul.

All Christians want their human spirit to be saved for eternity, many want the salvation (healing) of their bodies, so wanting the salvation (deliverance/ cleansing) of our souls should not be strange for us to desire, especially when the Word commands it.

(ii)   JESUS IS OUR MODEL

In many places in the Word of God we are instructed to pursue sanctification (holiness) and Christlikeness (perfection), because there is such a huge gap between Christ's **sinlessness** (2 Cor. 5:21, Heb. 4:15b) and our **sinfulness** (Rom. 3:23, 5:12 etc.).

There are times when we Christians feel quite spiritual, righteous and pleased with ourselves but we are brought up with a jolt when we look at the person of the Lord Jesus and His perfection. Pioneer Renewal speaker **Bob Mumford** records how he was walking along a beach and talking to the Lord. He was feeling quite pleased with himself and so he asked the Lord to show him how He (the Lord) considered him.

Within moments he was reduced to a weeping, snivelling wreck on his knees in the sand.

That's how it should be for all of us when we measure OUR righteousness against the inner beauty of Jesus, because, as John writes, Jesus said **"... he (satan) has NOTHING IN me"** (John 14:30 lit.). This is not true of normal human beings, of course.

> *"Jesus himself did not trust himself to them because He knew all men, and needed no one to bear witness of man FOR HE KNEW WHAT WAS IN MAN".*   *(John 2:24-25)*

It is strange that the **apostle John** did not simply say Jesus knew of the SIN within men. The obvious reason is the Holy Spirit caused this to be left open-ended so the old man (the strong man) could be revealed later and, in God's good time, the Man of Sin also (2 Thess. 2:3-9). Certainly the **apostle Paul** called this pollution in man "SIN" but even he went further and left the door open for more understanding or revelation. He wrote:

> *"For I know that no good thing dwells within me..."*

- and then, he remembered he had been filled (topped up) with the Holy Spirit in his soul, so he clarified what he meant:-

> *"... that is, in my flesh!"*   *(Rom. 7:18a)*

What a powerful statement this is! It is the exact opposite of what Jesus said about Himself in John 14:30b. Paul says that nothing good (only pollution) dwells in his flesh and makes him do what he doesn't want to do. This pollution is not an abstract, airy-fairy, questionable theory or possibility. **It is spiritual, very much alive, active and controlling.**

If the mighty, Spirit-filled apostle Paul can admit to having spiritual pollution dwelling in his flesh, and controlling him, then **where does that leave us?**

It seems the apostles John and Paul are of one mind in this matter, with our Lord Jesus Christ.

(iii) HISTORICAL VIEWS

Do you remember the quotation from the **Oxford Dictionary of the Christian Church** in our Introduction?

> *"Since the end of the 17th Century there has been little further development of the doctrine of sin... More recently the recognition of demonic forces in contemporary civilisation has led to a renewed theological emphasis on the gravity of sin ..."* (page 1260).

Of course, our understanding should not have to change if it is right. What has been understood by Bible loving Christians is and was right - as far as it went. It just did not take into account what the **spiritual** nature of sin unmistakably implied.

Therefore every SINNER has a SPIRITUAL problem; that is the teaching of the Bible. We need to go one vital step further.

5.2 SIN IS DEMONIC

(i) A NEW TEACHING ???

Let me make it very clear that the teaching in this chapter may be new to many Christians but it is as old as **Cain** and **Abel**, the sons of **Adam** and **Eve**. Hollywood may have taught it for many years and some Churches may still have to accept and teach it, but it goes right back to the beginnings of mankind. I don't know where **you** place man's beginnings in time, but the Bible records that **SIN IS DEMONIC** in **Cain's** day

There are two definitions of SIN given to us in the Bible, one at the beginning and one at the end. They are as follows:

> *Gen. 4:7 Sin is a demon (lit. Hebrew)*

> *1 John 3:4 Sin is lawlessness (lit. Greek)*

—but we are getting ahead of ourselves here.

It should not surprise us the Bible says everyone who has a root of sin in their heart has unclean spirits, because the church has always (to my knowledge) defined "sin" as **the spiritual disease of the human heart**. Now, "spiritual" is further defined as "of the spirit", that is, **sin is spiritual**, which must obviously mean inspired by spirits, or a spirit. It is really so simple. It seems incredible the church could overlook that *spiritual things (problems) are caused by spirits* all these centuries - especially the spiritual nature of the human heart. (cf. Eph. 1:17-18)

Neither should we be surprised the same powers of darkness the early church had to contend with are still around today. They have had eighteen centuries to infiltrate the world and the church with virtually NO OPPOSITION! Even the denominational churches had lost sight of their existence and their method of operation until now. In the past every wrong-doing has been blamed by the church on SIN, the spiritual disease of the human heart, but *we have now been taught the spiritual disease of sin was made up of demons or unclean spirits.* This should not have surprised us, but it did. It was so simple yet so profound and SO un-traditional.

One key Scripture to help us is, of course, Ephesians 6:12,

> *"We do not contend (wrestle) with blood and flesh, but against rulers and authorities, against the rulers of this darkness, against spirituals of wickedness in the heavens". (lit. Greek).*

You may remember me discussing this briefly in Book 1, and I want to underline again that if you are a Christian who believes this Scripture for its plain and obvious meaning you are in the minority (at this time of writing) in the Body of Christ. The vast majority of Christians don't believe it in their hearts. If they did they would have no serious problems with the revelations in this chapter and this book.

While I do not know of any Bible student who denies that RULERS and AUTHORITIES here refers to SPIRITUAL rulers and authorities (rather than earthly, physical rulers and authorities) it is also true that I know of no Bible student who has questioned why Paul wrote we contend with spiritual rulers and authorities rather than we contend with "sin" or "the flesh".

When I first began to experience deliverance victories in my Anglican parish in the inner-city of Sydney I experienced several surprising "mysteries". Little did I realise the good Lord was about to demolish a number of nice, neat little evangelical traditions in my life. Some of the things I could not immediately understand were:

(a)   the huge RANGE of types of spirits that could be located and removed from the souls of Christians.

(b)   the huge NUMBERS of spirits that could be removed from the souls of Christians - even with the same name (e.g. anger).

(c)   the amount of MINISTRY TIME required to obtain the complete loosing of a Christian from just one type of spiritual kingdom.

(ii) MORE ON MAN'S "DARK SIDE"

The terrible state of man's inner condition is very well attested to us in the Word of God, and neither is it totally hidden from those who do not know the Word.

For example the **Dalai Lama**, the world leader of the Tibetan form of Buddhism, is quoted as saying:

> *"The real destroyer of our inner peace is not our external enemy but our internal enemy"*

Even the ancient Chinese, long before they saw a Bible, coined a proverb **"Beware the wolf in every man."** and today the secular psychiatrist talks about man's **"dark side"**.

By kind permission of Ian Jones, Pearly Gates Promotions
Email:pgp@interworx.com.au

The Word of God tells us:

> *"The heart is deceitful above all things and is desperately wicked"* (incurable - by man).   **Jer. 17:9**

OLIVER WYON: One of the first things for which we have to pray is a true insight into our condition.

That is a very powerful statement - isn't it? The Lord Jesus said:

> *"But if your eye is evil, all your body will be dark. If, therefore, the light in you is darkness, how great is the darkness!"*
> *Matt. 6:23*

This tallies with John's letter:

> *"For all that is in the world, the lust of the flesh, and the lust of the eyes, and the vain - glory of life is NOT of the Father, but is of the world."*
> *1 John 2:16*

We already know that **the world lies in (the power of) the evil one** (1 John 5:19) and that, of course, means *the powers of darkness control the world,* through the STUPOR of men and women.

The lust of the flesh and the eyes and man's vain glory (pride) all spring from WITHIN man - his heart, mind, soul, and through his flesh.

Well meaning politicians who call themselves "internationalists" and many other people share the generous, but incorrect, belief that mankind is basically good and, as a consequence, Law and Order (Justice) in "Western" nations has become a shambles. What does the Bible say?

> *"If you therefore, being EVIL, know how to give good gifts to your children, how much more will the heavenly Father give the Holy Spirit to those who ask Him?" (Luke 11:13, cf. 18:19, Rom. 3:18)*

So the good Lord who sees into all our hearts confirms that we are inwardly evil - all through. This teaching was called *"total depravity"* by the **Puritans,** which basically means that every part of man, - spirit, soul and body - was polluted or affected to a major degree. This does not mean man won't give good gifts to those he loves (cf. Matt. 5:46-48). So also our Father God will give us the **HOLY** Spirit to replace and wage war in amongst all our **unclean** spirits if we ask Him.

MAN'S SPEECH

> *... "Do not swear (by an oath) at all ... But let your word be 'Yes, yes' or 'No, no', for more than these is from the evil one."*
> *Matt. 5:34,37 (cf. James 5:12)*

> *"... and all which is not of faith is sin."*
> *Rom. 14:23 (cf. James 4:17)*

These are very challenging scriptures most of us prefer to slide over. Certainly we can say sins are inspired from the evil in our hearts (cf. Mark 7:21-23) and our mouths speak out of the abundance of our hearts (Matt. 12:34).

So it seems that our unclean speech (e.g. blasphemy, profanity) comes from the evil one through his agencies that reside in our hearts. Our unclean speech coming from the evil one (satan) is also confirmed by Jesus' clash with the disciple **Peter.**

You will remember how Jesus commended Simon Peter because he had identified the Lord, *"You are the Christ, the Son of the living God!"* But soon after Peter attempted to rebuke the Lord for talking about His coming suffering and death. It troubled Peter so much he did not have the ears to hear Jesus mention the Resurrection to come, or understand what the Lord was saying.

So when Peter exclaims *"Mercy to you Lord! This shall never happen to you!"* - What does the Lord answer?
> ***"Get behind me satan! You are an offence (stumbling block) to me, because you do not think the things of God but the things of men".***
> Matt. 16:24

What a revealing passage! There are TWO powerful revelations here:

(i) The Lord says it is **the indwelling inspiration of satan** (the evil one) that caused Peter to get it wrong! (Remember that satan is a spirit being). — And Peter did not mean evil - he meant well!

(ii) This inner inspiration is common through all mankind because Peter thought **like MEN normally think**. This is consistent with the wisdom of this world which is **earthly, soulish, demonic** (James 3:15).

So, if we think like men of the world, or we think like non-Christians about philosophical matters we have a BIG problem! Thank God for His Word of truth that cuts through like light into darkness!

(iii) EVIDENCE TODAY?

We have already shared a good deal of evidence from the beginning of this book. In addition to spiritual enemies like **fear, rebellion,** and **stupidity**

DWIGHT L. MOODY: I have more trouble with D.L. Moody than with any other man I ever met.

etc. there are **sexual lusts** galore (hands up those who have never lusted), plus **sorrows,** emotional hurts and griefs, which we know the Lord Jesus defeated for us by bearing such sorrows on our behalf on the Cross of Calvary (Isa. 53:3-5).

Of course, when we are hurt emotionally by someone, there are two very common responses we make. We can either:

(i)   allow ourselves to be crushed, wilt and withdraw from our attackers

OR

(ii) allow **bitterness** and **resentment** to flood our hearts. We think of ourselves as toughening up, not being a victim any more and giving as good as we get and, of course, **hate** makes us a force to be reckoned with.

Either of these situations is an opportunity for unclean spirits to flood into us and take control, IF we allow it!

(iv) CHILDREN

Legendary Australian radio talk-back host **John Laws** reported that the **NSW Bureau of Crime Statistics** has done a review of all the national and international research into juvenile delinquency.

> *Dr Don Weatherburn, director of the **Crime Statistics Unit,** had this to say: "**Kids are not born good.** The willingness to curtail your impulse to take what you want is acquired, not inborn. Concern for others, concern for others' property, is acquired, not inherited."*

The cruelty of some children to other children should tell us something. There is a simple spiritual experiment which will confirm the Christian teaching on **original sin** and the truth that sin is born in us. It requires praying with a little child.

Simply teach the little one the LORD'S PRAYER. They may be in the bath-tub or in bed, but ask them to pray the Lord's Prayer. Somewhere during the prayer they will probably emit a yawn.[2] It will only be a weak, worker-class

---

2. Please remember that a yawn is an involuntary expulsion of gases (breath/wind/spirit) from the lungs, quite outside the control of the conscious mind.

   VANCE HAVNER: The church is so subnormal that if it ever got back to the New Testament normal it would seem to people to be abnormal.

spirit which was sitting on the top of their personality, but it won't be able to put up with the child saying the Lord's Prayer and will flee.

"But", you say, *"That yawn was probably a sign of tiredness as bedtime approaches. It doesn't prove a thing!"*

Okay then, try again the next night, only teach the child to recite a nursery rhyme like *"Mary had a little lamb"* or something like that. See if you get any yawns from that! If you do it will be caused by tiredness, because no demon, no matter how weak, is frightened off by Mary's lamb, only the Lamb of God!

If you remain doubtful or sceptical, or the results are confusing, try the experiment for several nights and draw your conclusions at the end, after a fair run.

Don't be alarmed at children being spiritually polluted; we all arrived in this world with more than enough unclean baggage from our ancestors. Little children are not sometimes called KIDS (rebellious baby goats) for nothing!

(v) SIN IS DEMONIC - SERIOUS BIBLE STUDY

What has happened is that, **through the ministry of deliverance, the Lord granted a revelation of the TRUE SPIRITUAL NATURE OF SIN,** which, in brief, is as follows:—

1.   The Bible teaches us man and woman are created *spirit, soul and body* (1 Thess. 5:23) and although the terms *"spirit"* and *"soul"* are sometimes used as if they mean the same thing, nevertheless **there is a clear distinction between them** which can be arrived at from studying the Word of God, which is *"sharper than any two-edged sword, piercing to the division of soul and spirit."* (Hebrews 4:12 RSV).

2.   The Bible indicates **the human soul** (the area of the emotions) **can contain many indwelling spirits in addition to the human spirit** of life (Gen. 2:7; Heb. 12:23), e.g. the man who had the Legion of spirits. When the spirit(s) said to the Lord Jesus *"my name is Legion for we are many"* (Mark 5:9), it/they did not know how revealing this would be for us today.

In EXTREME cases of multiple personalities (M.P.D.) our secular society has viewed such conditions in the past as "emotional instability", schizophrenia or even insanity, but the truth of the matter is the Bible teaches that **EVERYONE is born with spiritual kingdoms of sin and death reigning[3] in their souls,** normally thought of in Christian tradition as *"original sin"*, and when this basic spiritual condition is worsened by continuing enquiry into occult practices, crime or immorality for example, noticeable (public) activity of the spirits of these kingdoms in the soul is not unusual.

3. In addition, when we become a Christian we receive the **Holy Spirit (of Christ)** into our souls (Rom. 8:9) so that our **human spirit,** which was dead (drowning) in trespasses and sin (Eph. 2:2), is born again (or anew, or from above). Our dead spirit is made alive by the Spirit of the Lord Jesus and we are transferred from the kingdom of darkness into the Kingdom of God (Col. 1:13-14). The indwelling Holy Spirit is our seal and guarantee that we belong to God (2 Cor. 1:21-22), and He not only revives the human spirit, but helps us to wage war against all that is unclean in the soul as well. Praise the Lord!

4. The Bible teaches that everyone is a sinner (Rom. 3:23) and has **a deposit of sin and death** transmitted down to them from generation to generation (Rom. 5:12; 1 John 1:8). The Bible also teaches that **the transmitted disease of original sin is inspired by an unclean spirit** (Eph. 2:2; Matt. 12:33-45) within the human soul and is referred to as the **strong man,** the **old man** or **old nature,** because it strives to rule over the human spirit—before—**and after**—we are converted to Christ.

The very first reference to sin in the scriptures, when the subject is introduced, personalises sin. Sin is not some nebulous, airy-fairy, abstract "it" but a "he" and I believe the **New American Bible—Catholic Edition**—gives us the best translation:—

> *God speaks to Cain: "If you do well you can hold up your head, but if not, **sin is a demon** lurking at the door; **his** urge is towards you, yet you can be **his** master".* (Gen. 4:7).

The footnote of this translation tells us the words **"demon lurking"** are translated from the literal "crouches", and allude to the similar **Akkadian[4]** term to designate **a certain kind of evil spirit.**

---

3. Sin and death REIGN (as Kings over Kingdoms) in the hearts of mankind (Romans 5:12, 14,21).
4. Semitic language of Akkad in ancient Babylonia.

(vi) SUPPORTING EVIDENCE

Perhaps you may find this literal translation a revelational shock to your thinking and suspect the **Roman Catholic** translators of some inaccuracy, but let me assure you they are not the only ones who have perceived this revelation that **SIN is a living personality,** and a **demonic personality** at that. I offer you five supporting pieces of testimony:

(i) **"The Analytical Hebrew and Chaldee Lexicon"** (p. 674) lists the Hebrew word for "crouching" or "lurking" as an active singular MASCULINE participle and therefore warrants references to SIN as a HE or HIS (N.A.B.-Catholic Ed.) and HIS and HIM (R.V.) etc. rather than an IT.

(ii) Also the same lexicon (p. 779) indicates that the Hebrew noun for "desire" has a masculine suffix, warranting the translation "HIS desire" rather than "ITS desire". Furthermore the Hebrew word for the phrase "over it" has a masculine suffix (p. 70). This warrants the last part of Genesis 4:7 being translated as "and you shall rule over **him**".

(iii) The **New International Version** of the Bible is also very supportive of the N.A.B. version but the translators here were not quite bold enough to put the literal translation into the text, but did the next best thing. In the Study version of this Bible translation of Genesis 4:7 they put in a vital explanatory footnote:

*"4:7 **sin is crouching at your door.** The Hebrew word for "crouching" is the same as an ancient Babylonian word referring to an evil demon crouching at the door of a building to threaten the people inside. **Sin may thus be pictured here as just such a demon,** waiting to pounce on Cain—it desires to have him. He may already have been plotting his brother's murder."*

The only comment I wish to make on this footnote is to say that **sin IS to be seen and understood as a demon,** not simply MAY be so pictured. That seems to be the plain meaning of the text.

(iv) The most powerful support for the N.A.B. translation that *"SIN IS A DEMON lurking ..."* comes from the Lord Jesus Christ Himself. In Matthew Chapter 12, verses 38 to 45, the Lord explains something of the unclean inspiration behind the evil and adulterous generation that craves a sign. Once we understand that sin is a demon which was crouching at the door of Cain's body and soul, and that his response to God's warning would dictate whether or not the demon could enter Cain to "possess" him, that is, his (Cain's) house, we can immediately see that *Jesus was alluding to the Genesis passage* and its revelation of the operation of the sin demon upon, outside and within a man's house (body). This is what the Lord Jesus actually said:

*43: "Now **when the unclean spirit goes out from a man,** he goes through dry places seeking rest and does not find (any).*

*44: **Then he says 'I will return into my house** from which I came out'. And when he comes he finds it standing empty, swept and furnished (ready for occupancy).*

*45: Then he goes and takes with himself seven other spirits more evil than himself, and **they enter and dwell there; and the last state of that man** becomes worse than the first. **So it will be also with this evil generation.**"* (Matt. 12:43-45 lit. with added words in parenthesis).

So the Lord explains Cain's experience VERY clearly! It is about time we began to believe some of the descriptions of the Word of God about our innermost pollution.

(v) The **apostle Paul** repeatedly refers to our **Old Man** (Rom. 6:6, Eph. 4:22, Col. 3:9) which is corrupt, while the Lord Jesus refers to the **Strong (man)** who rules his "house" (Matt. 12:29). *Clearly the pollution within us is a spiritual personality*, as covered earlier.

You can see from all the evidence that **the natural minds of men are spiritually polluted** (cf. James 3:15). They don't have a clue about God's mind even though they are surrounded by the witness of His creation, because their minds and hearts have become darkened (Rom. 1:18-22). **It is only through the Word of God, made alive by the Spirit of God, that mankind can begin to understand the truth of the mind of God.** (Isaiah 55:8-11; John 6:63, 8:31-32, 14:6, 17:17; 1 Cor. 2:10-16; 2 Cor. 3:6; Eph. 1:17-18).

Two questions for you:

(a) Do you believe Jesus' teaching?

(b) Can you see that in referring to a man as a house with a demon or unclean spirit lurking outside, looking for a suitable place (house) to

---

"(Whoever is) slow to anger is better than the mighty, and he who rules his spirit (is better) than he who takes a city." Proverbs 16:32

enter and rest or dwell in, **Jesus was referring to and expanding the literal meaning of Genesis 4:7**, where *sin is a demon* lurking at the door of Cain's body and soul?

5.3 SIN, FLESH AND DEMONS

(i) ANSWERING THE CHALLENGE

In early days in ministry the few brothers in Christ that were prepared to talk with me usually did so while we passed as ships in the night. That way they didn't get too involved, or hear something they didn't want to hear.

One incident went like this:

Brother X approached me, *"Hallo Peter".*
I replied, *"Hallo X, how are you?"*

Brother X (still walking), *"How do you know when a sin committed by someone is inspired by:*
    (a) the (kingdom of) sin in their heart/soul? or
    (b) an unclean spirit? or
    (c) the flesh?
"I don't know...."

then as brother X moved safely out of earshot, I add:

> *".... but every time we test the spirits and name the sin, a spirit responds to that name and is removed."*

By the grace of God I believe I now know the answer to the question asked. Let me explain by illustration.

Let us assume that you are a Christian who is moving forward in Christian things. You fellowship with other Christians, read the Word of God and pray etc. Now and again you witness about what the Lord Jesus Christ means to you and what He has done in your life. Occasionally, to your great delight, a sinner responds to your testimony and is converted to Jesus - praise the Lord!

Although you are a full-on Christian you are not yet perfected (except in a legal positional sense) and you enjoy some of the works of the flesh (Gal.

WILLIAM PENN: Right is right, even if everyone is against it; and wrong is wrong, even if everyone is for it.

5:19-21). You occasionally get angry with an anger that is not of the Holy Spirit and sometimes you sense your desire to serve God and be important in the Church is not always pure but driven, in part, by selfish ambition. (Jas. 3:16).

So there are two sides to your nature/soul - what the Scripture describes as being double-minded (literally, two-souled - James 1:8, 4:8). The **New man** in Christ in you is always being opposed by your **Old man.** (Rom. 6:6)

Let us consider the importance of what we have just written, and with which I hope you agree.

When you led someone to Jesus you may have involved three different parts of you.

(i)   Your **flesh** - you used your **tongue** to speak and possibly your **eyes** (to read the Word of God) and your **hands** (to impart the Holy Spirit with prayer).

(ii)   Your **soul,** which includes your mind and heart.

(iii) - and you would be the first to give glory to God and say that you (your **spirit**) was **led and inspired by the indwelling HOLY Spirit in all that you said and prayed and did!**

Can you agree with this analysis? If so, say AMEN! Because now I can tell you that **these same PRINCIPLES are involved when we commit sin.** If we get angry with a fellow motorist who happens to be driving slowly in front of us, and abuse him, it involves three different parts of us, in the same manner as when we do a good (Godly) work.

(i)   Your **flesh** - you use your **tongue** to abuse, and your **hands** to sound your car horn in frustration.

(ii)   The **Old Man of sin** in your heart/soul would get a measure of temporary satisfaction from harassing the other motorist.

(iii) - and all this **inspired by an unclean spirit of anger.**

So you see, when we seek to make a distinction between:
    (a)   the (Kingdom of) sin in our heart/soul/mind
    (b)   an unclean spirit, or
    (c)   the flesh

- we are very largely wasting our time. **The only distinction to be made is that of FUNCTION because they all work together. They are all part of the same problem.** The unclean spirit is part of the spiritual disease of sin in the human heart/soul (which is part of the Old Man) and manifests itself through the flesh by actions. That is why Paul takes away the veil of misunderstanding from our spiritual eyes and can write, under the inspiration of the Holy Spirit, that *we are not contending with .... flesh, but with rulers with authorities!*

These rulers and authorities reign over the kingdoms of SIN and DEATH, which dwell **IN THE FLESH!** (Rom. 5:12, 6:12, 7:17-18,20,23-24,8:3).

No other explanation comes close to satisfying all the evidence!

(ii) BLAME?

Some Christians don't like blaming human weakness on unclean spirits because they are concerned that human responsibility will be removed or weakened. Just as **Adam** blamed his wife **Eve** and Eve blamed the **serpent** it seems too easy for foolish sinners to blame the devil for all their transgressions and then blatantly wear a tee-shirt with the slogan **"The Devil made me do it."**

However, we all know there is no excuse, because **Adam and Eve and the serpent ALL received the judgement of God**. Let us face the truth first, and get that right, and consider the flow-on consequences after.

Here is a suggested Bible Study for you:

(iii) MANKIND and DEMONS

Eph. 2:1-3	**All are born with a spirit of disobedience (rebellion) by nature.**
Eph. 6:12	**All attacks on Christians (and others) are sourced in the spiritual world - no exceptions.**
1 John 2:16	**These attacks are often from within man.**
2 Cor. 11:4	**They continue after conversion - and further pollution is possible.**

Rom. 7:18-21	**Sin is in all -no exceptions (cf. Rom. 5:12, 1 John 1:8).**
Gen. 4:7	**Sin is demonic (cf. Matt. 12:38-45).**
Matt. 12:28	**Deliverance brings the Kingdom (Rule) of God, replacing the unclean rule.**
Matt. 15:26	**Deliverance is bread (basic spiritual diet or food) for the children of God FIRST. Christians first and then (maybe) pagans!**
	Praise the Lord!

5.4 CONSEQUENCES OF THIS TEACHING!

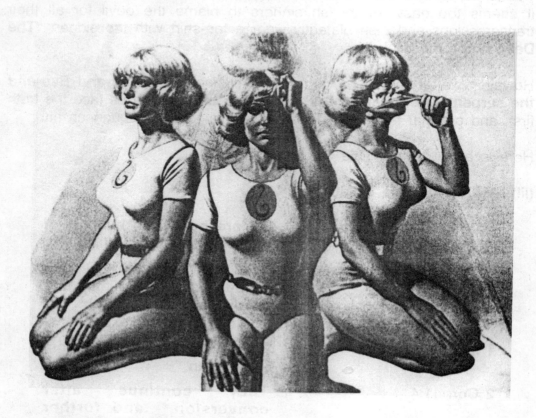

"You Can't Judge a Book by its Cover!" (Old English Proverb)

a)   The soul disease of SIN is spiritual and therefore DEMONIC.
b)   Therefore SIN is REMOVABLE (at this time in God's time-table for history).
c)   Now the Body of Christ (the Church universal) has the means to prepare herself to become the beautiful, spotless Bride of Christ (Eph. 5:25-27).
d)   This is the Salvation to be revealed in the End-Time (1 Peter 1:5).

This is the Bible's message. Beware of unbelief and rationalism. *With men, it is impossible.....!.*

SUNDAY, 24TH JULY, 1988
DELIVERANCE AND RESTORATION MEETING

PROPHECY: (PETER)

MY PRECIOUS CHILDREN, AS YOU TRAVEL ALONG THE ROAD OF YOUR CHRISTIAN LIFE, THERE ARE MANY THINGS I DESIRE TO TEACH YOU AND TO SHOW YOU WHICH ARE UNEXPECTED, AND WHICH MAY SURPRISE YOU, AND THE FURTHER YOU TRAVEL WITH ME THE MORE I CAN CONFIDE IN YOU THE SECRET THINGS OF THE KINGDOM OF GOD. AND AS YOU ARE ABLE MORE AND MORE TO BE LED BY MY SPIRIT WITHOUT MIXTURE; AS YOU ARE ABLE TO WALK IN THE FOOTSTEPS OF MY SON JESUS, SO I CAN SHARE WITH YOU THE MOVING OF MY SPIRIT UPON THE EARTH, AND THE THINGS THAT ARE NECESSARY TO BRING ABOUT THE BEAUTIFUL BRIDE FOR MY SON.

TRULY THE WORK TO BE DONE IS OF GREAT MAGNITUDE. AS YOU LOOK ABOUT YOU TOWARDS YOUR BRETHREN IN THIS CHURCH AND IN THAT DENOMINATION, YOU CAN SURELY SENSE IN YOUR SPIRIT THE WORK TO BE DONE IS OF GREAT MAGNITUDE. EVEN THE WORK I AM DOING IN YOU IS FAR GREATER THAN YOU COULD EVER HAVE IMAGINED BEFORE YOU SET OUT ON THIS PATH. AND THE FURTHER YOU TRAVEL WITH ME THE GREATER MUST BE THE REVELATION OF YOUR NEEDS. THE FURTHER YOU TRAVEL WITH ME THE GREATER MUST BE THE COMMITMENT THAT YOU HAVE MADE TO ME. FOR WE COME TO THE PLACE WHERE WE MUST DEAL WITH RULERS AND AUTHORITIES IN YOUR LIVES.AND IF I HAD BROUGHT YOU THIS WAY SOONER, THEN YOU WOULD HAVE NOT BEEN ABLE TO STAND AND OBTAIN VICTORY. SO I ASK YOU, EACH ONE OF YOU, TO CONTINUE TO TRUST ME AS YOUR HEAVENLY FATHER. TRUST MY FATHERHOOD OVER YOUR LIFE, EACH ONE (OF YOU). CONTINUE THE WALK OF FAITH. LOOK TO MY SON JESUS, AS THE AUTHOR AND TRULY THE FINISHER OF YOUR FAITH, FOR WHEN HE IS FINISHED MOULDING YOU, YOU WILL BE LIKE HIM, AND THAT TRULY IS A GREAT AND MIGHTY TRANSFORMATION.

SO DO NOT BE ALARMED THEN, IF YOU COME TO OBSTACLES ALONG THE WAY WHICH SEEM TO BE BEYOND YOUR CAPACITY, BECAUSE THEY ARE BEYOND YOUR CAPACITY BUT NOT BEYOND **MY** CAPACITY. SO LOOK TO ME, LOOK TO MY SON JESUS, STAY CLOSE TO HIM, AND ME, AND THE OBSTACLES THAT SEEM LIKE GIANTS, THAT SEEM LIKE MOUNTAINS, THEY SHALL BE BROUGHT DOWN. THEY SHALL BE LEVELLED BEFORE YOU; **BUT YOU MUST** DRAW CLOSE TO ME THROUGH MY SON. **YOU MUST DO THIS,** IF THE MOUNTAIN IS TO BE REMOVED.

I AM WITH YOU. I WILL NOT FAIL YOU NOR FORSAKE YOU. AS THESE WORDS WERE SPOKEN TO MY PEOPLE AS THEY PREPARED TO ENTER THE PROMISED LAND, SO ALSO THEY WERE SPOKEN TO MY PEOPLE OF THE NEW COVENANT IN THE EARLY APOSTOLIC DAYS OF GREAT TESTING AND DRAMA AND VICTORY, SO I SPEAK THEM TO YOU TODAY ALSO, IN THIS HOUR. I WILL NOT FAIL YOU NOR FOSAKE YOU, AND EVERY MOUNTAIN SHALL BE BROUGHT LOW AS YOU CONTINUE THIS WALK WITH YOUR LORD JESUS, BECAUSE HE WILL GO BEFORE YOU.

CHAPTER 6
REINCARNATION

6.1 THE REINCARNATION CHALLENGE

The legendary Indian philosopher and sage, **Mahatma Ghandi** is reported to have said *"The burden of reincarnation is too great to bear!"* This may seem strange to those who are attracted to the notion of this form of eternity but when some of my son's Buddhist friends promote this theory to him, he replies *"Why would you want to come back to this (world) and go through all the stress, grief and pain again. Thanks, but NO thanks!"*

Timothy has come to understand that reincarnation theory does not offer hope, as first thought, but makes all existence hopeless, in reality, because we human beings can never attain the goal of paradise through THAT system.

In recent years the newspaper media have regularly featured articles on **spirits, ghosts** and **poltergeists,** presenting the evidence and claims of reincarnation: that is, the notion that the human spirit or soul dwells in many different bodies from generation to generation, reincarnating itself in a new body in some way, prior to or in the event of the death of its present "home".

Incarnation is the clothing of a soul or spirit with a body of flesh. By definition then, **re**incarnation means the re-clothing or re-birthing of a soul or spirit (which has departed from an earlier body) with a fresh form or body. Hence it has come to popularly mean the transference of a soul or spirit-being from creature to creature when the death of the flesh takes place.

It follows, of course, that the soul laid bare under *the occult practice of hypnosis* enables the unclean spirit (masquerading as the human spirit) to show off its knowledge of history and various languages, such as in the **Bridey Murphy** case where the lass concerned reportedly gave accurate details of an earlier lifetime in France during the French Revolution, and also spoke French, under hypnosis.

Reincarnation theory is, of course, a concerted and critical attack upon the true Christian faith, so that what the Bible teaches about spirit, soul and body needs very careful consideration indeed. However, when we do focus our attention on the Scriptures in order to find the truth it is most rewarding. But let us make no mistake. It is as **Mr. Greg Tillett, Tutor in Religious Studies at Sydney University** was quoted as saying:

"If reincarnation is true the whole idea of people being resurrected on the day of judgement, so their bodies are re-united with their souls (spirits) is thrown out. Ideas like sin, forgiveness, judgement and baptism become irrelevant if reincarnation does exist."

The article went on to say that these themes are essentials of the Christian faith and Christian theology would have to be completely rewritten if re-incarnation exists (the way it is commonly understood). Mr. Tillett is quite right in this assessment so we can see this subject matter presents a most serious challenge to the Christian faith.

Another reason why the reincarnation theory is such a serious challenge to Christianity, quite apart from its totally anti-christian teaching, is that it seems so ATTRACTIVE. Most of mankind would like to think we go on living additional lives after experiencing death. To most non-Christians in western countries death is widely thought of as nothingness- *"when you're dead you're dead!"* So when a considerable mass of evidence is presented that seems to "prove" we can have new lives-continuously - generation after generation - and there is no judgement in the biblical sense, which removes any immediate threat of Hell, it can seem most appealing. My son Timothy's view is not the common one.

ADAM AND EVE

This confidence trick is not new. In fact it goes back to the very beginning of human life on earth, as far back as **Adam and Eve.** And it worked then too! It worked then and unfortunately it continues to work today upon those who are looking for an easier way to escape the judgement of God, other than by repentance and commitment to our Lord and Saviour Jesus Christ.

God told Adam he was **not** to eat of the fruit of the knowledge of good and evil, for in the day that he did so he would surely die. However the Scriptures indicate Eve wasn't even created when that command was issued (Gen. 2:15-22) and as she did not hear this command directly from God but indirectly through Adam (Adam being responsible for the teaching of God's Word to his family) - when the time came for **the serpent** to tempt Adam and Eve, he cleverly worked through the weak link Eve, weak because she had not heard the original command but had only her husband's word for what had taken place. This is further indicated by the serpent's opening attack, sowing seeds of doubt as to what God had really said:

"Did God say (??) 'You shall not eat of any tree in the garden?' "
                                                          (Gen. 3:1).

Having sown the seeds of doubt ("your husband must have got it wrong") the serpent comes out with a very appealing barefaced lie:

"You will not die ...." (Gen. 3:4).

- how many would like to hear those words and BELIEVE them true!

And so Eve disobeyed her husband, and therefore God also. She may have been just plain rebellious or she may have thought her husband was mistaken or exaggerating. Surely the God who had been so generous to them would not be so severe over one little fruit that looked so good? In any event she began the tradition of woman's liberation or, I should say, woman's rebellion.

So you see, there is nothing NEW about the reincarnation deception - it simply says "You will not die!" Satan rarely changes his tactics, and unfortunately this one has been working very successfully for him since the beginning of mankind. Most of us would like eternal life but the kind we would like to have can only be obtained on God's terms, through Jesus Christ, not through satan's lies.

Then what is the truth? That is to say, what do the Scriptures really teach? We will need to remind ourselves what we have established about the demonic nature of sin with which we are all born (Rom. 5:12, 1 John 1:7-9). Indeed all the previous chapter is vital, so let us now begin to apply those truths of God's Word to the phenomena and situations which the reincarnationists present to us.

6.2 EVALUATING REINCARNATION EXPERIENCES

The Bible says that *it is appointed unto man(kind) to die once, and after that, the judgement* (Heb. 9:27). Therefore **it is the human spirit that goes on into eternity (Heb. 12:23)** and there is NO reincarnation of the human spirit.

There can be no question that much of the evidence the reincarnationists put forward is genuine, i.e., the experiences or words of hypnotised subjects for the most part have been recorded accurately by professional men and women of integrity but the BIG question is, what spirit is producing the manifestations and information from an earlier life? Is it the **human spirit?** The **Spirit of God?** An **unclean spirit? Our assertion is that the spirit manifested is unclean!** Why? There are three main reasons as follows:

(i)   Can the spirit contacted be the Spirit of God?

There are many spirits that pass themselves off as God or Christ from within a person, but so far as I know no reincarnationist claims to be contacting the Spirit of Almighty God (that is, the HOLY Spirit) INSIDE a person; that is not the claim being made. Some may think there is no God or Holy Spirit and that the human spirit is a "god."

(ii)   Can the spirit contacted be the human spirit?

As we have seen, the Scriptures tell us that since the Rebellion of Adam and Eve the human spirit is dead (drowning) in trespasses and sins (Eph. 2:1). Is it likely then, that the hypnotist can get past the ruling spirits of sin to the human spirit? No way! The hypnotist will be fed what the unclean rulers give him.

A moment's reflection will help confirm this. If our **human** spirit was very much alive and well and active, and if it was our **human** spirit that had travelled down through centuries of history in many different bodies, you and I today would have an enormous wealth of knowledge *carried into this life* and available for our *conscious* minds to use daily, since in the original and perfect design of God *the human spirit was provided with a brain, memory and a conscious mind as tools to use (cf. Eph. 4:23).* However, the Bible also teaches that since sin and death entered the human race through the Rebellion of Adam and Eve, our minds and hearts have been polluted and our human spirit suffocates in sins until released by the Holy Spirit, through the forgiveness of our sins. There is a distinction then, between the human spirit of a non-Christian which is dead in sins, and the spirit of a Christian which has been born again, made alive by the Spirit of God - a kind of personal resurrection from death to life of the human spirit within the human soul (Rom. 6:4-5).

Clearly then, Christians and non-Christians will differ in their understanding, because the non-Christian does not know that his/her human spirit is dead in sins, and they unknowingly have an identity problem. The point is that if the reincarnationists' theory they are contacting an alive and **fully operational human spirit** is correct, it seems strange our CONSCIOUS minds are not fully conversant with all the experiences of our alleged previous lives.

Also the fact that it usually requires the unclean occult practice of hypnosis (charming, spells-Deut. 18:11) to open up what is called our subconscious mind or soul, in order to explore alleged past existences, is surely another very strong indication that we are confronting something other than the human spirit.

(iii) Can the spirit contacted be an unclean spirit?

Yes, of course it can. Spiritualists, hypnotists, psychiatrists, witches, mediums and all kinds of occultists contact them all the time. Every time you read "Your Stars for Today" in the local newspaper you are seeking information from unclean spirits, according to the Bible (Deut.18:9-12). But what about reincarnationists? We have seen that the Scriptures reveal we have all been affected by original sin and its spiritual causes, hard to accept though it may be. We have also seen that there is only one life given to the **human** spirit but that **unclean** spirits seek reincarnation down through history (Matt. 12:43-45). This enables them to speak any number of languages, give any number of verifiable historical incidents and data, and also parade their historical experiences through human bodies today. Such spirits are experts at deception and allow their imaginations to run riot when they know there is little chance of detection and their lies being challenged effectively. Because they are 'unclean' their role is totally that of anti-christ though some may cunningly appear "religious" in order to deceive.

CONTROL SPIRIT "FAHREEM"

Some of the experiences recorded by hypnotised subjects themselves reveal the unclean nature of the spirits manifested, and again some plainly admit to NOT being the human spirit. Consider the newspaper report of the spirit named "Fahreem" within a young woman - "Fahreem" reportedly claimed to be "a spirit on the go"; "a guide for all" and "a being of a higher plane" (typical arrogance). Then what, we may ask, is "he" doing as an inner voice in the same body and soul as the young woman's own human spirit?

The implication and essence of this situation is that by her own testimony she (her own human spirit) was allowing herself to be controlled by "Fahreem", an intruder. Such domination (lordship) should only be exercised by the Spirit of Christ, the Creator of all things and thus by definition the spirit of "Fahreem" is an usurper, a spirit of anti-christ, operating in the place of, and thus usurping the role of the Spirit of Christ.

Options open to people in this kind of situation are to either:

(i) allow this situation to continue and pay the inevitable price, which is to allow oneself to be dominated until one self-destructs,

OR

(ii) seek help from a section of the Christian church which is alive to spiritual warfare and is empowered to minister the appropriate ministry in the manner of the apostle Paul (Acts 16:16 -18) and be set free.

6.3 JOHN THE BAPTIST IS ELIJAH?!

Many people who believe in reincarnation point to the fact the Lord Jesus Christ seemed to confirm that **John the Baptist** was a *re-appearance* of the Old Testament prophet **Elijah** who had come to earth a second time. However this view in no way alters the truth that man only dies ONCE on this earth, because ELIJAH NEVER DIED at the end of his Old Testament life-time, but was translated by a whirlwind into the heavens *while alive* (2 Kings 2:11). Therefore when John the Baptist was beheaded that was his (and Elijah's) *first and only experience of death.* Confused ... ??

Let us take a careful look at what the Word of God has to say about these two men of God:

(i) God promised Israel that Elijah would re-appear on earth again before the great and terrible day of the Lord came:

"Behold, I am going to send you Elijah the prophet (again) before the coming of the great and terrible day of the LORD." (Malachi 4:5).

(ii) John the Baptist IS Elijah who has come again. The archangel Gabriel said of John before his birth that he would:

".... go Before Him (The Messiah) with the spirit and power of Elijah ..."
(Luke 1:17, compare this verse with Mal. 4:5-6).

(iii) Also Jesus said, ".... if you are willing to accept it, *he (John the Baptist) is Elijah who is about to go (or come)".* (Matt. 11:14). and, "But I say to you that *Elijah has indeed come* (again) and they did to him what they wished, as it has been written of him." (Mark 9:13).

Compare also their clothing and life-style (2 Kings 1:8 with Mark 1:6). John the Baptist IS Elijah because he has Elijah's (human) spirit and Godly power, if not his body of flesh. However, *much more needs to be said:*

1. *This is the only reincarnation of a human spirit recorded in God's Word and is quite unique.* Its uniqueness is so outstanding that it required a whole range of other circumstances, some of which were also unique. For example it became necessary in the foreknowledge of God for Elijah to cheat the normal experience of death, and this was accomplished by translation into heaven WHILE ALIVE (2 Kings

2:11), thus becoming a forerunner of **the Rapture of the Living saints** when the trumpet blows (1 Thess. 4:17).

2. It was necessary Elijah should escape the experience of death altogether because:

    (i)   God had ordained that he should return to earth one day, and

    (ii)   If he had died, he would not have been able to return again, because of GOD'S UNIVERSAL LAW that *"it is appointed to man to die ONCE and after this, judgement."* *(Heb. 9:27).*

3. This meant the wicked **Queen Jezebel** of the Old Testament was thwarted in her plan to execute Elijah (1 Kings 19:2-3).

4. But the unclean spirit of Jezebel (not her human spirit but her familiar spirit), millions of which operate through people's lives today, executed the plan of Jezebel, Queen of Israel, through a modern Jezebel whose name was **Herodias,** and John the Baptist was put to death (Mark 6:19, 22-27).

5. So, when Jesus spoke of John the Baptist's execution He referred to it as if it were Elijah's execution, with the words:

"... and they did to him what they wished, AS IT HAS BEEN WRITTEN OF HIM."   *(Mark 9:13).*

Now it is plain that NOWHERE IN THE WORD OF GOD is the death of **John the Baptist** foretold, so what did the Lord mean? He obviously meant the Old Testament record of Jezebel's threat against Elijah when she vowed:

.... *"So may the gods do to me and even more, if I do not make your life as the life of one of them (the slain prophets of Baal) by tomorrow about this time."*   (1 Kings 19:2).

This text is what was written of John the Baptist, that is, Elijah who came again, and the "they" who did what they wished obviously refers to *the powers of darkness operating through Jezebel and Herodias.*

In conclusion we can say that the references to Elijah and John the Baptist do not help the reincarnation theory at all UNLESS one can guarantee avoiding the experience of death. As no one can guarantee they will not die, and the mathematical likelihood of you or me being another Elijah/ John the Baptist is inconceivable, the biblical case for reincarnation of the HUMAN spirit today becomes non-existent.

JOHN THE BAPTIST WAS AND IS UNIQUE. Perhaps we could clear away a lot of confusion if we said it is not a matter of LIVING more than once that we Christians challenge, because we believe in Eternal Life through Jesus Christ, but rather it is a matter of DYING more than once in the flesh[1], according to the Word of God.

6.4 DEJA VU

Very much an "in" experience with some people today, this subject can be reduced to the same principles as reincarnation. The best way to describe DEJA VU is by illustration.

You enter a certain room for the first time in your life and although you know you have never been there before, it seems familiar. You FEEL that you **have** been there before - perhaps in an earlier lifetime. Or perhaps if you meet strangers you feel sure that you KNOW them, although in this lifetime or present body it is not possible. Again, it is not the **human** spirit that has been around before and gives one that "familiar" feeling, but the unclean spirit.

Worldly people are encouraged today to develop their latent (soulish) powers - i.e. their psychic gifts and awareness. This is simply an invitation to develop your ability to gain knowledge by means of the supernatural uncleanness within you. Extra Sensory Perception is another case in point. E.S.P. is well-named because by it the human being is persuaded to perceive things that cannot be perceived by the normal senses of *touch, sight, smell, hearing or taste.* Instead, information is perceived (or received) by means of the spirit world. It is not the Holy Spirit or the human spirit that is the prime agency used in E.S.P. but the agency satan has residing within us which links with the powers of darkness around us. The same principle applies to telepathy, fortune telling, clairvoyancy and all occult practices. These are simply satan's range of gifts which counterfeit the true and good gifts of the Holy Spirit listed in 1 Cor 12:7-11. The non-christians think these occult gifts are gifts from God above and are evidence of His favour, but the Word

---

1. The second death is, of course, a spiritual death that takes place after the Great Judgement and is experienced by non-Christians only (Rev. 20:6-15).

of God says they are unclean gifts which are an abomination to God (Deut. 18:9-14) and come from the "god" of sin within. How deceptive these gifts and powers can be, may be gauged from the esteem which **Simon the Magician** held (Acts 8:9-24), which story will repay careful study.

6.5 CONCLUSIONS

Is reincarnation an elaborate hoax, or a revelation of truth? It is not so much an elaborate hoax premeditated by PEOPLE, as a hoax by SPIRITS that even hoaxes its researchers.

The great deception for human beings is that there is a sense in which reincarnation is a fact, but for UNCLEAN SPIRITS only! They do indeed leave their "homes" on the death of a creature and look around for an alternative body, preferably human, but an animal will sometimes do.

This is in contrast to the HUMAN spirit, which the Word of God tells us must face the judgement of God after a man has died ONCE (Heb. 9:27).

The deception of the reincarnationists is caused by their confusion about the true meaning of the terms **"soul"** and **"spirit"**. As we have already seen, the distinction between soul and spirit is not an easy one to make, nevertheless the Bible does make such a distinction and enables us to do the same. For example, the man with the Legion numbered 4000-6000 spirits, Mary Magdalene had seven demons and another had blind and dumb spirits removed. Thus it is plain from the Word of God that many different types of spirits can inhabit the human soul alongside the human spirit, as we revealed in chapter one.

Now we can see how the reincarnationist has been deceived. A recent *Hare Krishna* publication quotes as follows:

> *"As the embodied soul continually passes, in this body, from boyhood to youth, and then to old age, the soul similarly passes into another body at death."*
>
> ("Bhagavad Gita" 2:13)

You may be surprised to know the above quotation is both deceptive and yet contains truth - that the SOUL, that is, ALL THE UNCLEAN SPIRITS IN IT, will seek to reincarnate themselves continuously until their judgement day. That part is true, but it is not so for *the human spirit* which goes to God. Of course, that is NOT the way the reincarnationist understands it or is intended to understand it. For "soul" he or she reads "human spirit".

In this lies the key to the deception - *the reincarnationist uses the terms "soul" and "spirit"* interchangeably for they have never understood the basic threefold make-up of human beings; **spirit, soul and body** as revealed in the Christian Bible by the Maker Himself (1 Thess. 5:23).

The truth that it is the "beggarly and elemental spirits of the universe" alone (Col. 2:8, 20) which can be considered to be reincarnated should not surprise us because the commandment tells us that God shall *"....VISIT THE SINS OF THE FATHERS upon the children, unto the third and to the fourth generation of those who hate me and show mercy unto thousands of those who love me and keep my commandments."* (Exod. 20:5-6).

Now it is plain that God is not setting a limit in naming the third and fourth generations. If he had been setting a limit He would have said "THIRD" **OR** "FOURTH" definitively. However, the third **AND** fourth expresses continuity. If we go back four generations we have to bear in mind that the fourth generation then goes back another four generations and so on. I can verify that spirits going back to TEN generations of island witchcraft have manifested themselves and been removed by the power of Christ while I looked on.

Therefore it is not the **evidence** put forward by the reincarnationists that is in question but the **conclusions** drawn from that evidence. It is so easy to misinterpret spiritual phenomena if we do not have the full truth of God's Word to guide us.

Allusions to Moses and Elijah appearing with the Lord on the mountain of transfiguration only prove that God is a God of the living, including spirit beings, but says nothing about reincarnation in the flesh.

The Bible teaches that unclean spirits are restless if they are in a discarnate state, i.e. *spirits without a body of flesh* through which to operate and manifest themselves. They don't like water (they remember the great flood only too well!) and they don't like being discarnate (Matt. 12:43-45), hence they will even accept dwelling within animals if there are no humans available, rather than remain discarnate (Mark 5:12). **THUS UNCLEAN SPIRITS ARE REINCARNATED** in body after body, generation after generation, century after century. When death brings to a close an earthly life, the soul and everything in it leaves. **THE HUMAN SPIRIT RETURNS TO GOD FOR JUDGEMENT and THE UNCLEAN SPIRITS OF SIN BEGIN THEIR SEARCH FOR SOMEONE NEW** to welcome them in, someone who is experimenting with or already enjoys their own particular brand of sin. Thus the so-called "liberated" society becomes a nightmare as great numbers of these foul spirits find places to dwell in those who ignore the Law of Christ and do what is right in their own eyes. (Deut. 12:8, Jud. 17:6, 21:25).

The Bible tells us that *the "liberated" humanistic society is in reality itself enslaved* and the unrighteous endeavour to entice weak and immature believers with promises of *"freedom, but THEY THEMSELVES ARE SLAVES OF CORRUPTION, for whatever overcomes a man to that he is enslaved."* (2 Peter 2:9-19).

We enter so many dangerous fields of activity, going where perhaps even angels fear to tread because we are both curious and ignorant of the spiritual realm. It is bad enough walking this path of danger ignorantly but it is disastrous to CONTINUE in it, having been advised of the warning of the Word of God.

If ever we needed evidence that the dark nature of sin within man is **SPIRITUAL** and therefore **DEMONIC,** we only have to consider the evidence of the reincarnationists.

SUNDAY, 21ST OCTOBER, 1990.

PROPHECY: (PETER)

THUS SAYS THE LORD:

Gen. 1:2 Isa. 31:5 Rom. 8:20-21 Rom. 5:12 Isa. 24:3-6 Rom. 8:11 Ezek. 37:1-14	MY SPIRIT HOVERS OVER MY CREATION TO BRING LIFE, AND EVEN THOUGH THE CREATION IS DEFILED, POLLUTED WITH SIN AND DEATH, DESTROYED AND LAID WASTE BY THE ABUSE OF MANKIND, YET DOES MY SPIRIT HOVER OVER THIS CREATION. MY SPIRIT BRINGS LIFE TO THE DEAD. MY SPIRIT WILL DRAW TOGETHER THE BONES OF ISRAEL AND BREATHE THE LIFE OF CHRIST INTO THOSE BONES, AND IT (THEY) SHALL STAND FLESHED AND STRONG AND BECOME A MIGHTY ARMY.
1 Cor. 3:12-13 2 Peter 3:7,10 Joel 2:28-32 Rev. 7:9 Matt. 9:37-38	MY SPIRIT SWEEPS OVER THE SOULS OF MY CHILDREN TO CLEANSE AND TO PURIFY, FOR MY SPIRIT IS A REFINING SPIRIT AND WILL BURN THE DROSS AND THE UGLY FROM MY CREATION. AND YET MY SPIRIT WILL CALL AND WILL ALIGHT ON THOSE WHO DO NOT YET KNOW ME, FOR MANY ARE YET TO BE CALLED AND COME INTO MY BLESSING. FROM EVERY TRIBE AND TONGUE AND NATION WILL I CALL THE HARVEST UNTO MYSELF.
Isa. 24:20 1 Thess. 4:16-17 1 Cor.15:51-52 Rev. 21:1-4 Isa. 34:16-35:10 Zech. 13:2 John 7:37-39 Isa. 44:3	AND WHEN MANKIND HAS DONE WITH HIS DESTRUCTIVE WAYS AND BROUGHT THE EARTH TO A STANDSTILL, EVEN THEN AT THE SOUND OF THE TRUMPET WILL THE DEAD IN CHRIST RISE TO BE CAUGHT UP, TOGETHER WITH THOSE WHO ARE ALIVE. MY SPIRIT SHALL DO IT. AND THEN SHALL MY SPIRIT RESTORE THE EARTH AND ALL THAT I HAVE CREATED. THE UNCLEAN SPIRIT SHALL BE REMOVED FROM THE

Joel 2:28
Isa. 35:1
Rom. 8:19
Rom. 8:21
Isa. 25:7-8
1Cor. 15:54 57
Ps. 98:8
Isa. 40:4-5
Luke 3:5-6
Ps. 150:6
Rev. 21:1-22:5
Isa. 25:8
Rom. 6:9
Rom. 6:14
Rev. 1:18

LAND AND THERE WILL BE RIVERS OF LIVING WATER, NOT ONLY FLOWING FROM THE BELLIES OF MY PEOPLE, BUT ACROSS THE NATIONS... AND THE DESERTS SHALL SPRING TO LIFE AND ALL CREATION SHALL REJOICE AT THE REVEALING OF THE CHILDREN OF GOD. THE BONDAGE TO DECAY SHALL BE FINISHED AND DEATH SHALL HAVE NO MORE DOMINION.

THE FLOODS WILL CLAP THEIR HANDS AND THE HILLS SHALL REJOICE AT THE GLORY OF THE LORD. THE MOUNTAINS SHALL BE MADE LOW AND THE LOW PLACES SHALL BE RAISED, AND THE GLORY OF THE LORD SHALL BE REVEALED IN ALL THE EARTH AND (IT) SHALL PRAISE MY HOLY NAME.

AND THE RESTORATION SHALL BE COMPLETE, FOR I THE LORD HAVE SPOKEN IT.

SUNDAY, 11TH NOVEMBER, 1990 -
CONTINUED FROM 21ST OCTOBER, 1990.

PROPHECY: (PETER)

THUS SAYS THE LORD:

Heb. 2:3
Matt. 5:6
Jonah 1:1-3
James 4:7
Luke 4:17-21
Luke 12:20
Rom. 13:11
2 Cor. 6:2
Ps. 103: 1-5
Luke 11:9-10
Rom. 8:14
1 Pet. 1:4

.....SO THEN YIELD TO MY SPIRIT AS IT MOVES ACROSS THE EARTH. AND AS MY SPIRIT MINISTERS TO YOU, BE FULLY PART OF MY GREAT RESTORATION. HUNGER AND THIRST TO BE A PART OF IT.

DO NOT SAY TO MY SPIRIT - "NO" - BUT SUBMIT TO HIM; ALLOW HIM TO MINISTER TO YOUR DEEPEST NEEDS. DO NOT PUT IT OFF FOR ANOTHER TIME - FOR THERE MAY NOT BE ANOTHER TIME, FOR YOU. RECEIVE NOW, ALL THAT MY SPIRIT HAS FOR YOU AND BE GRATEFUL. PRAISE THE LORD YOUR GOD FOR HIS PROVISION FOR YOU AND SEEK ALL THAT HE HAS FOR YOU, TODAY.

ONLY AS YOU FLOW WITH MY SPIRIT CAN YOU BELONG TO MY MIGHTY PURPOSES, AND RECEIVE THE INHERITANCE THAT I HAVE STORED UP FOR YOU IN HEAVEN.

CHAPTER 7

THE MAN OF SIN REVEALED

7.1 WHAT IS "THE TEMPLE"?

Let me first introduce to you the main theme of this subject as simply as possible. It is all about understanding that the **TEMPLE** referred to by the apostle Paul in his second letter to the Thessalonians (chapter 2 and verse 4) may **NOT** be referring to the rebuilding of the Temple in Jerusalem, which is a geographical, physical Temple of stone, made by men's hands. Its PRIMARY and perhaps ONLY meaning is referring to man and woman, made in the image of God (Gen. 1:26), made as a house for God to dwell in (Gen. 4:7, Matt. 12:43-45) and thus become individually His Temple(s) (1 Cor. 3:16-17).

So when an unclean control spirit enters into where it ought not and rules us from the Throne of God within us, it misrepresents itself as God (2 Thess. 2:4).

The Word of God calls these control spirits, these usurpers, **"rulers and authorities"** (Eph. 6:12 etc.), and this explains why many New Age followers believe they have God within them and/or that they are God or a god.

It is all deception of course, but it seems a logical idea and can "feel" right. Unfortunately these ruling "gods" are NOT the almighty and ever-lasting God, creator of heaven and earth (1 Cor. 8:5-6, Gal. 4:8-9). *"There is a way that seems right to a man/woman but the end of it is death"*. (Prov. 14:12).

7.2 CONDITIONS FOR THE DAY OF THE LORD!

Two conditions must be fulfilled before the Day of the Lord comes (2 Thess. 2:2-3). They are:

(i) **The great Apostasy (back-sliding)[1] must take place**. The "Western" (Christian) nations are now so morally sick and busy pursuing he-donism (pleasure) there is strong evidence they are already greatly

---

1. I choose the translation "back-sliding" rather than "departing" for three (3) very good reasons which will be presented in our booklet on this subject.

backslidden from the faith of Jesus Christ. **Christian fundamentalism,** which was the foundation stone of western civilisation and is basically a belief that the Bible is the Word of God, and the New Testament is our final authority in matters of faith and morals, is under constant attack from sections of the Media.

The good guys are now considered the bad guys in western cultures today, so arguably this first condition has already been met.

The second condition to be met is:

(ii) **The Man of Sin (the Lawless One) must be revealed.** I intend, by the grace of God, to reveal him now so **both essential conditions will have been met for the return, the coming, the presence of Christ Jesus!**

Praise His Holy Name!

7.3   THE TEMPLE REVELATION

The revelation, very simply, is this:

(i) **Every human being** is created in the image of God and is intended to be a temple or shrine of God (John 2:18-22, 1 Cor. 3:16-17, 6:18-20, 2 Cor. 6:14-16), made without hands (Acts 7:47-50) and filled and ruled by the Holy Spirit.

We are created **spirit, soul** and **body** (1 Thess. 5:23) - three specific areas, just like **Solomon's Temple**, each area having a specific function.

(ii) **The Holy of Holies** is where only our High Priest can enter - the place reserved for the Lord Jesus (Heb. 3:1, 9:24-25 etc.). *Our spiritual hearts become His Throne* and because He is both God and our High Priest, He ALONE is the **true** occupier of our Holy of Holies. However this area in us was given over to the Man of Sin by Adam and Eve when they rebelled, and sin and death flooded into them (Rom. 5:12) and thus infected their descendants - the whole human race!

(iii) **The Holy Place** is *our soulish area (including the mind)* wherein the human spirit of born again Christians does battle (with the help of the Holy Spirit) against every unclean thing deposited at conception (in our mother's womb) and afterwards. When the human spirit is born again or made alive by the Holy Spirit it **should begin** to win the battle and clean out the soulish area. Before being born again the human spirit is drowning in trespasses and sins. To all intents and purposes it is "dead" in filth and spiritual excrement, but when the human spirit is made alive the cleansing of the WHOLE Temple should begin and continue (Eph. 2:1-10) until Christlikeness is attained.

(iv) **The Outer Courts** of the Temple (e.g. Ezek. 40:17) are the members of our human body. Our bone and flesh, even our blood stream, shows forth the evidence of what is going on in our soulish area. This is why perhaps 90% of medical doctors acknowledge the huge effect that the **soul (psyche)** has on the **body (soma).** And so label many infirmities as **psycho-soma-tic, that is,** bodily ailments produced by soulish (emotional) causes.

(v) **Explanation**

So, three part man (spirit, soul and body) is in reality designed to be a **Temple of God** made without (human) hands (Acts 7:47-50), with a **Holy of Holies,** a **Holy Place** and **Outer Courts,** after the manner of the Old Testament tabernacles and temples.

I submit that when sin (which is known as a spiritual disease) and death (which is known to be a spirit) entered Adam and Eve at their Fall from grace, all this evil, spiritual pollution took over their temples producing **"total depravity"**, as the **Calvinists** call it.

Their **Holy Places** and their **Outer Courts** were filled with Rulers and Authorities (Eph. 6:12) which even usurped the Throne of Christ Jesus in the **Holy of Holies!** (Rom. 7:18, Eph. 6:12, 2 Thess. 2:4).

So please now burn the following conclusion into your spirit!

The ruling unclean spirit that resides in a human being, setting itself up where it ought not to be, on the Throne of Christ in God's Temple is the Man of Sin (2 Thess. 2:4).

Please read that again - slowly - with understanding!

7.4 GETTING THE VICTORY OF RESTORATION

The Man of Sin (or ruling unclean spirit) has sometimes been called the **Strong Man** (Matt. 12:29) and the **Old Man** (Rom. 6:6, Eph. 2:13, 4:22, Col. 3:9), but he is a usurper and has to make way for the Spirit of Christ when **He** comes into **His** Temple(s). However this does not happen automatically or immediately at conversion. The order of events is something like this:

(i)   In the un-converted non-Christian, the **Man of Sin** rules from the throne in the Holy of Holies, while the **human spirit** is dead in trespasses and sins (Eph. 2:2), drowning in sin and death (Rom. 5:12).

(ii)   The preaching of the Cross of Christ (1 Cor. 1:17-18) breaks through all the spiritual barriers of uncleanness to reach, revive and convict the powerless human spirit.

(iii)   Faith (trust) in Christ is followed by the seal and deposit of the Holy Spirit (2 Cor. 1:22) being shed abroad in our hearts (Rom. 5:5).

(iv)   The human spirit is **made alive (born again)** by the operation and power of the Holy Spirit (Eph. 2:1-10).

(v)   Although the newly converted Christian may have expressed repentance and total commitment to Christ these are desires that have yet to be realised through continuing spiritual warfare. All the uncleanness in the soulish area will resist the "intrusion" of the Holy Spirit and the made-alive human spirit, and be constantly seeking to regain the throne again.

(vi)   Deliverance ministry will be necessary, together with other Christian disciplines (prayer, testimony, Bible study etc.) to **remove ALL the unclean opposition,** including the Ruler - the Man of Sin.

(v)   Then will the Christian be FULLY filled with the Spirit, without spot or blemish, inside and outside. Then will the Christian have made himself/herself ready for the Bridegroom, and be without fear of the Day of the Trumpet of God!

If I have made it sound easy, it isn't! But it is what LIFE is all about! Hallelujah!

End of Revelation!

If you have been able to receive this, then a lot of what follows will simply tidy up some loose ends for you. However if this revelation cuts across what you have previously believed, I ask you to continue to work through this material carefully in the hope and expectation your queries will be satisfied.

The good news about all this is that we do not have to know all the administrative details, which will probably remain known only to our Creator - praise His Holy Name. We know what we need to know - that **we ALL** *need to be cleansed - spirit, soul and body - from ALL the pollution of the enemy, spiritual and physical.* (2 Cor. 7:1)

Then perhaps we might see a little more Christlikeness in the Church of God! — Both ministry and character!

7.5 A POLITICAL MAN OF SIN

This revelation of a SPIRITUAL Man of Sin residing in every heart and now being exposed in God's time for the purposes of his removal (cleansing the Temple(s)) does not necessarily conflict with an historical political figure being raised up to lead the United Nations (the wicked tenants - Mark 12:1-11) against the Father's anointed Son (Psalm 2).

If a political Man of Sin appears he will obviously promote anarchy, because he is described as the Lawless One - Laws will basically be aimed at Christians and against true Christianity, that is, the Bride of Christ. On Jan 6, 1995 the **Law Society of Australia's new president** stated on Channel 9 television station that he believes heroin should be supplied to addicts, and homosexuals should be allowed to marry and adopt children. His reasoning? Morals are irrelevant, he said, and these situations are a fact of life and should be permitted (legalised).

Here we have the President of the Law Society saying that if something exists it should be legalised! I suppose that applies to child sexual abuse, wife bashing, stealing and murder also? Already we see the foundations of an anarchistic, amoral society being laid, and most of us are powerless to stop it. However we are comforted that the Lord Jesus has warned us in advance (Matt. 24:12). Sections of the **media have locked up all forms of mass communication** and exercise a cynical censorship over and against almost all forms of expressions of the righteousness of God. How hard it is for political media people to enter the Kingdom of Heaven (cf. Matt. 19:23).

7.6 A "SPIRITUAL" MAN OF SIN

The link between (i) a **political** Man of Sin and (ii) the **spiritual** Man of Sin within the human heart could be achieved by a political figure who was also spiritually gifted by the powers of darkness - **according to the working of Satan with all power and signs and wonders,** as the Word of God puts it (2 Thess. 2:9).

As a charismatic leader (that is, with **counterfeit** gifts) of the New Age movement he would promote the false notions that:

(i)   **soul** and **spirit** are the same thing (1 Thes. 5:23, Heb. 4:12 etc.)

(ii) God is within ALL of us
      (Confusing the breath or spirit of life with the Spirit of God)

(iii) Therefore EVERYONE has the Holy Spirit indwelling them
      (Confusing the first birth - Gen. 2:7 - with the second birth - John 3:3).

(iv) YOU are God, or a god.
      (Made in His image - yes! Children when "born again" - yes! God? - No!)

(v)   There is no Judgement or Hell;
      (When some find out this is wrong - it'll be too late!)

(vi) God is love - no need for repentance;
      (Repenting is **accepting** His love and changing as He requires.).

(vii) You will be reincarnated until perfected.
      (Straight out of fantasy-land!)

The notion of a **political** Man of Sin and the rise of the New Age movement today in no way conflicts with the revelation of a **spiritual** Man of Sin residing in every human heart, until he is removed by Christ's deliverance ministry and cleansing program. I believe the Bride of Christ for which the Bridegroom comes will have been cleansed of every Man of Sin and his followers. Impossible? Perhaps we do not know the Scriptures well enough, nor the power of God? (Matt. 22:29).

7.7   CONCLUSION

In summary let us ask ourselves three questions:

(i)   How does Christ Jesus rule His Kingdom on earth?
      The answer is, **through His Spirit in human hearts.**

(ii) How does Satan rule his kingdom on earth?
      The answer again is, **through his spirits in human hearts.**

(iii) Where is the Temple of God today?
      Certainly one answer from the Word of God is the physical bodies of Christians. (1 Cor. 3:16-17, 6:19)

It seems to me that the **exposing** of the Old Man, the Strong Man, i.e., the Man of Sin as ALREADY RESIDING IN EVERY HUMAN HEART should precipitate an enormous inner cleansing of Christians by the ministry of Deliverance which MUST take place prior to the Return of Jesus for His Bride.

The full salvation of God will be experienced by all those who want to put off from themselves every shackle and chain of Satan, that they might be cleansed and made fitting to be a member of the beautiful Bride for which the Bridegroom is returning. (Ps. 45:13 - The King's daughter is all glorious WITHIN! - lit. Heb.).

There may be a physical Man of Sin as head of the United Nations, leading a physical world government dedicated to anti-Christ but I remind you again that such a leader will control the inhabitants of the world THROUGH THEIR HEARTS, where a spiritual MAN of Sin reigns by means of daily hypnosis and subliminal mind control through modern air waves (media) technology (cf. Eph. 2:2). But not the true Church - she knows her Lord and though the love of many may grow cold, those who endure to the end shall see the Great Salvation of their God. (Matt. 24:12-13, Heb. 2:1-3).

Now is the time to preach a FULL SALVATION to both Church and world, and receive and minister INNER cleansing to the Body of Christ, through **Deliverance and Restoration programs,** that the Bride of Christ might come forth out of the mess without spot or blemish (2 Peter 3:13-14).

And may the good Lord abundantly bless you!

THE BATTLE FOR THE SOUL

WITHIN A NEW CHRISTIAN!

The Man of Sin control spirit in the human soul has to be de-throned and replaced with the Holy Spirit of God.

The kingdom of Sin - **Manifesting the tip of the iceberg e.g. ANGER, INFIRMITY**

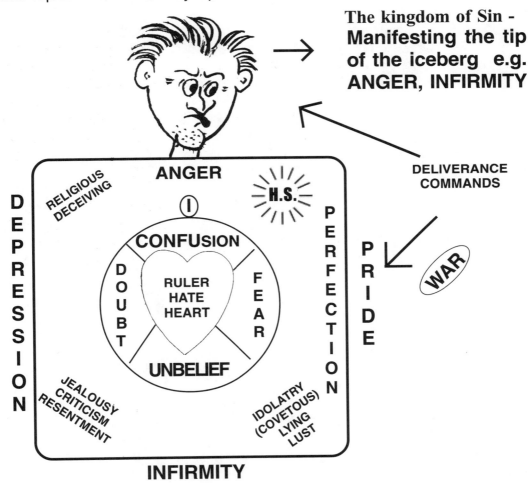

DELIVERANCE COMMANDS

WAR

ANGER

RELIGIOUS DECEIVING

H.S.

D E P R E S S I O N

CONFUSION

I

DOUBT

RULER HATE HEART

FEAR

UNBELIEF

P E R F E C T I O N

P R I D E

JEALOUSY CRITICISM RESENTMENT

IDOLATRY (COVETOUS) LYING LUST

INFIRMITY

SIN + DEATH ☞
(satan's "jericho" fortress)
in the <u>human soul</u>

I = EGO (HUMAN SPIRIT)
H.S.= HOLY SPIRIT

The Holy Spirit is in the soul (the Holy Place) and linked with the born again human spirit, but not on the Throne (the Holy of Holies) - yet! You can place the spirit of death anywhere!

CHAPTER 8

MORE ON THE MIND

There is so much more that could be added to a book with the title **"We All Have Our Demons"** but we have to finish this message somewhere. I have been concerned about writing a book so large it would be too costly to buy, too large to carry and too heavy to mail - just too much for anywhere, except a public library!

So may I refer to important matters here very briefly indeed, and also refer you to chapters in our other publications. For example the chapter **"The Invisible Problem - Elemental (Creation) Spirits"** in **"Sex, Demons and Morality"** deals with the animalistic sexual behaviour of humans (and that's probably an insult to the animals), caused by **the stoicheia** (the elemental spirits of the world—Gal. 4:8, Col. 2:8,20). The variety of sexual lusts is further evidence that **"we all have our demons"**, and this area required a separate publication.

8.1   MUSICAL HYPNOSIS

Recently in Sydney, authorities concerned with the rise of violent crime in a central area introduced a program of soft, sweet, gentle music to be played in and through the shops. The reduction in violent incidents was amazing and reminds us of **David's** ministry of music to soothe the troubled **King Saul:**

> *"Whenever the (evil) spirits from God came upon Saul, David would take his harp and play. Then relief would come to Saul; he would feel better, and the evil spirit would leave him" (1 Samuel 16:23).*

This, of course, is the positive side of music and simply confirms that much music is spiritual/soulish in inspiration and contributes to human feelings or behaviour, good and bad. Informed Christians have expressed alarm over the destructive nature of heavy rock music for many years.[1] The evidence, from the days of suicidal **Janis Joplin,** is overwhelming and need not be repeated here in detail.

Drum beat noise is by far the most common and greatest evil influence because of its hypnotic effect. I quote from an earlier publication:[2]

> *"Drum hypnosis (charming) is unclean and an abomination to the Lord (Deut. 18:11). There is no reference to the use of drums being*

---

1. "Satan's Music Exposed", Lowell Hart, etc.
2. **"Toronto and the Truths You Need to Know"**

*used in worship in the whole of the Bible, yet pagan cultures have
used them for thousand of years. That should tell us something!"*

It is true that many Christian drummers try to be sensitive to the Holy Spirit and can be used by Him but I suspect these occasions are far outnumbered by their unclean, hypnotic use. It is better, I think, to use guitars for gentle, rhythmic support and timing, although hypnotic misuse is possible.

Drum beats control our minds hypnotically, often inducing hysteria and destructive behaviour, and in the rock music scene almost inevitably lead into drug use and increased demonic control.

8.2 MIND CONTROL

During World War 2 the propaganda "machines" of both antagonists were really geared up to using selective information in news reports, so as to keep up good morale throughout their civilian populations. I remember as a young boy saying to my parents, when hearing a news item that **Benghazi** or **Caen** had fallen to allied troops: "But we took that city two weeks ago!" When our side had a victory we heard about it, but when we lost a city they didn't bother to tell us.

Misinformation was also developed into an art form during the **Falklands** conflict, when media reports deliberately misled the Argentinian forces.

There is an old saying that if you repeat a lie often enough it will be believed and I suppose that is the basis of all brain-washing, which I prefer to re-label brain-controlling or brain-polluting. And, of course, a medical definition of hypnosis is **"a rhythmic stimulus** (drums?) **accompanied by the repetition of carefully worded suggestions "**[3]

There can be no doubt that in a Democracy, where laws exist to punish crime and corruption, a free media can be enormously effective in exposing the truth. Alternatively, where the media is controlled by a dictatorial government, exploitation and corruption seem to engulf the nation. The powerless poor remain that way.

However a free press is not free from its own dangers. Today we experience enormous media influence to the extent that it fills our homes and minds with a whole range of views, from politics to religion. Journalists ex-

---

3. "Daily Mirror" Medical Roundsman.

press their worldly views to millions of readers and get paid for it - what a powerful and awesome privilege and responsibility! It is not only the print media but radio, television and the Internet are impacting on us and this means we are being swamped with opinions and information moment to moment, almost without ceasing, from non-Christian or misinformed Christian sources. Christians who have compromised Biblical truths are those who are given most space and coverage.

So it comes down to realising that the powers of darkness don't need to use the hypnotic method of **subliminal indoctrination** to pollute and control human minds because our daily diet of media mental saturation is more than successful. It is as the apostle **John** wrote, **"The whole world lies in (the power of) the evil one"** (1 John 5:19).

8.3   MULTIPLE PERSONALITY DISORDER (M.P.D.) AND DISSOCIATE IDENTITY DISORDER (D.I.D.)

Either **Multiple Personality Disorder** is spreading at an unprecedented rate, or it has always been a significant condition which is no longer closeted but being exposed.

I believe BOTH the above activities are true. The levels of demonisation are rising at a rapid rate in western societies AND there is much greater awareness of the need to seek professional help.

Why do you think there is so much domestic violence, even homicides, so much divorce, greed and corruption throughout societies that were once Christian? It is so common today for a man and woman to live together **before** marriage in order to find out what their partner is really like. Otherwise one might find oneself marrying a street angel who is also a house devil (demon).

The truth is the Bible says we ALL suffer from M.P.D., but for most of us it hasn't shown up or been diagnosed in years past.

I was reminded of the involvement of psychiatrists and psychologists at a **Festival of Light Conference** in January 1999. One of the main speakers was eminent psychiatrist **Dr James Quinn,** who had been brought into a severe case of M.P.D. by Salvation Army **Major Marina Randall.** Major Randall had "hung in there" for more than two years, trying everything she knew and refusing to give up.

Illustrating M.P.D. at a level recognised by the medical profession.

Reproduced courtesy of Kookaburra Products Pty Ltd
Fax (61)7 3353 9805

And again, the **Health Care in Christ** seminar in Sydney (October 2000) featured a special speaker **Sally Grant** who spoke on subjects related to **Dissociate Identity Disorder** such as the effect of trauma on the brain, and false memories.

The vital thing to notice is that the change in the subject title from **Multiple Personality Disorder** to **Dissociate Identity Disorder** is not simply a playing with words but reflects a major change in diagnosis, and therefore treatment. Whereas MPD allows for a diagnosis of demonisation, the label DID seems much more supportive of the current trends in therapy which treat the various personalities as **memory fragments** and as a PHYSICAL problem, not spiritual.

Our contribution of course, is to now look at the spiritual nature of this condition, and to perhaps say a few things hard to receive, with no offence intended. There are truths that hurt and there are truths we can't handle (immediately) but the good Lord helps us to face them, sooner or later.

(I) HEARING VOICES

When we try to add up all the unclean spirits that make up the kingdoms of sin and death (Romans 5:12), we begin to understand why people become neurotic, schizophrenic, psychotic, and hear voices. We have probably all heard of the rather cruel explanation of a **neurotic** and a **psychotic** which says:

> (i)   *A neurotic builds castles in the air*
> (ii)   *A psychotic lives in them*

I am more interested in **schizophrenia** (in the sense it is used today, being applied to a wide range of mental illnesses, including the two referred to above - refer chapter 1.14).

One of the more amazing errors ever ministered to the mentally ill is the medical practice (still in vogue) of trying to persuade patients who complain of "hearing voices" they are imagining things. Qualified, educated, sane scientists promoting denial!

Patients who suffered from hearing voices were first told they were imagining, then because this "treatment" was plainly unsuccessful and unconvincing, they were then told the voices were real enough but were produced by the torment or illness of the mind. This was at least partly true but of little comfort because the treatment prescribed was usually drugs or sedation.

It seems incredible that even Christian psychiatrists who are familiar with the Gospels could not add two and two together and diagnose cases of demonisation. Unclean spirits understand only too readily the stupor of mankind in general (because they are responsible for it) and so they brazenly chatter away in our soulish area (which includes the mind) driving the sufferer into great distress, confident the human race will not diagnose the problem correctly and expose them.

Chatter, chatter, chatter! They can be as bold and as open and as brazen as they like. They can be as cruel to the sufferer as they like. The only thing that happens is the sufferers get drugged up, which limits the spirits marginally for a short time. They are so convinced of the stupefied nature of man (cf. Rom. 11:8) and his inability to perceive or threaten them in any effective way they even begin to direct and rule their "house". Barely a week goes by without a newspaper report of someone who murdered someone else because *"the voice(s) told me to do it".*

Mark Chapman who killed **John Lennon** (the Beatle's singer and composer) in December 1980, said on television he blamed a voice in his head telling him to do it.

Twenty one years old deaf mute **James Curtright** used sign language to explain to a Lincoln Court in Nebraska how he had an argument with someone claiming to be God, before he stabbed his mother and sister to death. *"I'm God",* the voice said, *"Do you believe me? Kill the devil".* He told the court that he now believed it was satan who gave him the instructions to kill the women.[4] Two months later a part-Aboriginal woman named **Joan Racnil** told a Perth court how she battered her de-facto husband repeatedly over the head while in a drugged sleep, tried to strangle him and slit his throat. She then cut out his eyes, sawed off his arms and legs, and cut off his head because *"the angels ordered her to do it for the black people of the world." "I had to kill a white man to set the black people free,"* she said, *"Voices were telling me to kill a white man."*

A senior psychiatrist from Graylands Hospital, **Dr Sanath de Tissera** said Racnil was a classic case of **relapsing paranoid schizophrenia.**[5]

And so we could go on. However **instead of being taught to utterly ignore head voices** many people in the occult actually encourage them. They call it having a **spirit-guide** where one spirit guides them every day, all day.

---

4. Daily Mirror 21/4/86
5. Sydney Morning Herald 17/6/86

Quite recently we had a New Age leaflet dropped into our letterbox headed *"Have You Discovered Your Spirit Guide?"* This of course, is an offer to help us discover satan's counterfeit of the Holy Spirit of God whom Christians should allow to guide them every day, all day.

(II) MULTIPLE PERSONALITY DISORDER (M.P.D.)

(a) SOUL AND SPIRIT (HUMAN)

> *"... may all of you, your spirit, soul and body, be kept blameless by the presence of our Lord Jesus Christ." (1 Thess. 5:23)*

It goes without saying that Christians who believe "**soul**" and "**spirit**" are synonymous or interchangeable terms in the New Testament are going to have problems with this chapter. I attended a Christian Conference at a Sydney University where we were all encouraged to play down the distinction between **soul** and **spirit** by the respective Principals of a conservative Theological College and a charismatic Bible College.

I was obliged to point out in question time that if we do not distinguish between the *human spirit* and the *human soul* when confronting a person with M.P.D., we might easily find ourselves trying to cast out the HUMAN spirit instead of the unclean intruder(s) in the soul.

What a waste of time that would be!

Every spirit within us, human, Holy or unclean, resides within our soulish area, which is where there is so much battle, and why our minds and emotions need so much cleansing and renewing for Christ-likeness! (Eph. 4:23)

(b) THE WORLD

Sensing the increasing confidence of unclean spirits in parading themselves before a stupefied world without fear of being exposed for what they are, I noticed Hollywood was beginning to dabble into witchcraft and split personalities, even **Multiple Personality Disorder (M.P.D.).** Consequently I wrote a caution to the producers of **L. A. Law** in California in anticipation. I received a very courteous reply from **Steve Bochco** and later **Patricia Green** (Executive Producer) and it seemed to me that when the anticipated segment on M.P.D. appeared they handled it very sensitively and well, with no hint of mockery, blasphemy, flippancy or bad taste.

M.P.D. has appeared in a number of television courtroom scenes and there has been a suggestion that murderers may plead innocent because only one of their personalities/demons committed the crime. Who did the dirty deed? Was it Dr Jekyll or Mr Hyde? Can we execute one without the other? This is similar to an insanity defence, but Christians should be quite clear there is no such thing as a plea of insanity before the Judgement Throne of God. Earthly courts may have lost direction in this matter but when we appear in the Court that really matters the only defence possible is the plea for mercy on the grounds of repentance towards God and an active and obedient faith in the Son of God. The mission of unclean spirits is to bring us into death and hell, and if we live Christless lives - they succeed, whether we are judged sane or insane.

Soon after, television news documentaries in Australia (which usually follow the main evening news at 6.00 pm) got into the act. One produced a person with 27 personalities. Not to be outdone, a few days later a rival television station produced a person with 41 personalities, and then, lo and behold, the American show **Sally Jesse Raphael** produced a woman, in company with her psychiatrist and/ or counsellor, who claimed to have had over 1700 personalities, which had since been reduced to 1450 plus. (She confessed to have been involved in heavy witchcraft and satanism). This greatly interested me because, as far as I know, the only ways to get spirits to leave are as follows:

(i) **Shock treatment**
It seems that unclean spirits do not like electric shock treatment and will leave for a season, during which the patient seems to improve.

However, because they are still "free agents" to do what they want undetected and unopposed, they quickly move back in, and *"the last state of the sufferer can be worse than the first"* (Matt.12:43-45).

(ii) **Occult exorcism**
The occult's method is to do deals with unclean spirits and consequently any benefit gained is offset by even greater disability and slavery, whether hidden or obvious. **Pastor Dennis Teague** told me once (in the Philippines) that *"the devil always trades up."* When we do business with him, it only tightens his grip on us.

(iii) **Christian deliverance**
"My name (singular) is LEGION for we (plural) are many". And he/it (singular) begged Jesus earnestly not to send them (plural) out of the country (Mark 5:9-10)

This is the best and only way for a true Christian to **get free and stay free** - Hallelujah!

When the psychiatrist/counsellor was asked how he had reduced the number of personalities from 1700 plus to 1450 plus, he said something very interesting (honest man that he was). He said, in effect, that he could NOT REMOVE any personality, only INTEGRATE them. I take that to mean his method of helping the sufferer was to harmonise the "personalities" so that if two had previously been in conflict, they would now exist in the soulish area united as one, so that in effect, one would "disappear". In any event this number still doesn't get close to the LEGION quantity which would be a MINIMUM of 4000 (soldiers).

(c)   BIBLICAL AND SCIENTIFIC PSYCHOLOGY

Different personalities are often described as Alters (memory fragments caused by trauma) and the notion that Alters are NOT demons has been presented by **Dr. James D. Friesen,** the author of **"Uncovering the Mystery of MPD"**, a monumental pioneering work by one who is both a professional psychologist and a minister.

He argues thus:

> The second anti-therapeutic reaction to the material in this book is *when the sufferer concludes that the only problem is demons*. When people come to their therapist saying they are suffering from "demon possession", that is a highly suspect claim. Only a careless clinician would accept such a claim without careful scrutiny. I have found that where too much hope is placed in a quick spiritual solution, serious disappointment usually follows..... Serious damage has to receive more than a deliverance and more than only a prayer for healing.

While we can agree with much of what Dr. Friesen (the minister) has written, I can only say that his assessment of the human soul needs updating because **"We All Have Our Demons!"** Counselling, unearthing past traumas and renouncing them, rebuking the unclean spirits that took the opportunity to enter at trauma time and commanding them out, then praying for "closure" and healing from the effects of all their damage - all this may be necessary for a complete work of restoration for the whole person.

And what a great step forward it is for a sufferer to be filled with the HOLY SPIRIT!! - and come into and under HIS control/rule/reign/Kingdom, rather than the enemy. We record here for study some important comments from the books of notable Renewal author **Dr. Neil Anderson.**

There is much with which we can agree, for example:

(a) *"Psychological versus spiritual .... creates a false dichotomy. Our problems are always psychological (to some degree) .... Likewise our problems are always spiritual".*

(b) *"I personally have never come across a true Multiple Personality Disorder who doesn't have severe demonic problems as well."*

(c) *"It deeply troubles me that well-intentioned Christians are actually encouraging victims to lose mental control by getting in touch with fragments of their minds WITHOUT RESOLUTION".* (We shall soon see that at least two eminent psychiatrists support this concern).

Those comments with which we differ (in italics); and WHY!

"Command satan in the Name of Christ to release the person ..."

We cannot COMMAND satan (Jude 9) but we do have **authority** over his **power** (army of demons - Luke 10:19). Some unclean spirits are so stupid they will obey such a command given in Jesus' Name but the smarter rulers and authorities will just laugh.

"Their problem may not have had demonic origins ..."

This seems to be in conflict with **(a)** above. *We do not contend with blood and flesh but with .... (spiritual) rulers and authorities ...* (Eph. 6:12). This scripture is absolute. Check the whole verse and, if you need to, read this book again!

"Satanic ritual abuse (SRA) victims cannot always discern whether the voices in their heads are demonic or other personalities".

What other personalities??? (See section **(vi)**)

I cannot understand how spirits that control or influence people's lives can get away with "blue murder" in front of mature Christians.

"(It is a serious mistake) trying to cast out a personality .... It can't leave. It is part of them. Such rejection will only further alienate the already damaged personality."

I don't mind in the slightest alienating a rebellious unclean personality. I say give it hell on earth, until it obeys and goes to its appointed place.[6] The so-called *"psychological damage"* some therapists are afraid of causing is simply a batch of demons panicking because they have been given the boot by someone who is using their Christian authority resolutely.[7] When victory is in sight, it is no time to quit!

---

6. Book 2, **"Engaging the Enemy"**, Chapter 5.4.
7. Book 1, **"Make Yourselves Ready"**, Chapter 1(vi) (c).

Too many Christians give up on strong rebellious rulers without entering serious, protracted prayer and fasting (Mark 9:29).

" In other extreme cases I believe there is a combination of a spiritual stronghold and a fragmented mind caused by severe traumas."

Even if a person who suffers with a so-called fragmented mind has **physical** brain damage, perhaps due to an accident or shock treatment, we still come back to the two essential ministries with which the Lord Jesus supported His messages - **Deliverance** of the soulish area from demons and **Healing** of the body from physical imperfections. *Is the "fragmentation" spiritual or physical ???*

The answer to this question is absolutely vital because our ministry/ therapy/attention given to each problem hangs on it.

Neil has already written that our problems are ALWAYS spiritual (remember?) but seems to shift his position on this. **Sally Grant,** who has a Masters degree in Social Work, says they are physical. I agree with Neil's original position although, of course, a spiritual presence does not exclude physical damage (Luke 13:10-13). The so-called manifestations of fragmentation, I believe, are simply a parade of all the control spirits seeking centre-stage - anything to keep the born again human spirit from functioning under the control of the HOLY Spirit!

"Nowhere in Scripture are we told to ... heal the flesh."

Christ's command to His disciples to **heal the sick** (Matt. 10:8), and the biblical ministry of the elders in a local church (Jas. 5:14-15) would seem to differ. We are not ASKED to heal the sick, we are COMMANDED! (Refer chapter 1:13).

"Dialoguing with demons is always wrong ..."

I have covered this fairly thoroughly[8] and the way the Lord Jesus dealt with *Legion* should not be overlooked (Mark 5:7-13). Certainly dialoguing with demons should not be engaged in for flippant or self-promotional motives. **What if Alters are demons,** as we believe? Because talking with so-called Alters seems to be normal within therapy.

---

8. Book 2, **"Engaging the Enemy"**, Chapter 5.3 (iv).

The huge learning curve continues for ALL of us in these vital ministry matters. We learn little from a victory and so much from a failure. There are many occasions when it is difficult to express ourselves accurately and in a way that will not be misunderstood.

Praise the Lord, He overrules (Rom. 8:28).

(d) MORE PROBLEMS FOR MPD COUNSELORS

It ought to be noted that Deliverance ministers would not be the only stream of healers who have problems with the MPD/D.I.D. diagnosis and therapy. Some reputable psychiatrists such as **Dr. Paul McHugh**, Chief of Psychiatry at John Hopkins Hospital, Baltimore, and **Prof. Herbert Spiegel**, Columbia University, New York have grave doubts as to the validity and effectiveness of M.P.D. therapy. To quote **Dr. McHugh,** *"MPD is a distraction from the real problem. It is a dead end."* And **Dr. Spiegel** said: *"The danger of taking alters seriously and increasing them is to add to the confusion and the anxiety and even the depression that the person has. I see nothing therapeutic about that at all."*

However we should make a clear distinction between (i) the scientific practice of M.P.D. or D.I.D. **therapy** and (ii) the Christian **ministry** to sufferers based on prayer to the Lord Jesus Christ.

Sally Grant says her work is not a therapy, but a MINISTRY. The former may well be a dead end, but the latter? Who knows how the good Lord will lead both counselor and counselee? Sally agrees with Neil Anderson that any contact with "Alters" should result in some resolution or progress in the condition of the sufferer.

The bottom line is to *get rid of these rotten, controlling usurpers no matter how attractively or sympathetically they present themselves!*

(e) HOMOSEXUALITY AND TRANSVESTISM

It would be remiss of me not to mention that many folk who have a confusion of gender identity and are not sure whether they want to be a man or a woman, are actually suffering from a form of M.P.D., although it may be known today as gender identity disorder (G.I.D.).

God doesn't make mistakes. He puts a male human spirit in a male body and a female human spirit in a female body. Even when we allow for scientific mistakes where drugs etc. can so deform a foetus that its body is a gender mix-up we should recognise that transvestites, for example, suffer from a measure of M.P.D., in as much as they experience at least one control spirit seeking to deny the gender of the body which they inhabit.

We say more about this in *"Sex, Demons and Morality."*

(III) DISSOCIATE IDENTITY DISORDER

D.I.D. is a different area of infirmity to M.P.D., so the workers in this field of medicine tell us.

I can agree it is a **new diagnosis** but believe it to be the same old problem where someone appears to have multiple personalities manifesting in his life. However this latest theory also describes the personalities as Alters, which are memory **fragments**, not personalities or demons at all.

Although the psychiatrists, psychologists and social workers who practice this form of therapy are often fired-up, caring Renewal Christians who put a lot of time and effort into their counselling, and appear to have a level of success in reducing the "memories", I have to say that at the time of writing I am highly sceptical of this diversion from casting out demons and moving onto a "new" track.

(IV) FALSE MEMORY SYNDROME

It may be wise to reflect how "effective" and "beneficial" the unclean practice of hypnotherapy is supposed to be (see 6.1–6.2), even being used by some well meaning Christian psychiatrists.

The BBC Television documentary HORIZONS also revealed that hundreds of those once convinced of being victims of child abuse during therapy (through that great evil of hypnotherapy which was strongly presented in the program) now believe these memories were FALSE. This has been so prevalent it has resulted in yet another new psychiatric syndrome - *the False Memory Syndrome.*

Certainly one can feel "good" or "better" after hypnotherapy. It has been used to defeat nicotine addiction, for example, but at what price? The mind is forever held captive to another human and/or demon. It deals in lies and deception, and may be responsible for many so-called *"Recovered" Memory* cases where counselees suddenly recall they were sexually abused as children by their father or mother.

Until hypnotherapy they had no knowledge of those events. So where do these "memories" or deceptions come from? The father of lies (John 8:44)?

Entertainers who use hypnotism make a fortune by making us laugh at the strange antics their volunteers exhibit on stage. We see people stroking an old shoe because they believe it is a lovely little puppy dog. The natural senses are shut down by mind control and a huge dimension of deception exists. Good feelings or humour are no guarantee that the Almighty is at work.

There may be a lesson here for us in regard to D.I.D. People may feel good after a session (who wouldn't, with prayer to Christ and so much caring, personal ATTENTION!). I think we need a lot more evidence than better feelings, especially from the Word of God, before we give this ministry direction the "thumbs up" approval.

(V)   CHRISTIAN MINISTRY TO "ALTERS"

Courtesy of Sally Grant, who has processed a wealth of research, we have material produced by **Dr. Ed Smith** of **Theophostic Ministries.** He has produced a list of ten (10) distinctions between Alters and demons and, as I understand them, they are along the same lines already covered in this chapter but in more specific detail.

The distinctions are impressive in their reasoned presentation, but quite unconvincing for me personally. I expect to respond fully in a separate booklet on this subject.

After viewing something of the considerable research on how the brain functions and gets fragmented, I ask myself the question, *"Did the Lord Jesus teach his disciples (who were simple fishermen etc.) all this psychological data?"* Even the apostle **Paul,** who added brains to the apostolic team, writes nothing about this stream of hypotheses, although he himself was no slouch when it came to healing the sick or casting out demons (Acts 19:11-12).

Even allowing for *(i) the explosion of revelation at the close of this Age, (ii) the greater works to be done by true disciples of the Lord (John 14:12) and (iii) that ALL truth would become available through the Holy Spirit (John 14:26, 16:13),* the whole D.I.D. scenario re Alters is too intellectual[9] (Jas. 3:15) and un-apostolic for me.

Again I say, the SPIRIT who controls the mind should be a more important focus for us than its natural ability (Eph 4:23).

---

9. See Book 3 **"Walking in Victory"** 2nd Ed. pp 87-88 re the removal of **intellectual spirits.**

(VI) THE BOTTOM LINE

You may remember from Chapter 4.3 there are up to seven (7) demons recorded for us in the Bible which are associated with MIND control. And that number does not include jealousy, pride, fear, disobedience and bitterness, all of which could be argued as belonging to our mental functioning.

That makes a possible total of TWELVE! Twelve out of seventeen! The mind is such a huge area of demonic activity, affecting our speech and behaviour throughout each day. No wonder we are exhorted in the Word of God to be renewed in the SPIRIT of our minds.

Now we are being asked to believe there can be strange voices and controlling personalities manifested through humans, but they are only memory fragments (Alters), not spirits.

Give us a break!

It seems to me that:

(i)   **the Legion account is being ignored** (Mark 5:1-12).

(ii) the apostle Paul is being ignored when he wrote: **"We do not wrestle blood and flesh but with (spiritual) rulers and authorities"** ... (Eph. 6:12).

iii) we are going back to **"the healing of the memories"** again (a la **Agnes Sanford's** great contribution of forty (40) years ago) but more than that is necessary today.

(iv) **the high rate of suicide**[10] associated with D.I.D. sufferers strongly suggests demonic inspiration.

In the final analysis people will choose for themselves how to deal with extra personalities. D.I.D. therapy or D.I.D. prayer ministry may seem the softer options but only because they are uninformed about (and perhaps a little fearful of) Christian deliverance ministry.

It may be difficult to imagine but a Deliverance and Restoration meeting, with its cleansing power and refilling with the HOLY Spirit, is quite a blessing to ALL present, including the ministers.

It is all a matter of TRUSTING the Lord and applying His appropriate ministries.

In the meantime I wish the D.I.D. counsellors, both secular and Christian, every success in their efforts to help the sufferers.

---

10. **"Health Care in Christ"** newsletter Nov./Dec. 2000

CONCLUSION

I believe the MPD and/or the DID diagnoses have been grasped and settled on because nobody (at least, not many) in the psychiatric and psychological professions wants to horrify or frighten their patients with a seemingly heavy diagnosis of *"demon-possession"*. Also many practitioners would not want to face up to demonic situations. In days gone by you could not even find Christian ministers facing up to such issues. It was a case of facing the truth as a very last resort! - And then sending your sheep to a psychiatrist - such misunderstanding of the Great Commission (Matt. 10:8, 28:20)!

Thank God that is changing!

For the uninformed sufferer such a diagnosis can be very devastating, with a potential for a breakdown or even suicide. However, hiding the truth results in miserable progress (if any) and the same risks exist. A true diagnosis is essential if a healing is to be obtained (by the grace of the Lord), so how can we gently convey the truth?

The sufferer has to be made to see they are NOT a freak or a walking disaster without hope, and there is no need for any of these dear people who believe they have MPD or DID to be shocked or horrified at the thought that Alter personalities may be demons because, as this book has proven, I trust, to all who have an open mind, *"WE ALL HAVE OUR DEMONS"*. And the good Lord can remove them. Hallelujah!

For you and me the words of the old chorus still remain true:

> **"Jesus is the answer**
> **For the world today."**

The solution is:

- so simple (if you read and believe the New Testament)
- so free (of financial cost)
- so beautiful (Matt. 12:28)

and so available to all who believe and are prepared to put their hand to the deliverance plough and persevere without looking back (Luke 9:62).

What is it again?

*Get rid of the unclean spirit(s)!
*Get FILLED with the HOLY Spirit!
*Move into true discipleship (John 8:31-32)

- and ALL your so-called Alters will be crucified with Christ! (Rom. 6:6, Gal. 2:20, 5:24, 6:14).

Hallelujah!

SUNDAY, 27 SEPTEMBER, 1987
DELIVERANCE AND RESTORATION MEETING

CONSIDER THE CROSS!

PROPHECY: (Peter)

"My children, as you travel through this path of grace, this path of restoration, keep your eyes on my Son Jesus; and with every difficulty that you encounter look to the sacrifice of the Cross. Consider the agony in the garden of Gethsemane. Consider that which is described by men as the passion of the Son of God, through that long, dark night of interrogation. Consider the treatment - the scourging of His flesh. Consider the bearing of the curse of the crown of thorns. Consider the crucifixion itself. Consider the Blood which was shed. Consider the shame and the humiliation. Consider the price of your redemption. Consider what was necessary to purchase your salvation, and then look upon your pride and crucify it. Look upon your complaints and put them to death. Look upon the measure of suffering into which you have entered in this restoration period, and be ashamed. For the Son of God gave Himself for YOU. Despise the shame. Do not waste that sacrifice. Do not measure your own suffering against it in any sense of justification, but go to your knees and honour Him who saved you. As far as it lies within your power, and I will supply that power, you must walk in His footsteps. Despise the shame. Be crucified with Him and become the new creature that I have ordained for you to become; and never let me hear you complain without first considering Jesus my Son.

And when you have considered Him, bring your petitions to me, not in anger but in gratitude, and I will make a way of escape for you."

THE UNRECOGNISED M.P.D IN THE "NORMAL" PERSON

S-232

I'M BEGINNING TO REALIZE THAT THERE ARE MANY TREVORS...

THERE'S THE MACHO, ONE-OF-THE-BOYS TREVOR

THEN THERE'S THE ROMANTIC SENSITIVE TREVOR AROUND HIS GIRLFRIEND...

AND THERE'S THE PSEUDO INTELLECTUAL TREVOR AT ART GALLERIES

THE CONSERVATIVE, RESTRAINED TREVOR IN A PUBLIC PLACE

AND THE CARE-FREE UNINHIBITED TREVOR AMONGST FRIENDS

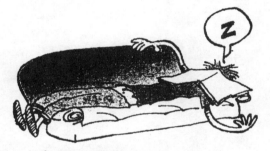

THERE'S THE LAZY, DON'T-GIVE-A-DAMN TREVOR ON ANY SATURDAY AFTERNOON...

I WONDER WHICH TREVOR IS THE REAL ONE...

G'DAY..."BURP"... I RECKON THE 'FIRST-THING-IN-THE-MORNING' TREVOR IS YOUR TRUE SELF..."YAWN"

SCRATCH SCRATCH

I DEMAND A RE-COUNT

CHAPTER 9

ACTION STATIONS!

9.1 THE FORGOTTEN VICTORY

Most Christians would agree that EVERYONE (Christian and pagan) needs the victory of the Cross of our Lord Jesus Christ to be appropriated in their lives for themselves.

In effect, this means that EVERYONE needs to be:

(i) born again in their human spirit by the Holy Spirit (John 3:3-5)

(ii) healed with many healings, emotional, mental and physical (Matt. 8:16-17, Acts 5:16).

But healing includes the third salvation ministry of DELIVERANCE for which many Christians do not see the need for the victory of the Cross at all, even for a few, let alone EVERYONE (Matt. 15:16, Acts 10:38, Col. 2:14-15).

When the **Holy Spirit Renewal movement** got under way in the historic denominations some thirty years ago many Renewal Christians thought of it as a re-discovery of the Person of the Holy Spirit. He was considered the forgotten member of the Trinity of the Father, Son and Holy Spirit for much of the twentieth century.

So also, I suggest, has **Christ's defeat of our ever-present spiritual enemies (Eph. 6:12) been the forgotten victory of the three-fold victory of the Cross.**

> *By His **blood** we are REDEEMED for ETERNITY!*

> By His ***"Bruise"*** (sometimes translated *"wound"* or *"stripes"*) we have been healed (1 Peter 2:24), and that includes both bodily healings and soulish deliverances (Matt. 8:16-17, Acts 5:16).

Through His mighty victory on the Cross of Calvary the good Lord has obtained for us a Full Salvation through THREE SALVATION MINISTRIES:

(i) **Evangelism** for the saving (reviving) of the human **spirit.**
(ii) **Deliverance** for the saving (cleansing) of the human **soul,** and
(iii) **Healing** for the saving (restoring) of the human **body (flesh).**

Martin Luther's Reformation battle-hymn, *"A Mighty Fortress is our God"*, has a wonderful third verse which says it for me:

> *"And tho' this world with demons filled*
> *Should threaten to undo us.*
> *We will not fear for God has willed*
> *His truth to triumph thro' us.*
> *Let goods and family go,*
> *This mortal life also.*
> *The body they may kill,*
> *God's truth continues still.*
> *His Kingdom is for ever."*

9.2 THE POWER OF OUR VISION

"Write the vision and make it plain ... that he may run that reads it" **(Hab. 2:2).**

The Vision, simply stated, is:

... the perfecting of the saints (believers)
... to the measure of the stature of the fullness of Christ (Eph. 4:12-13).
... through spiritual (inner) cleansing (James 4:8, 2 Peter 3:13-14)
... by Deliverance and Restoration programs (Rom. 12:2, 2 Cor. 7:1),
... in the Name of the Lord Jesus Christ (Col. 3:17).

We have done all we know how to do in seeking to share our Vision with the Body of Christ. It is a **powerful vision**, perhaps because it is an **urgent vision** which touches upon the life of **EVERY Christian.**

Many people have a vision for themselves, which they can keep to themselves or share with a very limited number of believers. Not a problem. Others have a vision for their work or ministry, and this is shared by all those who have a part in that ministry. However it is not necessary to share or push that vision upon others in the Body of Christ, locally, nationally or internationally, because it is a group vision. Again, no problem.

However in F.S.F. *we have been given an international Vision for the universal Body of Christ.* This puts us in the awkward position of having to say to other groups, whether battling or successful, whether small, large or huge *"Hey, bretheren! You need to catch THIS Vision! You need to change! You are missing something absolutely vital! You have NOT got it all! Wake up!"* - as lovingly as we can.

9.3 THE POPULARITY OF OUR VISION

You can imagine how well such a message and vision is received, even if it is listened to. If we were a big group we might be listened to with some tolerance or even respect, but coming from a virtually unknown group it is about as popular as a pork chop in Jerusalem. Unfortunately the messenger often gets more scrutiny than the message.

Yet what we say is a central message of the New Testament - a message that has been ignored for 19 centuries. It is a message of Salvation (pastors and evangelists please note). It answers the question asked by a Renewal pioneer **Rev. Alan Langstaff** in September 1975, **"WHERE IS THE CHARISMATIC MOVEMENT GOING?"**

9.4 THE "TORONTO" BLESSING

Thanks be to God that He has broken into the traditions of the churches with a fresh wave of power, apparently flowing from **Toronto, Canada,** and later **Pensacola, U.S.A.**

What we in F.S.F. could never do (by ourselves) the good Lord has done sovereignly, pouring out His power and flattening people, with attendant healings and deliverances. This is not new, of course. Most **Renewal churches have known this power for about twenty five years,** but I have no hesitation in saying that they have not known what to do with it. It has been used as a gimmick to attract crowds into churches. It has been used to exalt the ministers with this "gift". **What it has NOT yet been used for is the reason for which it has been given, that is, to begin the serious cleansing of the saints**, ALL who wish to be included in the Bride of Christ.

The sad, unfortunate but inevitable consequence of the so-called "Toronto Blessing" of the 1990's is the churches have become divided into those FOR and those AGAINST.

Those against the experience(s) of the T.B. include many fine and scholarly international teachers and evangelists. Their problem is that very few of them have any significant experience in ministering deliverance to others and even fewer have RECEIVED personal ministry. They are still loaded with garbage, ancestral and otherwise, and have little experience in the discernment of spirits (1 Cor. 12:10).

So the bottom line is those AGAINST the T.B. do not understand what is going on in a T.B. meeting, and they cannot help but be very wary. They see demons manifesting and overlook the work of the **Holy Spirit** forcing those manifestations and beginning the cleansing of God's people.

Those who are FOR the experience and the meetings are also on a huge learning curve and cannot always explain to the opposition what is happening in biblical terms. Many of these ministers also lack deliverance experience, both giving and receiving ministry, but they are seeing lives changed and praise the Lord for what He is doing.

Because whole congregations are sometimes flattened under the power of God the notion they ALL need deliverance seems preposterous or impossible but really, all the good Lord is saying AGAIN (to those with eyes to see and ears to hear) is

WE ALL have our demons!

9.5 THE TIME HAS COME!

All of this means that we should be preparing ourselves for our place in the Army of the Lord. While the Lord may use locusts as His Army (Joel 2:25) He also exhorts us as His soldiers to arm ourselves with the whole armor of God - to take up our spiritual weapons (Eph. 6:10-18, 1 Cor. 12:4-11) and fight a spiritual war, in Jesus' Name!

The time has come for the Renewal Church to grow up. The time has come to leave behind our "teenage", the froth and bubble of thinking only of having a good time in the Lord. The time has come to put an end to being satisfied with clapping and dancing and noisy celebrations as if they were the ultimate achievement of our Christian lives. These things are not necessarily wrong, and when they are inspired by the Spirit they are very right. But the Church of God is essentially an ARMY! It is an ARMY equipped in many ways and each soldier is to be girded with TRUTH (Eph. 6:14).

The time has come to make straight the way of the Lord in our personal lives and to face up to crucifying our sins (misdeeds) and our DEMONIC SIN heart condition.

The time has come for pastors and leaders to cease glossing over SIN and preaching only the "positive" things in the faith. People who sit under ministries where they only hear good things (smooth and pleasant things - Isaiah 30:10, Rom. 16:18, 2 Tim. 4:3-4) all the time are ill prepared for the times of testing and persecution to come. **It is better that we teach the WHOLE counsel of God,** so we be innocent of the blood of our hearers

(Acts 20:18-20, 26). **True men and women of God cannot escape persecution** (Acts 20:18-28, 2 Tim. 3:12), but great is their reward in Heaven (Matt. 5:11-12). On the other hand, smooth teachers, preachers and prophets who present only "positive" nice, popular themes are declared FALSE by the Lord Jesus (Luke 6:26).

DEMONIC SIN must be presented as the Christians' major weakness and Christians must realize they are SINNERS, albeit forgiven sinners! If the Church cannot face up to SIN and sins within herself how then can she purify herself, cleanse herself and make herself ready as a beautiful Bride for the Bridegroom?

The time has come for every Christian and every Church desirous of being numbered among the *five WISE maidens* (Matt. 25:1-11) to immediately get involved with a regular *Deliverance and Restoration* (cleansing and healing) *Program.*

What has the Lord got to do to wake up His shepherds to the need for inner (soulish) cleansing for EVERY ONE OF GOD'S CHILDREN - INCLUDING THEMSELVES!?

We are talking serious, week by week refining in the fire of God's deliverance and restoration programs for everyone in every Renewal group and church making up the five wise maidens!

> *Therefore having these promises, beloved, let us cleanse ourselves from all pollution of flesh and of spirit, perfecting holiness in the fear of God. (2 Cor. 7:1)*

30TH MARCH 1986

PROPHECY: Peter

I AM THE RESURRECTION AND THE LIFE SAITH THE LORD AND WHOEVER BELIEVES IN ME SHALL LIVE, AND THE LIFE THAT I HAVE PREPARED FOR MY PEOPLE IS THE LIFE OF CHRIST HIMSELF.

I WOULD HAVE MY PEOPLE TRANSFORMED BY THE RENEWING OF THEIR MINDS. I WOULD HAVE THEM CONFORMED TO THE IMAGE OF THE SON OF GOD AND I WOULD HAVE MY PEOLE KNOW THAT TO BE CONFORMED TO THE IMAGE OF THE SON OF GOD IS INDEED A MIGHTY TRANSFORMATION. A TRANSFORMATION IS NECESSARY THAT IS FAR GREATER THAN YOU WOULD EVER IMAGINE. THE TRANSFORMATION THAT IS NECESSARY BEGINS FROM DEEP WITHIN YOU. IT REQUIRES **THE CLEANSING OF YOUR SOUL.** IT REQUIRES THE **FULLNESS OF MY SPIRIT.** IT REQUIRES THE **RENEWING OF YOUR MIND.** IT REQUIRES THE

HEALING OF YOUR BODY. IT REQUIRES A **TOTAL RESTORATION** OF EVERY PART OF YOUR BEING. IT REQUIRES THAT YOU BE **STRONG IN MY SPIRIT**. IT REQUIRES THAT YOU **SHED ALL THAT IS OF THIS WORLD**; THAT YOU PUT TO DEATH THE THINGS OF THE FLESH IN YOUR LIFE. IT REQUIRES THAT YOU **BE CRUCIFIED WITH THE SON OF GOD**; THAT YOU **SHARE IN THE FELLOWSHIP OF HIS SUFFERINGS**. ONLY THEN CAN YOU SAY THAT YOU ARE CONFORMED TO HIS IMAGE. ONLY THEN CAN YOU SAY THAT YOU HAVE BEEN TRANSFORMED, THAT YOUR MIND IS THE MIND OF CHRIST.

MY PEOPLE, **YOU KNOW THERE IS MUCH THAT IS TO BE PUT TO DEATH IN YOUR LIVES, MUCH THAT IS UNWORTHY OF THE SON OF GOD.** ARE YOU PREPARED TO BE CRUCIFIED WITH HIM? YOU CANNOT KNOW THE POWER OF HIS RESSURECTION UNTIL YOU HAVE SHARED IN THE FELLOWSHIP OF HIS SUFFERINGS. AND YET I CAN PROMISE YOU THAT IN THE MIDST OF THAT WALK, ALTHOUGH YOU SHALL KNOW WHAT IT IS TO BE GRIEVED IN YOUR SPIRIT, TO WEEP FOR THOSE WHO ARE REBELLIOUS, TO WEEP FOR THOSE WHO CONTINUE ON THE ROAD TO THE LAKE OF FIRE, THE BROAD ROAD THAT LEADS TO THEIR DESTRUCTION. YET IN THE MIDST OF ALL THAT YOU WILL KNOW THE JOY THAT IS SUPPLIED TO YOU FROM THE THRONE OF GOD. YOU WILL KNOW THE PEACE THAT TRULY DOES PASS UNDERSTANDING AND MY JOY SHALL FLOW IN YOU AND THROUGH YOU AND SUSTAIN YOU, FOR IN MY JOY SHALL BE YOUR STRENGTH AND YOU WILL BE ENABLED TO OVERCOME EVERY OBSTACLE.

EPILOGUE

This book has been in my spirit for years. Even in 1988 people were asking when it was going to be ready. Sometimes the whole package of teaching and revelation seemed to overwhelm me so that I did not know where to begin. It could have been twice as big, but I have tried to keep it simple and manageable.

We have also been able to comment on newish movements, changes and problems that have increased enormously over the last part of the twentieth century.

Chapters 3 and 8 are being expanded into separate booklets so if you are looking for fuller individual studies try to obtain a copy of:

1.   **"Religious Spirits - The Blight of the Churches"**
2.   **"Dissociate Identity Therapy - Help or Hoax?"**

Chapter 4 is also a separate and expanded booklet with a slightly changed title: **"We All Got Our Demons"**, for handier reference. We'll also try and get chapters 6 and 7 expanded into their own booklets.

We are happy to receive your genuine questions by mail, telephone or fax and wish you every success in Christ Jesus our Lord. Please see our Distributors and Enquiries pages.

Wishing you EVERY BLESSING in Christ Jesus, as you make yourself READY for Him!

Peter Hobson
CROWS NEST
May 1, 2002

APPENDIX "A"

STUDIES IN DISCERNMENT

Here is a brief outline of the subjects related to **discerning of spirits** already covered in Books 1, 2 and 3:

Book 1, Chapter 3
    Point 6 - Discerning of spirits
    Introduction
        (i)   Operation
        (ii)   Warnings:
                (a) Beware the Counterfeit
                (b) Beware Enemy Agents
                (c) Beware Pride
        (iii)   How to Develop Discernment
                (1)   The Personal Particulars Sheet
                (2)   Observation of external evidence
                (3)   Experience of groupings (kingdoms)
                (4)   A Word of knowledge
                (5)   Intercessory suffering
                (6)   Revelation

    Point 7 - Spiritual Hosts of Wickedness
        (i)   Creation spirits
        (ii)   Racist or Religious?
        (iii)   Infirmity spirits

Chapter 4
Point 4
(iii)   Hatred

Book 2   Chapter 5
    Point 3
    (iii)   Names, Characters and use of Discernment

    Point 9
    (ii)   Lack of Discernment

    Chapter 6
    Point I
    (iii)   (b) 2) Discernment

Book 3   Chapter 8 - Opposition
    Point 1
    (iii)   (f) A Common Deception

    Chapter 9 - Failures
    Point 3
    (ii)   Lack of Discernment

APPENDIX "B"

SINNER'S PRAYER

It is vitally important that YOU believe that God is working out His plan to judge the earth and save for Himself as many as will repent and ask for mercy, and YOU REPENT and ASK FOR MERCY—the sooner the better. How about right now?

If you are not a Christian or if you are a Christian who has been slack and failed to follow the Lord Jesus the way you know you should, then you can put things straight with the Lord by saying a prayer along the following lines:

Dear Lord Jesus,

I am a sinner and I now know that I have done things which have grieved you. I am truly sorry Lord, for my sins.

Please forgive me for ALL my sins. Wash me clean in your precious Blood. I renounce the devil, the powers of darkness and all their works.

I ask you, Lord Jesus, to break every foul curse upon my life, snap every unclean chain that binds me. Please FILL ME with your HOLY Spirit of power, and set me free to worship you and serve you as I should.

Thank you, Lord Jesus, for making it all possible for me on Calvary's Cross, my Lord and my God.

Hallelujah and Amen!

If you can agree with ALL these prayer points - that's great - get somewhere private and onto your knees and pray.

Don't READ this prayer out to the Lord but examine it and pray its PRINCIPLES out loud, from your HEART, using your own words.

If you can agree with some petitions but have difficulty with others you can at least make a beginning. As each day goes by your faith will increase and you should be able to pray more pettions. The Holy Spirit will help you - be persevering and patient.

This is a beginning, or a fresh start!

After this prayer has reconciled you to your Heavenly Father through the Lord Jesus Christ, you must move into contact with ALIVE Christians as soon as possible, preferably those who share the same kind of vision as in this book. There is not much point in joining a Church which belongs to the five foolish virgins group—they won't help you get clean and ready. If you have any difficulty or even if everything goes smoothly for you, please 'phone us or write to us and tell us what you have done.

We know that God will provide a way forward for you to enter into the move of God's Spirit today and possess all that you want to possess. The only limitations are what you yourself impose, perhaps by failing to link with others who have caught fire.

We are here to help you if you need us. Tel: (02) 9436 3657
                                         Fax: (02) 9437 6700
        MAY GOD BLESS YOU.   See Ministry and Personal
                                         Enquiries Page
        Peter and Verlie Hobson

P.O. Box 1020
Crows Nest 1585
N.S.W., Australia

APPENDIX "C"
ICONS and IMAGES

Here is a summary as given to us in **"Documents of the Christian Church" Bettenson:**

THE ICONOCLASTIC CONTROVERSY

The controversy began with the Iconoclastic edict of Leo III (the Isaurian) in 726. His motives included the desire to purify the debased Christianity of much of the East, and especially the Balkans, where the continual raids of Slavs, Bulgars, Saracens, etc., had demoralized the population and almost destroyed learning. Christianity here was fast becoming a degraded superstition, inferior, intellectually and morally, to Arab monotheism. The edict gave rise to rioting, Pope Gregory II denounced it, and the imperial cities of Italy rebelled. In 730 Leo deposed the patriarch of Constantinople, seized part of the papal lands, and placed the dioceses of S. Italy and Sicily under Constantinople; but incessant wars against the Arabs prevented him from enforcing his decision in the West.

The Second Council of Nicaea, held under the influence of the Empress Irene, when the emperor was a boy, was followed by a temporary healing of the breach between E. and W., but it broke out again in 815. This breach, since it left the papacy without protection against the Lombards, was one of the causes of the founding of the Frankish Empire; though Charlemagne took the side of the iconoclasts, repudiated Nicaea II, and asked the Pope to excommunicate the Emperor; a request which Hadrian I refused.

Definition of the Second Council of Nicaea, 787: Actio VII. Mansi, xiii. 378 D sqq.

We define, with all care and exactitude, that the venerable and holy images are set up in just the same way as the figure of the precious and life-giving cross; painted images, and those in mosaic and those of other suitable material, in the holy churches of God, on holy vessels and vestments, on walls and in pictures, in houses and by the roadsides; images of our Lord and God and Saviour Jesus Christ and of our undefiled Lady, the holy God-bearer, and of the honourable angels, and of all saintly and holy men. For the more continually these are observed by means of such representations, so much the more will the beholders be aroused to recollect the originals and to long after them, and to pay to the images the tribute of an embrace and a reverence of honour, not to pay to them the actual worship which is according to *our faith, and which is proper only to the divine nature: **For the honour paid to the image passes to its original, and he that adores an image adores in it the person depicted thereby ....***

THE WORD OF GOD

So much for the wisdom of men, which wisdom is often earthly, soulish and demonic (James 3:15). The Word of God says:

> *"Take careful heed to yourselves, for **you saw no form** when the LORD spoke to you at Horeb out of the midst of the fire, **lest you act corruptly** and make for yourselves a carved image of the form of any figure: the likeness of male or female ...." (Deut. 4:15-16. cf v. 12).*

Clearly the Lord explains why He keeps Himself INVISIBLE. *It is to prevent us acting corruptly and making images.* But does that stop the unclean religious spirit? Not on your life! We make images anyway, even though we have no idea what the originals looked like in the first place!

And to add insult to injury, we surround our images with a pious, religious rationale to justify our rebellion. All the cleverness of careful phrasing and explanations cannot hide the fact that the Second Council of Nicaea, 787, greatly erred in authorising the making and use of images for ANY purpose, and thus misguided centuries of Christians to the present day.

Let us receive this warning and, when the Church(es) experience the mighty SHAKING of God's Truth as this Age draws to a close, let us heed the warning of the apostle John, *"Little children, keep yourselves from idols"* (1 John 5:21).

APPENDIX "D"

TO DEAN LANCE SHILTON - CHAIRMAN

2nd July '75

2/7/75   Peter Hobson resigns from the Occult Enquiry in view of its comments in the report on "Exorcism" as under:-

"Dear Dean Shilton,

The Anglican Commission of Enquiry into the Occult

Further to my intimation yesterday I now confirm that I wish to withdraw my name from the list of members of the Commission.

Inasmuch as the final report and recommendations have a good deal to say about the ministry of deliverance (exorcism) and as it would appear that I am unfortunately the only Commission member with any degree of skill in that specialised area of counselling and ministry, the obvious conclusion to be drawn by readers of the Report would be that I am responsible for that area of the Report.

As the truth is that I have been permitted to make very little contribution, I do not believe it would be honest for me to give that impression. You must be aware that I am the only member of the Commission to have been consistently over-ruled in my own area of competency and I regret to say that there is very little on the subject of deliverance in the Report with which I am in full accord.

The wording of the final draft implies that some careful consideration and expertise has been applied to the question of deliverance. Again I suggest this is less than accurate and would urge you to eliminate this "Achilles heel", lest it cast a shadow of suspicion on the valuable work accomplished by each member of the Commission in their appropriate field of competency.

Yours Faithfully,

Peter Hobson.

PUBLICATIONS BY THE SAME AUTHOR

This book is produced by FULL SALVATION FELLOWSHIP LTD., and designed to assist the people of God in their preparation for the drama of the End Time, which we believe has already begun on God's calendar.

The others published are:

"Guidance for Those Receiving Deliverance"
"The Reincarnation Deception" (out of print)
"Headcovering and Lady Pastor-Teachers"
"Christian Authority and Power"
"Toronto and the Truths You Need to Know"

Christian Deliverance series:

Book 1 **"Make Yourselves Ready"**
Book 2 **"Engaging the Enemy"**
Book 3 **"Walking in Victory"**
"Your Full Salvation"
"Surviving the Distress of Nations"
"End-Time Deliverance and the Holy Spirit Revival"
"Sex, Demons and Morality"

Others in the process of production and to be published are:

"The Stigmata of Jesus"

Booklets expanded from this publication:

"We ALL Got Our Demons"
"Dissociate Identity Therapy-Help or Hoax?"
"Religious Spirits"
"Sin is Demonic"
"The Man of Sin"

Ministry And Personal Enquiries

AUSTRALIA

Full Salvation Fellowship Ltd.
P.O. Box 1020
Crows Nest, 1585
AUSTRALIA

TEL: (02) 9436 3657
Fax: (02) 9437 6700
Website:wwwfullsalvationfellowship.com
Email: peter@fullsalvationfellowship.com

PHILIPPINES

Good News Kingsway Fellowship Int. Inc.
P.O. Box 6
CAGAYAN DE ORO CITY 9000
PHILIPPINES

Phone: 088 857 3485

Full Salvation Fellowship
Hillside, Purok 4-A Qusa
9000 Cagayan de Oro City
PHILIPPINES

UNITED KINGDOM

Ellel Ministries
Ellel Grange
Ellel, Lancaster, LA2 OHN
U.K.

Phone: (0) 1524 751651
Fax: (0) 1524 751738

U.S.A.

Impact Christian Books, Inc.
332 Leffingwell Ave., Suite 101
Kirkwood
Mo 63122 USA

Phone: (314) 822 3309
Fax: (314) 822 3325

AFRICA

SJBS Outreach Inc.
P.O. Box 4953 Oshodi
Lagos, NIGERIA
WEST AFRICA

Full Salvation Ministry
P.O. Box 3438 KISII
KENYA. EAST AFRICA

Fax to Box (254) 381 31194

Full Salvation Ministry of
Uganda
Ps. Grace Okurut
P.O Box 25643
KAMPALA
UGANDA

Phone: (077) 453 745
Email: okurutg@yahoo.com

Trade Enquiries

AUSTRALIA

W.A. Buchanan and Co.,
20 Morrisby Street,
(P.O. Box 206)
GEEBUNG, QLD, 4034

Phone: (07) 3865 2222
Fax: (07) 3865 2600
Email: paul@wab.com.au

NEW ZEALAND

Rise Up Marketing NZ
20 Goodall Road
Snells Beach
Warkworth, New Zealand

Phone: (09) 425 6900
Fax: (09) 425 6727
Email: info@riseup.co.nz

PHILIPPINES

Good News Kingsway Fellowship Int. Inc.
P.O. Box 6
CAGAYAN DE ORO CITY 9000
PHILIPPINES

Phone: 088 857 3485

UNITED KINGDOM

Ellel Ministries
Ellel Grange
Ellel, Lancaster, LA2 OHN
ENGLAND

Phone: (0) 1524 751651
Fax: (0) 1524 751738

U.S.A.

Impact Christian Books, Inc.
332 Leffingwell Ave., Suite 101
Kirkwood
Mo 63122 USA
Phone: (314) 822 3309
Fax: (314) 822 3325

AFRICA

SJBS Outreach Inc.
P.O. Box 4953 Oshodi
Lagos, NIGERIA
WEST AFRICA

Full Salvation Ministry
P.O. Box 3438 KISII
KENYA EAST AFRICA
Email: casiago@hotmail.com
fsm@pace-tech.co.ke

Full Salvation Ministry of
Uganda
Ps. Grace Okurut
P.O Box 25643
KAMPALA
UGANDA

Phone: (077) 453 745
Email: okurutg@yahoo.com